SPIRIT OF SIBERIA

CONTRIBUTING SPECIALISTS

Russian Museum of Ethnography, St. Petersburg
Natalia Kalashnikova
Valentina Gorbacheva
Irina Karapetova
Nina Margolina
Tatyana Sem
Karina Solovieva

Khanty-Mansisk Museum of Regional Studies,
Khanty-Mansisk
Olga Khudyakova
Tatyana Muldanova

Department of Northern Peoples,
A. I. Hertsen Russian State Pedagogical University,
St. Petersburg
Arkadi Gachilov
Alexander Petrov
Elrika Semeonova

Academy of Science, Moscow
Larrisa Aburtina
Ludmila Chubarova

SPIRIT OF SIBERIA

Traditional Native Life, Clothing, and Footwear

Jill Oakes and Rick Riewe

SMITHSONIAN

INSTITUTION

PRESS

WASHINGTON, D.C.

Published in association with the Bata Shoe Museum, Toronto, Canada

© 1998 by the Bata Shoe Museum Foundation

Published in the United States of America by Smithsonian Institution Press

ISBN 1-56098-801-0

Library of Congress Catalog Number 98-86778

02 01 00 99 98   5 4 3 2 1

First published in Canada by Douglas & McIntyre Ltd., Vancouver, British Columbia

Editing by Barbara Pulling
Design by Val Speidel
Front jacket photograph: Nenets mother and child by Maria Stenzel/National Geographic Image Collection
Back jacket photographs: *Left:* Chukchi seal skin summer boots by Vladimir Dorokhov. *Right:* Amur region seal skin winter boots by Antony Vecera
Pages ii and iii: Migrating reindeer by Rick Riewe. Page iii, inset: Nenets herder feeding an orphaned reindeer by Rick Riewe. Page vi: Nenets herder by Rick Riewe
Drawings by Frank Kazmerowich
Maps by Heather Warkentin and Isabelle Swiderski

Printed and bound in Canada by Friesens
Printed on acid-free paper

CONTENTS

*I*T HAS BEEN my good fortune to visit many parts of
the world, mainly in connection with our family shoe
business. Through my interest in footwear I have
become involved in the study of cultures and lifestyles and
have learned that shoes have much to tell about a wearer's
personality, activities, surroundings, status in society, cultural
traditions, and sometimes even religious beliefs. Over the last
fifty years I have built up a large collection of shoes and
related artifacts, which are now housed in the Bata Shoe
Museum in Toronto, Canada.

Through our museum's studies of the North American
Inuit, we were somewhat familiar with the footwear worn by
Siberian reindeer herders. Alika Podolinsky Webber, our first
curator, was instrumental in acquiring Siberian skin boots in
1983 through an exchange of Canadian Inuit boots with the
Bally Shoe Museum in Switzerland and the Shoe and Leather
Museum in Offenbach, Germany. Both European museums
had limited information on the provenance of their Siberian
boots. In 1989, we were able to acquire some Siberian boots
which had been collected in the field by Asen Balikci, a writer
and filmmaker, and Dr. Valery Tishkov, now director of the
Institute of Ethnography and Anthropology in Moscow.
Finding out more about Siberian footwear and culture was a
challenge, since very little has been written on the subject. Jill
Oakes and Rick Riewe, who had done extensive research for
our museum on circumpolar peoples, particularly the
Canadian Inuit, were keen to extend their field of study to
Siberia.

I originally met Jill Oakes in 1985, after she had completed
her Master's thesis on how the Canadian Inuit made their
kamiks. My first contact with Rick Riewe came when he
undertook a research project on narwhals for the World
Wildlife Fund, an international conservation organization in
which I have been involved for many years. Jill and Rick share
a deep love of the North and a fascination with circumpolar
cultures. Unlike many other researchers, they not only
observe people's lifeways and listen to their stories but
actually learn about certain Indigenous activities, such as
scraping and chewing skins and preparing sinew for sewing,
by carrying out the tasks themselves. Both appear to have an
unlimited curiosity about the spiritual value systems of the
peoples of the North, and they are also very interested in

how the natural environment invariably influences local lifeways and material culture. In 1990 the Bata Shoe Museum Foundation helped to fund their first trip to the Chukchi and Even regions of Siberia to collect footwear. Several of the boots they found are illustrated in this book.

But it was only in 1993, when Dr. Valery Tishkov arranged for me to visit the ethnographic collection in St. Petersburg, that I became fully aware of the richness and diversity of Siberian cultures. Thanks in large part to Dr. Natalia Kalashnikova, deputy director of the Russian Museum of Ethnography, and to her colleagues, I became totally fascinated by the artifacts I saw and by the stories the Russian researchers told me about them. As we opened boxes in the storage area and examined various items, I was overwhelmed by the realization that the Indigenous peoples of Siberia, with so few handmade tools, living in such harsh conditions, were able to create items of such beauty and craftsmanship for their daily use. A whole new world of knowledge opened up for me. My initial visit, followed by close co-operation between the Russian Museum of Ethnography and the Bata Shoe Museum, culminated in a loan exhibition entitled *Spirit of Siberia*, which opened at the Bata Shoe Museum and included many of the artifacts featured in this book.

The enthusiasm of the Siberian specialists at the Russian Museum of Ethnography and their willingness to share their knowledge was crucial to our research. I specifically would like to thank Dr. Natalia Kalashnikova, Nina Margolina, Irina Karapetova, and Karina Solovieva. The Bata Shoe Museum Foundation is most grateful to them for their assistance in preparing background papers and in identifying appropriate artifacts and archival photographs for our study.

In Siberia, as in other parts of the world, human ecology has always been anchored in very specific features of nature and the environment, reflecting a pragmatic approach to survival. While new technologies and communication systems have brought about many improvements in our lives, they also threaten to throw into oblivion age-old traditions. But even when older values seem more appropriate and in better balance with their surroundings, time cannot be turned back, and people and cultures cannot be isolated from change.

I hope that the research presented in this book will help to document aspects of Siberian heritage and contribute to the survival of some traditional knowledge. The Bata Shoe Museum Foundation is proud to be involved in initiating and sponsoring the publication of *Spirit of Siberia*.

Sonja Bata
Chairman
Bata Shoe Museum Foundation

1

*O*UR INTEREST IN footwear began while working
with Inuit seamstresses and hunters in northern
Canada thirty years ago. A continuing fascination
with traditional culture has introduced us to many northern-
ers in Canada, Greenland, Alaska, and Siberia since then.

In 1990 we travelled to Siberia to learn more from the
Even and the Chukchi, semi-nomadic herders who still live in
reindeer skin tents. Most of them had never seen a westerner,
but as they were feeling jeopardized by the resource extrac-
tion occurring in their traditional territories, these extremely
hospitable people requested that we document their stories
and their way of life. This experience enticed us westward to
the tundra and taiga of the Siberian lowlands, where we
learned new ways of interacting with the environment from
Nenets and Khanty people.

Our field work was supplemented with a review of the
large body of literature written in Russian on the Indigenous
peoples of Siberia. In addition, we conducted an intensive survey of Russian and European museum collections. Illuminated
by interpretations from Siberian scholars and Indigenous
people themselves, the artifacts we studied provided a wealth
of environmental, economic, cultural, social, and historical
information. The first phase of our work culminated in an
exhibition entitled *Spirit of Siberia,* which was hosted by the
Bata Shoe Museum in Toronto from May 6, 1997, to June 15,
1998. Organized with the assistance of specialists from the
Russian Museum of Ethnography in St. Petersburg, the
exhibit featured exceptional works of art—footwear, clothing,
tools, and other objects—from that museum's collection of
over 90,000 Indigenous artifacts.

This book explores in more detail the material culture
and incredible diversity in environment, lifeways, customs,
and beliefs among the Indigenous peoples of northern
Siberian and the Far East. It opens with a general introduction, then moves into individual chapters devoted to the
main cultural groups from each region. Many different terms
are used to identify Siberia's Indigenous peoples; we have
used the most common ones in the text, but the reader may
refer to Appendix I for a complete list of terms as well as
population figures for the various groups. The final chapter
of the book provides a key to the identification of Siberian
and Far Eastern footwear. A fuller discussion of skin

preparation techniques and a glossary appear in Appendices II and III.

We are very grateful to the many Russian specialists who shared their extensive knowledge with us in the course of our work. Sonja Bata's international vision and intense enthusiasm inspired our research significantly; opportunities to work with such an intellectually challenging colleague and mentor are rare. Funding was provided by the Bata Shoe Museum Foundation and the Social Sciences and Humanities Research Council of Canada.

Jill Oakes
Department of Native Studies
University of Manitoba

Rick Riewe
Department of Zoology
University of Manitoba

In researching this book, we examined Siberian and Far Eastern footwear in the collections of the following museums, working with both photographs and the artifacts themselves. All accession numbers in the text and captions refer to artifacts in these collections.

BSM	Bata Shoe Museum, Toronto, Canada
REM	Russian Museum of Ethnography, St. Petersburg, Russia
AM	Anadyr Museum of Ethnography, Anadyr, Russia
BM	Museum of Mankind, The British Museum, London
CU	Museum of Archaeology and Anthropology, Cambridge University, Cambridge, England
DL	Deutsches Ledermuseum, Schuhmuseum, Offenbach, Germany
EMB	Ethnographic Museum, University of Bergen, Bergen, Norway
EMO	Ethnographic Museum, Institute and Museum of Anthropology, University of Oslo, Oslo, Norway
KK	Kunstkamera, St. Petersburg, Russia
KM	Khanty-Mansisk Museum of Regional Studies, Khanty-Mansisk, Russia
MM	Magadan Museum of Ethnography, Magadan, Russia
MVB	Museum für Völkerkunde, Berlin, Germany
MVD	Museum für Völkerkunde, Dresden, Germany
MVH	Museum für Völkerkunde, Herrnhut, Germany
NMD	National Museum of Denmark, Copenhagen, Denmark
NME	National Museum of Ethnology, Leiden, The Netherlands
NMF	National Museum of Finland, Helsinki, Finland
NMS	National Museum of Scotland, Royal Museum of Scotland, Edinburgh, Scotland
PRM	Pitt Rivers Museum, University of Oxford, Oxford, England
RM	Centre for Native Culture, Roskinskya Museum, Roskinskya, Russia
SI	Smithsonian Institution, Washington, D.C., United States
SM	Salekhard Museum of Ethnography, Salekhard, Russia
SP	Scott Polar Institute, Cambridge University, Cambridge, England

History and Prehistory

- Nenets, Enets, Khanty, Selkup, Komi, Dolgan, and Nganasan reindeer herders travelling across moss- and lichen-covered arctic tundra;
- Mansi, Even, and Evenki hunters calling moose deep in the taiga;
- Even and Evenki riding reindeer as the sound of bells rings through stands of larch, birch, and pine;
- Yakut and Yukagir forging powerful spirit helpers from iron ore;
- Koryak dancers speaking to the spirits of the dead, wildlife, and the universe;
- Chukchi traders and warriors exchanging reindeer and seal products;
- Siberian Yupik hunters in walrus skin boats watching for whales to surface off the arctic coast;
- Nanai and other Amur River peoples fishing for salmon with the familiar cry of seagulls overhead along the Pacific Coast.

THESE ARE SOME of the amazing sights and sounds that greet the visitor to northern Siberia and the Far East, the vast northern territories of Russia, even today. The region covers more than 13.5 million square km, an area one-quarter larger than all of Canada. It encompasses the area from the midwestern Ural Mountains, which rise to about 2000 m, east to the Pacific Ocean and the Bering Strait, and from the islands north of Nova Zemlya in the Arctic Ocean south to the borders of Kazakhstan, Mongolia, and China (Noble and King 1992). These territories are closely associated with specific cultural groups who have inhabited them for centuries (Symmons-Symonolewicz 1972).

Ancient Beringian cultures may have existed along the coastal regions; however, the first evidence (A.D. 1000) is of Paleo-Eskimo inhabitants. The earliest confirmed use of the region, by predescendants of the Yupik people, occurs in the Old Bering Sea phase, followed by the Okvik, Birnirk, Punuk, Thule, and Late Prehistoric periods. The differences between artifacts from the Old Bering Sea and Okvik phases are minimal; decorative art, harpoon heads, and housing construction are the key identifiers. Geometric decorations continued until the late Punuk phase, when linear designs became common.

FIGURE 2
Overleaf: For generations, the Indigenous peoples of Russia and the Far East have lived an outdoor way of life working as reindeer herders, fishers, and hunters.
REM 1706.72

MAP 1
Siberia and the Far East

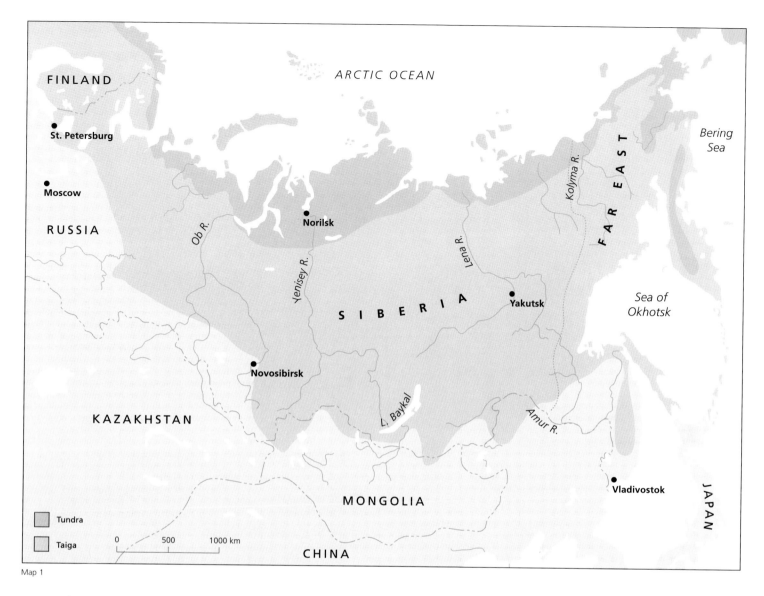

Map 1

During the Punuk and Thule periods, co-operative hunting and trading activities developed, and specialists such as shamans and warriors began to appear. These traits were the beginnings of contemporary coastal Chukchi, Koryak, and Yupik cultures (Okladnikov 1965).

Even, Evenki, inland Chukchi, and other Indigenous peoples in the central region of Siberia are likely descendants of ancient European and central Asiatic cultures (Ackerman 1984, 1988; Arutiunov and Fitzhugh 1988; Dikov 1965, 1968; Fitzhugh 1995; Mason and Gerlach 1995; Pitul'ko 1993). Archaeological evidence indicates a late Paleolithic phase existed in the region (Konakov 1994). This phase was possibly followed by a transitional Mesolithic phase, and then the Neolithic. During the latter phase, chipped or ground stone tools were used in a hunting and gathering way of life. Some of the oldest ceramic pots were made during this period by people in the Amur River region. Sedentary ocean- and river-fishing lifeways and large villages developed, especially in the Amur River region. The Bronze and Iron phases that followed led into the lifestyles and cultures of modern Indigenous

peoples in central Siberia (Arutiunov and Fitzhugh 1988, Fitzhugh 1995, Michael 1984, Mochanov 1969, Okladnikov 1970).

Approximately thirty distinct cultural groups reside in northern Siberia and the Far East of Russia. Most groups have populations of only a few thousand people (Vakhtin 1992). These groups can be divided into four major language families: Ugrian, Uralic, Altaic, and Paleoasiatic (Armstrong 1980, 1989; Arpen 1989; Bartels and Bartels 1986; Czaplicka 1914; Dahl 1990; Fondahl 1985, 1995; Gurvich 1988a; Lebedev 1988a; Northern Affairs 1993; Prokhorov 1976; UNESCO 1983). Komi, Khanty, and Mansi people belong to the Ugrian branch of the Finno-Ugric language family (Pentikäinen 1992). This family is distantly related to the Uralic group of speakers, which includes the Selkup, Nenets, Enets, Dolgan, and Nganasan. The Altaic language family consists of Turkic, Manchurian, and Mongolian speakers from Yakut, Evenki, and Even, as well as most peoples of the Amur River and Sakhalin Island region. Nivkhi are an exception in the Amur; they speak an isolated language unrelated to any other. The

3

Paleoasiatic language family includes Chukchi, Koryak, and Yupik speakers, although Yupik use a structure and vocabulary that is unique (Forsyth 1992, Gurvich 1988b, Krupnik and Chlenov 1979, Levin and Potapov 1961).

Yupik speakers in Russia and Alaska are directly related. Less direct ties between Asian and North American Indigenous peoples can be seen in their clothing styles, skin boots, basketry, and pottery (Hatt 1914 [1969], Wissler 1933 [1973]), as well as in their physical features (Dolgikh 1965, Jochelson 1926a, Levin 1958, Szathmáry 1984), housing styles, belief systems, and ceremonies (Boas 1933 [1973]).

Traditionally, the Indigenous peoples of Siberia and the Far East were sustained by hunting, fishing, and reindeer herding. Between the sixteenth and the nineteenth centuries, the non-Indigenous population of the region grew slowly, beginning with the fur traders who came to extort sable pelts. But under the rule of the tsars, and later the Soviets, hundreds of thousands of prisoners from all across Russia were exiled to Siberia (Prokhorov 1976). In the 1930s, the Soviets moved Indigenous peoples into sedentary communities on collective farms, where they were taught Russian lifestyles and language. Wealthy herders were imprisoned or executed, and their reindeer were given to herders working for collective farms. These Soviet measures were interrupted during World War II but were vigorously resumed in the 1950s (Armstrong 1965, Balzer 1980, Forsyth 1992, Ilyina 1990, Osherenko 1995b, Poelzer 1995, Saunders 1990, Savoskul 1978). By the 1970s, virtually all herders in Siberia and the Far East worked in collective farm brigades (Lebedev 1988b). These resettlement policies had a major negative impact on Indigenous cultures.

Over the last thirty years, millions of non-Indigenous people have moved into Siberia to work in the newly established mines and oil and gas fields (Riewe 1992). More than two hundred cities have been established in areas traditionally used by herders for reindeer grazing, thirty of them with populations greater than 100,000 (Bond 1991, Cherkasov 1982, Mote 1995). Air, rail, and road transportation routes and extensive communication systems have dramatically developed Siberia. Some Indigenous people still try to eke out a living as herders; however, most families have adopted urban ways of life. Their difficult living conditions are reflected in low birth rates, high mortality rates, and a shortened life expectancy (Lebedev

FIGURE 3
Shamans across Siberia call on helping spirits to improve their ability to journey safely and to communicate with spirits in other worlds. Metalworkers create figurines in the form of animals and elements of the universe to act as spirit helpers. Metal figurines are considered more powerful than those made from bone, wood, or skin. REM 5659.120

FIGURE 4
Large herds of reindeer are carefully managed to ensure that grazing grounds are kept in good condition.

4

1988b, Pika 1996). Some Indigenous people have completed training at technical schools and universities in order to gain the skills needed to work in urban settings (DeBardeleben 1990; Osherenko 1995a, 1995b; Sokolova 1988).

Throughout the centuries of change and development, Indigenous peoples of Siberia and the Far East have maintained a strong spiritual connection to their environment. Natural phenomena such as animals, plants, rivers, weather, stars, and other elements of the universe are believed to be inhabited by gods and helper spirits. Through shamans, people are able to communicate with these spirits and with the spirits of their ancestors to get guidance and advice which is critical

to their survival. Some spirits are treated as totem animals. Effigies are kept at sacred sites where groups of families congregate to perform ceremonies in order to avert disasters such as famine, disease, or war. The brown bear is considered the master of the forest, embodying justice on earth. Occasionally bears are killed ceremonially and their flesh is eaten.

For more than two hundred years shamanistic activities were prohibited, first by the tsars and later by the Soviets. Indigenous shamans were repressed or killed, and their clothing, effigies, and drums were confiscated. However, shamanism continued in remote regions, and today it is openly practised by many Indigenous peoples in rural settings.

The Environment

There are 53,000 major rivers and more than a million lakes in Siberia (Noble and King 1992). The mighty Yenisey, Lena, and Ob rivers alone account for 70 per cent of the entire river drainage into the Arctic Ocean (Riewe 1992). For thousands of years these huge rivers have been used by Indigenous peoples travelling by canoe, boat, reindeer, and dog sled, and on skis.

The Ob River, at 5500 km the longest river in Russia, drains western Siberia, the largest plain in the world, which extends from the Ural Mountains to the Yenisey River. This vast, marshy region is underlain by fragile permafrost, which takes centuries to recover when disturbed. East of the Yenisey River, hilly and eventually mountainous terrain extends to the Far East (Mote 1995, Noble and King 1992).

Siberia and the Far East are divided into several natural vegetational zones: polar desert, tundra, forest-tundra, taiga, and mixed forest.

Polar Desert

Due to scant precipitation, an extremely cold climate, a lack of soil, and a very short growing season, the vegetational cover in the polar desert is less than 5 per cent (Bliss 1990, Bliss et al. 1981). Only mosses, lichens, and a few vascular plants can exist in this barren region, and only an occasional lemming or arctic fox is encountered. Polar deserts are found on the northern end of the island of Novaya Zemlya and on other more northern arctic islands. This territory is virtually uninhabited.

Tundra

The tundra, located between the polar desert and the forest-tundra, forms a strip 300 to 500 km wide along the arctic coastline. This zone has poorly developed soil underlain with up to 1.5 km of permafrost. Frigid temperatures, high winds, and scant precipitation create a treeless environment covered with low-growing vegetation, including lichens, grasses, and sedges critical for reindeer grazing. Large areas of mosses, dwarf birches, and willows are also used daily by herders for their reindeer (Chernov 1985, Prokhorov 1976). Snowdrifts hard-packed by wind remain on the land for close to nine months of the year.

Permafrost and the associated swampy landscape inhibit many hibernating and burrowing animals. The tundra supports only a few species of mammals, including lemmings, shrews, voles, arctic ground squirrels, tundra hares, arctic foxes, red foxes, weasels, wolves, polar bears, brown bears, mountain sheep, and reindeer. Birds commonly found here are Lapland longspurs, snow buntings, various shore birds and waterfowl, ptarmigans, arctic loons, swans, snowy owls, rough-legged hawks, and peregrine falcons. The most common fishes are salmon, cod, whitefish, and sturgeon. During the summer months, the tundra swarms with dipterans, especially mosquitoes and blackflies, which provide an abundant protein supply for passerine birds and fishes.

Along the coast, colonies of sea birds, shore birds, and waterfowl and marine mammals, including polar bears, ringed seals, harbour seals, ribbon seals, bearded seals, grey seals, fur seals, walrus, beluga whales, and bowhead whales, are dependant upon the productive marine environment.

Forest-Tundra

This transitional zone between tundra and taiga is characterized by sparse forest, tundra bog, and meadow. Pine, spruce, larch, birch, and alder are intermixed with meadows along river valleys, and tundra bogs usually occur along river divides. Lichen-moss, bush, or scrub communities, including perennial grasses, grow between islands of forest and provide valuable forage for reindeer (Prokhorov 1976), which is the animal most important to the well-being of Indigenous peoples inhabiting this region. Other animals inhabiting the tundra and taiga are also found in this zone.

Taiga

The taiga covers more than one-third of Russia, stretching 12 000 km across Eurasia. In winter, the taiga experiences lower temperatures and less wind than does the tundra; the coldest temperature in the northern hemisphere, $-71°$c, was recorded in the taiga of eastern Siberia. Summer temperatures are generally above $10°$c, some days as high as $30°$c. Snow may accumulate up to 125 cm, remaining powdery in calm forested areas (Mote 1995).

The taiga is divided into dark-coniferous and light-coniferous forest. Dark-coniferous forest, which is most typical, grows on acidic soil covered with lichens, mosses, or

5

a layer of decaying conifer needles. The spruce, fir, and stone pine species that grow here have needles capable of photo-synthesizing at low light levels. Dark-coniferous forest often has little or no underbrush. The more open light-coniferous forest of eastern Siberia is characterized by larch trees with underbrush of dwarf stone pine, scrub birch, and various herbaceous species (Prokhorov 1976).

The taiga possesses a fauna richer than that of the tundra but less rich than that of the mixed forest to the south. In addition to tundra mammals, the taiga supports river otters, sable, beavers, muskrats, pikas, tree squirrels, flying squirrels,

FIGURE 5
The spiritual and physical well-being, philosophies, and world views of Siberian herders, including this Nenets woman, Zoya Russkina, are completely dependant on reindeer.

chipmunks, red-backed voles, field voles, wolverines, lynx, musk deer, and moose. Some species usually found in mixed forests also occur in the taiga, including the hedgehog, marten, mink, red deer, and roe deer. The reindeer is extremely well adapted to both taiga and tundra. Typical taiga birds include turkey-sized capercaillies, hazel hens, Siberian jays, crossbills, nutcrackers, and several species of owls and woodpeckers. The taiga has only two species of reptiles, the common viper and the common lizard, which are more numerous in the southern mixed forests. Several species of whitefish and salmon are the most common fish in the area. Bloodsucking insects are prevalent; various species of ants, long-horned beetles, and bark beetles are less obvious. In southern areas, especially in the mountains and along coast-lines, the taiga displays even greater biodiversity. For example, in the Amur River region, larch and pine dominate the taiga in some places; in others, Yeddo spruce and Khingan fir prevail (Prokhorov 1976).

Mixed Forest

The Amur region of the Far East is covered by mixed forests of conifers and broadleaf trees as well as by taiga. Here mixed forests are influenced by a unique combination of monsoon winds and torrential rain from the Pacific in the summer, and frigid, sunny, dry weather from central Siberia in the winter (Noble and King 1992). Spruce, Daurian larch, several species of pine, Mongolian oak, Korean cedar, Amur cork, and woody creeper predominate in the mixed forest, often with hazel underbrush. At lower elevations the forest includes oak, maple, walnut, ash, and lilac (Forsyth 1992, Prokhorov 1976).

The Amur region possesses an extremely rich fauna, including the Manchurian hare, muskrat, tree squirrel, pika, red fox, wolf, raccoon, raccoon dog, weasel, marten, sable, mink, river otter, wolverine, badger, Himalayan black bear, Eurasian brown bear, the rare Amur leopard, the Siberian tiger, the lynx, wildcat, wild boar, Manchurian red deer, roe deer, reindeer, spotted Sika deer, moose, and chamois. There is also a rich assortment of waterfowl and shore birds, as well as game birds such as black grouse, cuckoo, and azure-winged magpie. The most important riverine fishes are long-snouted sturgeon, burbot, and carp.

Reindeer

Reindeer are one of the most important resources for Indigenous peoples throughout the vast tundra and taiga regions. Reindeer meat, blood, viscera, and fat provide superb nutrition. Tame reindeer are used for riding, for pack animals, to lure wild reindeer during hunting, and for breeding large herds which migrate thousands of kilometres. Wild reindeer are stalked and ambushed on their annual migration between tundra and taiga. Some marine-mammal hunters and fishers have few or no reindeer themselves, but they trade with their herder neighbours for essential reindeer products.

The durable and highly insulating skins of reindeer are used for clothing, bedding, and tent covers. Reindeer sinew is employed as a high-quality sewing thread, and antlers and bones are used for tools and carved into amulets and works of art. The peoples living on the land today are as dependant as ever upon the reindeer, and their belief systems, clothing traditions, and ways of life are directly linked to the well-being of domesticated and wild herds.

Traditional Clothing

Indigenous peoples continue to wear their traditional clothing for special events and winter travel. Skin clothing is like an unwritten text depicting wealth, age, marital status, and other cultural identifiers. For example, while a wealthy person can kill enough reindeer with hair of matching colour, length, and density to complete a sewing project, poorer seamstresses usually build their collection of skins over several years, because their reindeer may die at different times of the year, when the hair is at different lengths or densities.

Environmental issues also influence the availability of good-quality skins. Until recently, reindeer skin clothing lasted many years. Most clothing was made initially for winter wear, then used in spring and summer after it became worn and less insulating (Muller 1882). Some people—the Evenki, for example—transformed winter clothing into summer clothing by shaving off the fur. But significant changes have been observed by Khanty and other groups since the oil industry moved into traditional herding grounds. Herders report a decline in the overall health of their reindeer herds; reindeer suffering from the effects of pollution produce skin that is too thin, does not wear well, and lacks a healthy lustre (Oakes and

Riewe 1996). Khanty reindeer herder Komtin Antonovitch (1996) explained:

> In the fall, reindeer skins were strong and the reindeer hair used to be nice to touch, but not now—it doesn't feel or look the same. The lustre and shine that used to be in reindeer hair is gone. Sometimes I see black soot and oil on the tips of the bull reindeer beards. If reindeer get oil on their fur they can't wash it off.

Skin Preparation

Skin clothing is made from a variety of different animals. Reindeer skins are most commonly used across Siberia and the Far East, but bird, fish, sable, squirrel, fox, dog, seal, otter, arctic hare, horse, and cow skins are also employed. Skins are carefully selected for their insulating properties, water repellency, wind resistance, hair coloration, and flexibility. For example, hides from reindeer killed in late summer or early fall are ideal for winter hunting parkas. Skins from reindeer killed in October are too thick for hunters and are either cropped or used for the clothing of less active older women (Kreynovich 1979).

Skins are prepared at different times of the year, by both women and men, depending on weather conditions and when animals are killed. Some people prepare smaller skins and skins that will be smoked, such as leg skins, on cool summer days, and larger skins in the winter when the weather is colder. Other groups, such as Khanty and Even, prepare skins in the spring when they return to their winter caches, where the previous summer's skins are stored.

Mammals are case-skinned (in which the skin is removed as a tube) or flat-skinned (by cutting along the belly and legs and then removing the skin). Clothing skins are dried, scraped, and softened using tools and techniques learned from previous generations. Animal species, season, end use, available materials, geographic location, and cultural traditions all influence the method chosen to prepare a specific skin. Commercially tanned skins are used periodically; however, they last for only about five years, whereas hand-tanned clothing lasts up to thirty years.

Skin Preparation Tools

Knives, scrapers, and softening tools are used to prepare skins for clothing and footwear. These tools are made by a

6

FIGURE 6
Two-handed scrapers are used by Chukchi women to complete the first scraping on animal body and leg skins.

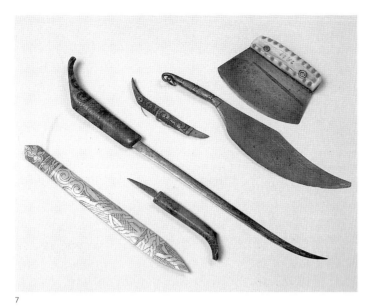

7

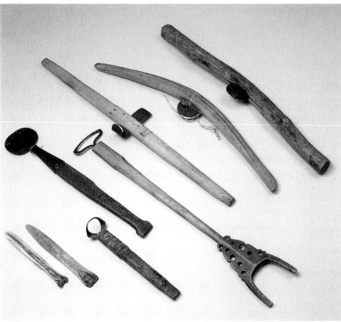

8

FIGURE 7
Siberian women use many different kinds of knives to prepare animal skins. Shown here, left to right, are examples from the Nanai (REM 1047.20, 100018.10); Nivkhi (REM 7006.103, 4978.27); Koryak (REM 10001.1); and Yupik (BSM 90.0143).

FIGURE 8
Two-handed scrapers used on animal skins are made with a variety of different blades. Shown here, from top to bottom, are a Chukchi scraper with a circular stone blade; an Even scraper with a circular metal blade; a Khanty scraper with an S-shaped blade; a Udege scraper with a circular blade and decorative handle; an Even scraper with a decorative blade; an undecorated Udege scraper; a Udege bone scraper; and a Nanai ivory scraper. BSM P90.0293, BSM P90.0264, BSM P96.0175, REM 7003.16, REM 730.34, BSM P96.0237, BSM P95.0143, BSM S97.0262

seamstress' husband, and she uses them for her entire life (Sartagov 1996). New tools are made when they are needed.

Large, medium, and small stone knives, often with bone, wood, or ivory handles, were traditionally used for skinning, food preparation, chiselling, and other activities. Today, blades are usually made from metal. A knife's shape, materials, and ornamentation vary across Siberia and the Far East. For example, Yupik, Koryak, and Chukchi women use semi-lunar knives, or ulus, to skin reindeer and seals (Chaussonnet 1995, Levin and Potapov 1956 [1964], Oakes and Riewe 1990, Rudenko 1961, Vasil'evskii 1969). Women in the Amur region use narrow long-bladed knives to skin fish and shorter-bladed knives to cut out the complex, curvilinear designs that decorate skins. Knife handles are often ornately decorated with stylized animal and plant symbols that improve one's ability to communicate with helping spirits (Black 1973, Shrenk 1883–1903).

Different types of dull and sharp scrapers, held with one or two hands, are used to soften skins (Oakes and Riewe 1996). Dull scrapers mechanically break up bundles of connective tissue in a dried skin; sharp scrapers create a soft, light finish by removing a thin layer of fascia (fibrous connective tissue). Often one scraper is used for both purposes, with the blade being sharpened as needed.

Nenets, Khanty, Selkup, Mansi, Enets, and Nganasan use both dull and sharp-bladed scrapers that have blades made from old scythes. A strip of strong fabric or rope is looped around one end of the blade and tied to the other; alternatively, the blade is embedded in a curved wooden handle, as is also done by people in the Amur region (Oakes and Riewe 1996, Shrenk 1883–1903, Vanstone 1985).

Two-handed scrapers are used by most groups. These are made by embedding a blade of stone or a rectangular piece of metal in the centre of a long (about 50 to 70 cm) handle (Hatt 1914 [1969], Levin and Potapov 1956 [1964], Sem 1997, Vasilevich 1963a). Blades have either a flat, a slightly curved, or a double-ended S-shape (Popov 1966 [1948], Vasilevich 1963a). Sometimes a circular blade is embedded on the end, rather than in the middle, of the handle. Many groups, including Nganasan, Dolgan, Yakut, Evenki, and Orochi, use this latter type of scraper (Oakes and Riewe 1996, Popov 1966 [1948], Vanstone 1985).

Other tools used to soften skins include a hinged "jaw"

and a hammer-and-platform combination. Even, Evenki, and Yakut construct large, hinged softeners featuring upper and lower jaws with serrated edges; a dried skin is repeatedly crushed between these jaws until it is softened (Karapetova 1997c). In the Amur region, skins are softened by repeatedly hammering them into a narrow slot cut into a wooden platform (Hatt 1914 [1969]). The size of the platform, slot, and hammer depends upon the size of the skin being prepared. The hammer is often elaborately decorated with hand-carved animal and plant symbols that help in communicating with the animal spirits, thereby improving hunting and fishing success.

Sewing

Once skins are prepared, they are ready for sewing. Beautifully sewn garments, as well as the actual process of sewing, provide spiritual and environmental protection for the wearer (Chaussonnet 1988). The power of sewing manifests itself differently across Siberia. For example, a pregnant Nivkhi woman ensures the safe birth of her infant by never sewing clothing or footwear that will be used outside the home or given to a stranger. When a Khanty person dies, the soul must be expelled from the body in order to protect against spiritual forces. To do this, a woman threads four strands of thread for a female, or five strands for a male, through a needle. She then walks around the corpse with needle and thread in hand, four times for a female corpse, five times for a male. After each circle is completed, one thread is put outside the tent. On the last circle the needle and thread are both left outside, and the soul has been expelled from the corpse (Golovnev 1994).

Sewing is done while looking after children, preparing meals, listening for reindeer, making tea, tending the hearth, or visiting. Women usually are responsible for sewing; however, men also know how to sew, and they repair their clothing when they are travelling without women. Most footwear and other clothing is sewn in August or throughout the fall and winter because skins are easier to work in cool temperatures. Stockings, boots, mittens, and other clothes that need to be smoked are sewn during the summer and then hung inside the tent over a smudge fire (Salender 1996c). Seamstresses usually sew small decorations and twist sinew on hot summer

9

FIGURE 9
Reindeer antlers are used to make hinged scrapers for softening reindeer skins. Different sizes of wooden hammers and notched platforms are used to soften skins in the Amur region. Skins are also scraped with tools with a metal blade at the end. *Clockwise from top:* REM 11603.17 (Even), REM 1998.309/1,2 (Nanai), BSM P90.0262 (Even), REM 8761.9149 (Nanai)

10

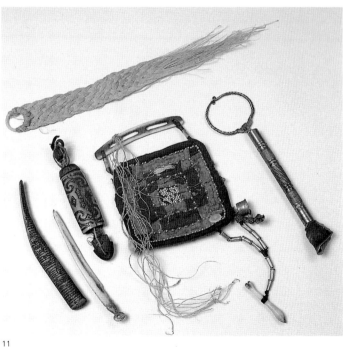

11

Nenets seamstress and herder Larrisa Salender (1996) explained:

> Usually I sew in the fall beginning at the end of August after all the skins are prepared, and when sewing doesn't make my hands sweaty. It's cool enough today to sew, as I can warm my hands by working with the reindeer skins.

Sewing Tools

Needles, awls, cutting boards, creasers, sewing baskets, and other items are required for sewing. Needles and awls were traditionally hand-crafted from reindeer, bird, and fish bones; ivory; or hand-forged iron; today, commercial steel needles are used. Historically, needles were carved with either an eye or a notch to carry the thread; the eye of the needle was drilled using a mouth bow drill. Tiny needles were used for sewing clothing, larger needles and awls for sewing thick skins such as walrus or moose (Apassingok et al. 1985; Black 1973; Chaussonnet 1995; Hatt 1914 [1969]; Oakes and Riewe 1990, 1996; Rudenko 1961; Vasilevich 1963a; Vasil'evskii 1969). Skin thimbles protect seamstresses' fingers. Most women wear skin cylinders on their index fingers (Hatt 1914 [1969]).

Variously shaped and decorated metal, bone, and ivory tubes are used as cases to carry needles, thimbles, and thread. Needle cases are worn on women's belts, attached to their clothing or sewing bags, or stored inside sewing bags to prevent them from misplacing these items while constantly making and breaking camp (Black 1973; Hatt 1914 [1969]; Oakes and Riewe 1990, 1996; Popov 1966 [1948]).

Needle cases, bundles of sinew thread, beads, buttons, pieces of skin and fabric, decorative trim, small bells, amulets, and an assortment of other items are stored in sewing bags or baskets. Women with large reindeer herds usually make reindeer skin sewing bags; women in the south, who have smaller herds, make sewing baskets or bags from cedar roots and birch bark. Flat, purselike birch bark containers are used by Nivkhi women in the Amur region to store elaborately decorated panels (Black 1973). Each cultural group has its own way of decorating sewing bags; brass bells are used for protection from illness or harm. After a death, mourners muffle bells used on reindeer, clothing, and sewing bags to prevent them from ringing for four months for a female and five for a male

12

FIGURE 10
Nenets prohibit women who are mourning from sewing or cutting out patterns. The person closest to the deceased is not selected to be the mourner if she is too busy sewing.

FIGURE 11
Needle cases made from metal, wood, bone, ivory, fabric, or skin are used to protect needles from breakage. Shown here are examples from Koryak (*far right*), Nivkhi (*third from left*), and Khanty (*bag in middle*). Khanty seamstress Varvara Sartagov used this Khanty needle bag for over fifty years. Tools used to press boot soles into shape and by shamans to warn hunters about potential danger may be elaborately decorated or left undecorated. A Nivkhi boot presser is shown at far left; a Udege tool is second from left. As shown at top, sinew is often braided by Khanty and stored with needle cases. *Top:* BSM P96.0195. *Left to right:* REM 7006.29, BSM P95.0142, REM 4798.155, BSM P96.0189, REM 2246.53147

FIGURE 12
The sewing bags of Nenets women demonstrate exceptional skin preparation and sewing skills learned from elders. A small piece of a newborn's umbilical cord is often sewn into a tiny pouch attached to the inside of the bag to protect the child from evil and illness and to link one generation to the next.

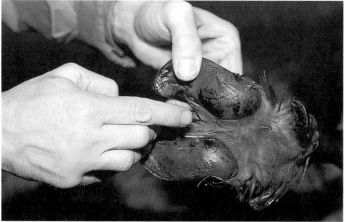

13

14

FIGURE 13
Boot soles are made by sewing together skins taken from beneath reindeer hoofs. Skin from this part of the reindeer is extremely durable and provides excellent traction.

FIGURE 14
Khanty herder and seamstress Varvara Sartagov cuts patterns from birch bark following ancient hand measurements.

(Golovnev 1994; Oakes and Riewe 1990, 1996; Popov 1966 [1948]; Sartagov 1996; Vanynto 1996).

Every woman has her own cutting board, which is often passed on to a daughter. The board, placed across the seamstress' lap, is used as a cutting table for doing tiny geometric-pieced skin work, for trimming seam allowances, and for cutting small sections (Oakes and Riewe 1989, 1990, 1996). Stone, wooden, ivory, or bone skin pressers are used to "iron" seams flat and to "press" sole seams to fit the shape of a foot (Vandimova 1996, Vokueva 1996).

The spiritual and cultural importance of sewing tools is evident throughout Siberia and the Far East. Tools are often attributed spirits that provide protection to the user; for example, both Nganasan and Enets consider scrapers and cutting boards to have spirits. Most groups regard scrapers as patrons of the hearth. The Even believe that cutting boards and skin pressers can transport people, including shamans, to different worlds in the universe. Both tools are highly treasured and are offered as sacrifices by many Indigenous peoples (Sem 1993, 1997).

Women, who possess innate powers because of their ability to reproduce, protect the spirits abiding in tools and clothing by not stepping on or over these objects. Because of their spiritual nature, tools may be called upon when a hunter is lost. By throwing a bone scraper into the air and watching how it lands, a woman can determine the location of her husband; the narrow end of the tool will point in the direction of the skins it has prepared, thereby locating the skin clothing and footwear worn by the hunter (Karapetova 1997a; Oakes and Riewe 1996; Popov 1966 [1948], 1984a).

Many groups consider a woman's tools, including scrapers, cutting boards, snow beaters, needles, beads, and sewing bags, to be grave goods, and they are buried with the women who owned them (Balzer 1980, Murashko and Krenke 1996). Many precautions are taken surrounding a person's death. Among the Khanty, for example, anyone related to the deceased is not allowed to use a knife or other sharp object for four days if the deceased person is female or five days if the deceased person is male. This protects the unattached soul of the deceased, which might still be clinging to the living, from being injured (Golovnev 1994). Some footwear and clothing is "tainted with death" and hung in trees near the graveyard to protect the living from coming into contact with the deceased (Oakes and Riewe 1996). Mourners dress up in their best clothing, wearing their scarves backwards, to participate in a remembrance feast for their deceased relatives (Balzer 1980).

Thread

Before beginning to sew, women prepare thread from either animal sinew, plant fibres, or fish skin. Animal sinew is used most commonly. It is strong, does not fray, and absorbs humidity at the same rate as skin clothing, unlike cotton or polyester thread. Sinew is collected from along the spine or the legs of reindeer. Leg sinew is often used for summer skin boots, because it lasts longer when wet. One reindeer provides enough sinew to sew a parka. Materials for thread are collected from other animals, including cows, moose (Sem 1997), birds, seals, walruses, and whales (Hatt 1914 [1969], Rudenko 1961), when reindeer sinew is unavailable. Heavier thread made from braided bowhead whale sinew is used for sewing covers on walrus skin boats (Karapetova 1997b, Vasilevich 1963a).

Sinew is prepared by removing the fat and meat, drying the sinew, rumpling it until it is soft and pliable, then separating it into thin, threadlike strands (Sartagov 1996). Chukchi use a bone comb for splitting dried sinew; the same tool is also used to prepare shoe grass (Hatt 1914 [1969]). Some people store strands of sinew by braiding them together into neat skeins; others spin the sinew first, using a cheek or a thigh. Evenki say they recognize hard-working women by the thigh of their right legging, which is worn smooth from continuously twisting sinew (Hatt 1914 [1969]).

When a woman is ready to sew, she twists the sinew, then dampens it with her lips and threads it into a needle. A knot is tied in one end. Tension is created by taking a stitch in a sewing bag and pulling the thread until it breaks at the knot. Once this has been done, the thread is ready to be used for sewing seams. Yakut rub the end of their sinew with wood pitch so that it can easily pass through the eye of a very tiny needle (Sem 1997).

Nettle or hemp fibres are collected from the taiga in the late fall. The stalks are peeled, and only the outside fibrous coating is kept. This material is carded with a clamshell, then bundled up and stored until winter. Then it is soaked in water until the connective tissue begins to dissolve and buried in snow for several weeks until the fibres start to separate. Fibres are spun into thread and then twisted into two-ply thread, netting, multi-plied yarn, or rope. Nettle thread is less durable than sinew thread but more readily available in some areas of the Far East. Historically, coloured thread was acquired through trade with the Chinese and used by Nivkhi for embroidery (Black 1973, Vanstone 1985).

Thin strips of fish skin are used for thread by seamstresses in the Amur region when reindeer sinew is unavailable. Fish skin thread is made by drying a skin, softening it slightly, then cutting it into one very long continuous narrow piece. It is coiled into a bundle and stored until needed (Hatt 1914 [1969]).

Footwear

The act of sewing footwear has many symbolic meanings. Through sewing boots, an individual gains support and strength for a prosperous life. Several groups, including Evenki, consider footwear to be a main supporting element of life; it is given human properties. Footwear is seen by Even as a critical point of contact between the sacred and the profane. Several ancient stories mention sewing footwear in relationship to shamanistic activities. In one story, an evil spirit enters the shaman's space while the daughter is making a pair of boots. The seamstress expels the evil spirit by sewing, which also has the power to cause the beating of the shaman's drum (Sem 1993, 1997; Vasilevich 1963a; Vasil'evskii 1969; Zakharova 1974).

Construction

The type and amount of material needed to make a pair of boots varies with size, style, and cultural group. Men's thigh-high leg skin boots require about twelve late summer or fall reindeer leg skins; women's boots use ten leg skins. One reindeer body skin is needed to make a pair of thigh-high stockings. Moose leg skins are much wider than those of reindeer, and fewer are required to make footwear.

Toe skins cut from between reindeer hoofs are sewn together into boot sole panels and then smoked. Sometimes pieces of leg skin are placed at the toe and heel. Toe skins provide traction and warmth and are extremely durable (Lapsoy 1996).

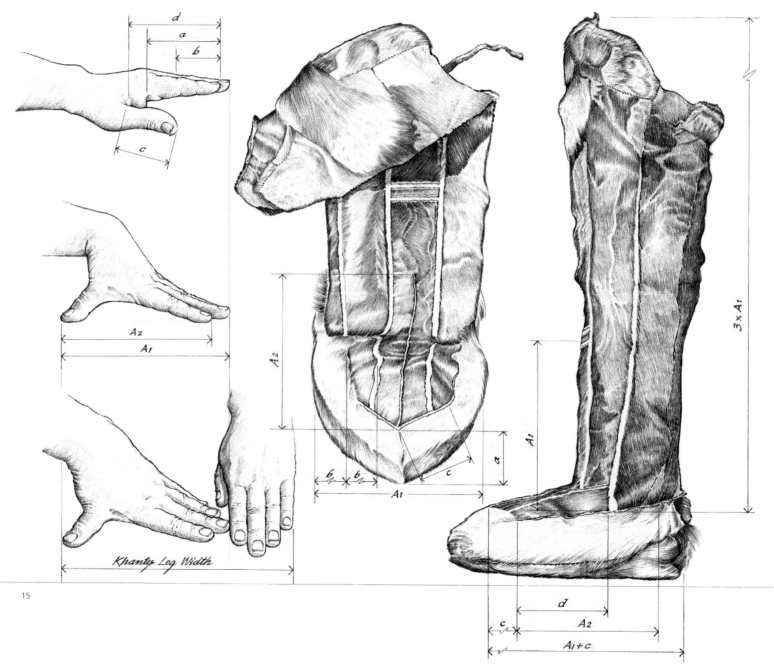

15

FIGURE 15

These patterns for a Nenets man's leg skin boot demonstrate the complex hand measurements used across Siberia. Each cultural group has its own variation. The line lengths marked A_1, A_2, a, b, c, and d correspond to the specific hand positions used as measurements.

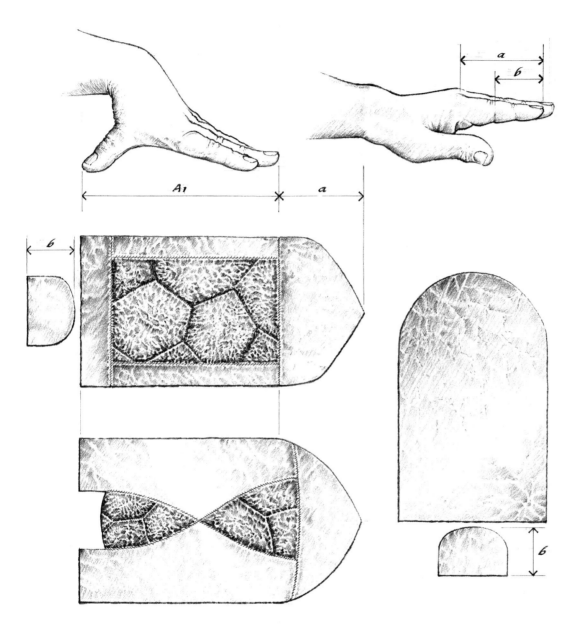

FIGURE 16
Nenets, Khanty, and neighbouring groups use hand measurements for their leg skin boot soles. Line *A1* is one hand measurement long, line *a* is the length of the index finger, and line *b* is two knuckles-length long.

Although it is very difficult, experienced seamstresses draw patterns directly onto skin using eye and hand measurements. Patterns from old boots that have been taken apart, or paper or birch bark patterns, may also be used (Sartagov 1996).

Different parts of the hand serve as a measuring device for patterns. For example, one handspan equals the distance between the tip of the outstretched middle finger and the tip of the thumb. The width of the leg section of a Nenets man's reindeer leg skin boot is one handspan plus the length of a thumb bent from the second knuckle, and the boot is three handspans high. Handspans are also used to measure the decorative inserts on the front leg section, and the sole length is one handspan plus the full length of an index finger (Vanynto 1996). Other groups make similar-looking leg skin boots using slightly different measurements. For example, Khanty leg skin boot patterns are wider than those of Nenets (Komtena 1996, Salender 1996a).

Leg skin boot patterns include a sole, an optional side strip, side gussets (number and length varies), and leg panels. Skin ties are attached at the ankle, knee, and upper edge on some boots. Pieces for the leg section are generally sewn first. The gussets and side strip are added next, and finally the sole is attached. The sole pattern may be either oval, oval with a point at centre front, or oval with a long extension at centre front. The back of the sole is fitted with either a few pleats, a slashed dart, or a separate piece.

On leg skin boots, side strips are often sewn between the sole and leg sections. The width, cut, and silhouette of the side strip varies. For example, Nenets use a wide side strip with an angular inner seam over the toes, creating a relatively low or flat silhouette. A short gusset just above the side strip is added by some seamstresses. This lenticular-shaped gusset usually extends to the beginning of the first or second leg skin panel of the leg section.

The leg section of leg skin boots is cut with a centre back and a centre front panel, plus either one or two side panels. Even, Chukchi, Koryak, and a few other groups only use one side panel; Nenets, Khanty, and others in the west use two. Nganasan are the only group who use three side panels. Some groups sew a skin thong at the top of thigh-high boots so they can be easily tied to a waistband or hung up to dry.

The overcast stitch is common across Siberia and is the only stitch used by Nenets, Enets, Nganasan, Khanty, Mansi, and Evenki. The Even and Chukchi also use running or tunnel stitches on some of their footwear. Yupik use the overcast stitch for most skins, but bird, rodent, and other fragile skins are sewn with a running stitch. An extra thread or strip of grass is placed on one or both sides of the seam and caught in each running stitch to provide more strength to the seam (Hatt 1914 [1969]).

Historically, Siberian Indigenous peoples placed long white hair from reindeer throats into their footwear seams. This evolved into the use of bleached skins, or of skins stained red or black, as welts in boot seams. Today red, and sometimes black, fabric is placed in seams. These welts make boots more watertight and add decorative details. Evenki, Even, and most groups in western Siberia now employ strips of stroud in footwear seams (Kocheschov 1989, Sem 1997, Vasilevich 1963a, Vasil'evskii 1969, Zakharova 1974). Yupik, Chukchi, and Koryak often use either a folded or a flat welt in the sole, and sometimes in the vamp and leg seams. Other common forms of decoration include skin mosaics used by Khanty, Chukchi, Koryak, and Yupik; and hair embroidery used by many groups, especially Evenki, Chukchi, Koryak, and Yupik (Chaussonnet 1988, Hatt 1914 [1969], Turner 1976).

People in the Amur region decorate extensively with fish skin appliqué and silk embroidery. Nivkhi cut out curvilinear designs from coloured pieces of fish skin, then glue these pieces onto fish skin of different colours to create beautiful patterns. Chinese threads, striped or unravelled coloured cloth, fish skin strips dyed blue or red, dyed birch bark, and reindeer, moose, and dog hair are all used by Nivkhi for embroidery thread (Black 1973).

Many Indigenous peoples and Russians in Siberia produce modern boots that combine a leg section made from leg skins with a sole made from mass-produced composite materials. The tops of these boots are usually decorated with simplified beading or skin decoration typical for one's cultural group. Ludmilla Alexandra (1996), a Nenets seamstress from the Tazovskiy collective, described the process:

> I sew the leg sections together and then take them to the shoemaker to get the rubber soles added. Patterns are picked up from the shoemaker and so it's easy to make the leg section fit the correct foot size, but I do it by eye. Leg sections are stiffened with glue before they are attached to the rubber sole. About 3 cm is left on the leg section to make sure there is enough leg material to glue to the correct rubber sole size. The shoemaker only puts the sole on my boots, but can also sew up the leg sections if I wanted.

Maintenance

Skin footwear is essential to herders, hunters, and fishers. Boots are carefully maintained to ensure effective protection against cold and wet conditions, as well as to provide spiritual protection. Plant material such as rotten birch or larch is crumbled into a fine powder and put inside newly constructed footwear, boots worn daily, and boots worn in wet conditions. A boot is shaken for several minutes to enable the wood powder to absorb moisture, then the excess material is poured out. If footwear or other clothing becomes wet it can also be dried slowly over a smudge fire.

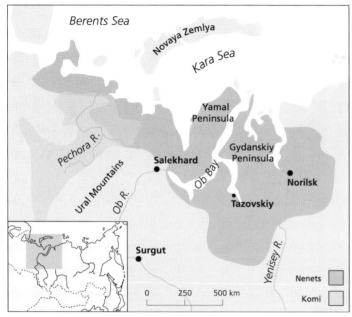

Map 2

THE NENETS OCCUPY the arctic tundra and forest-tundra region that extends from the Berents Sea eastward to the Yenisey River. In part because of their isolated homelands, Nenets managed to retain many aspects of their nomadic way of life well into the twentieth century. Until the 1960s, they were generally left alone as long as they supplied the reindeer and fish products demanded of them under the notorious Soviet Five-Year Plans. During the 1960s and 1970s, however, that isolation was rudely disrupted by the discovery of massive oil and gas fields in west Siberia (Bliss 1990, Clark and Finlay 1977, Forsyth 1992).

Prior to World War II, Komi people occupied the area west of the Ural Mountains. During the Soviet collectivization of the 1950s, Komi moved north into Nenets territory in such large numbers that they were as numerous as Nenets. Nenets also had extensive interactions with their other neighbours, the Khanty, Enets, Nganasan, and Selkup. In the forest-tundra region, Nenets were particularly influenced by Khanty (Forsyth 1992, Konakov 1993).

There are currently approximately 34,000 Nenets, made up of several subgroups speaking different dialects (Vakhtin 1992). In 1996, Nenets reported that there were a few thousand of them still living traditionally as nomadic reindeer herders and fishers. The remaining Nenets, particularly those living west of the Ural Mountains, live sedentary lifestyles in villages and cities (Oakes and Riewe 1996).

Reindeer Herding

Traditional Nenets are first and foremost reindeer herders, often travelling with their herds as much as a thousand kilometres annually on their migrations. Their lives are heavily dependant on reindeer for clothing, shelter, food, and tools. Herders move from one campsite to the next on graceful wooden sleds. During the winter, sleds are pulled by two or three trained reindeer. In summer, as many as five reindeer may be needed to pull the sleds (Levin and Potapov 1956 [1964]).

As do most Aboriginal peoples, Nenets maintain a strict division of labour between the sexes. Riding on lightweight sleds, men select the travel routes for their groups. They look after the reindeer herds, moving them to good grazing lands, protecting them from danger, and keeping them under control

FIGURE 17
Overleaf: Traditionally, all Nenets clothing was made from animal skins. Reindeer skins with dog trim were used most commonly.

MAP 2
Nenets and Komi homelands

FIGURE 18
Nenets travel by harnessing anywhere from two to five reindeer to each of their handmade wooden sleds. More than one hundred sleds are required to move a summer camp of approximately sixty people.

with herding dogs. Men also hunt and trap. Nenets women care for children, make meals, prepare skins, sew clothing, maintain their teepee-like tents (chums), and keep the hearth burning. When a group migrates, the women are also responsible for packing chums, wood stoves, clothing, and household possessions onto heavy freight sleds that are pulled by reindeer in a caravan. A woman always leads these caravans.

In winter, caravans for a group of about sixty Nenets may have twenty to forty sleds; in summer, one hundred or more. Camps are moved every couple of days to prevent reindeer from overgrazing the tundra. Rarely does a group remain at one campsite for as long as a week (Osherenko 1995c). Herders halt their migration only for a few weeks in spring, to separate pregnant cows, and again in autumn to slaughter reindeer. According to Nenets herder and seamstress Larrisa Salender (1996a):

> It gets boring; we're used to moving. As soon as the first snow appears we're happy. Too much time in the chum is uncomfortable. We want to get moving again.

In July and August mosquitoes, warble flies, bot flies, and other parasitic insects attack reindeer unmercifully. The constant movement this creates actually causes the reindeer to lose weight. During the summer months families consolidate their reindeer into herds containing thousands of animals. These amalgamated herds are kept so tightly bunched together that insects often have difficulty settling on individual animals. The herd is always revolving as animals force themselves into the centre.

Women act as veterinarians, providing medical services and keeping careful records of all animals through notches made in ancient wooden counters, or "books." Different marks are used to indicate the numbers of riding reindeer, untamed reindeer, young males, young females, and other categories needed to manage the herd (Forsyth 1992, Hajdú 1968, Salender 1996b).

Seasonal clothing and other supplies are stored at spring and fall caches located in the same general area. In the spring, warm clothing, bedding, and winter sleds are cached and lighter clothing, canvas chums, and smaller summer sleds

19

are collected. Bags of all sizes are used to carry sewing supplies, clothing, and other items from one camp to the next. These bags also allow young women to practise and demonstrate their complex sewing skills.

Fishing

During the period of Soviet collectivization, many Nenets along the lower reaches of the Ob River lost their reindeer herds and were assigned to commercial fishing brigades. Fish-processing plants were built in the administrative centre of Salekhard to handle the catch. Fishing Nenets, camping along the major river systems in west Siberia, are far less mobile than their herding relatives. They depend upon dogs, rather than reindeer, as beasts of burden; three to five large dogs can pull the same weight as one reindeer. Fishing Nenets, however, often own a few reindeer which are tended by their herding relatives. There is considerable co-operative interaction between herders and fishers.

Chums

Nomadic herders as well as fishers live in portable chums. The chum is the centre of life—from birth to death, it is the place of storytelling, lovemaking, food preparation, eating, and sleeping, and it is the beginning and end of all journeys (Osherenko 1995c). Inside the chum the woman is always in charge; on the tundra, it is always the man. The Nenets have a saying:

> Where it is warm, there is always an old woman; where it is cold, there is always an old man.

FIGURE 19
Nenets women provide veterinary services, feed orphaned calves, and offer solace to their reindeer. Reindeer often bond with women herders, communicating through eye contact and body language.

FIGURE 20
Some Nenets depend mainly on fishing. Those who do may have a few reindeer being looked after by herding Nenets.

Chums are covered with canvas in summer and reindeer skins in winter. Winter chums are made with thirty-two supporting poles. However, during the snow-free months it is too difficult to carry so many poles from one campsite to the next, so eight poles are cached and the summer chum is erected with twenty-four. Winter chums last about eight or nine years; when the skin cover is encased in lightweight nylon fabric, a chum can last up to fifteen years. Summer chums last about ten years if they have a waterproof cover (Vanynto 1996).

Chums are about five to seven metres in diameter, with a fire pit in the centre for cooking, smudging, and smoking.

Sleeping areas are collapsible tentlike compartments created with fabric or skin. It takes several specially designed sleds to carry all the components of one chum (Crowell 1988, Faegre 1979, Levin and Potapov 1956 [1964], Vanynto 1996).

Inside the chum, women organize the space into sleeping, visiting, and cooking areas. Women's parkas with the fur up are spread out as blankets along one side of the chum to create an area that is used both as a couch, when occupants are awake, and as a sleeping chamber. Skins, food, and clothes that need to be smoked are hung from or tucked around wooden tent poles.

Babies in cradles are also suspended from the chum poles. Rotten birch bark, a layer of skin and hair from a reindeer's throat, and then hair shed by reindeer calves in spring are placed on top of the sphagnum moss used in baby cradles. When a baby urinates or defecates, all soiled rotten birch, sphagnum moss, and calf hair is discarded. The reindeer throat skin is cleaned, dried, and reused. Older children and adults use shaved pine or willow as toilet paper and pads. Large bags filled with shavings are used as absorbent material.

It takes about fifteen days for women to sew a chum cover. About twenty-five to thirty-five reindeer body skins are

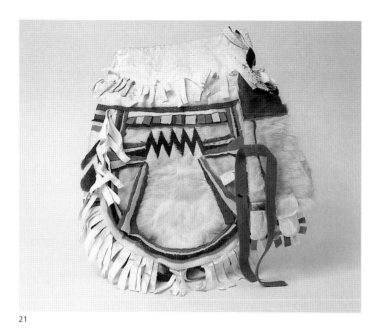

21

needed to make the inner or outer layer of a winter chum, depending on the size of the chum and the size of the skins. When there are not enough reindeer skins, the lower portion is made from canvas or another type of skin. Larrisa Salender (1996a) recalled:

> In the past sturgeon skins were also used for the lower one to one and a half metre of the inside layer. They weren't used all the way to the top because it took too many sturgeon skins. Now three layers of canvas are used. Grandpa told me this. It was long before my time.

Chums made with too few reindeer skins are not warm enough, and children may perish from the cold.

Women receive all or part of a chum for a dowry. Newlyweds without a chum may move into the chum of the groom's parents, or the groom's parents may cut their own chum in two and give one half to the new couple. If the groom has no parents, the bride's family will help the young couple.

Traditional Beliefs

Ancient traditions are still respected by contemporary Nenets herders. Women are extremely powerful. To prevent disturb-

ing the spirits, they do not walk around the back of the chum, nor do they encircle the inside; in this way, their powers are stopped from coming between the hearth and a sacred sled positioned off in the distance. This sacred sled is distinguished by its uneven number of upright supports. To show respect, Nenets set food on the sled for the spirits (Salender 1996a, 1996b; Vanynto 1996). Occasionally the sacred sled is placed up against the back of the chum, and herders use the space surrounding it to communicate with spirits and to ask for protection from illness, starvation, or dangerous situations. Reindeer antlers are cached in sacred places in order to strengthen communication with the spirits, bringing good health to the reindeer and herders (Levin and Potapov 1956 [1964]).

Women must enter and exit chums only through the doorway, but men may crawl out under the sides if that is the fastest way to the herd. Women cannot stand on bedding or step over tools left lying on the ground.

It is reported that in the eighteenth and nineteenth centuries Nenets women had a very low status in their society. This was the case in all Samoyed groups, including Selkup, Enets, and Nganasan. Women were considered so "unclean" that they were not allowed to give birth in the family dwelling. Consequently, babies were often born on sleds during migration or in an unheated temporary shelter (Krupnik 1985).

Traditionally, families selected husbands for girls when they were about six or seven years old; today who she marries is a young woman's own decision. The importance of skin preparation and sewing skills is demonstrated in both the bride price (the payment made by the groom) and the dowry. If a bride does not know how to make footwear, her family and friends provide her with skin boots for her dowry, and once she is married her family will continue to supply her with skins until she learns how to prepare them herself. Today, even women who are twenty years old may not be able to prepare skins and make skin boots; in the past, fifteen-year-old women were experts at these tasks. When a bride has no skin-sewing talents, her father is obliged to ask for fewer reindeer as the bride price. It is important for a young man to have well-developed herding skills if he wants to marry a talented woman. Grooms from wealthy herding families are able to pay higher prices to secure marriage with the woman they choose.

Dolls are one of the numerous items women pack from camp to camp. They serve several purposes: to recall the dead, as effigies; to protect the home; and to act as toys for children. Remembrance dolls are placed in the sitting area of the chum, given food and drink, and included in the conversation for four or five years after a person's death, depending on whether the deceased was a woman or a man. Holes are cut in the footwear of both the corpse and the remembrance doll to allow the soul to escape.

Protective dolls are placed at the entrance of the chum to keep out evil spirits. These dolls also participate in sacred sled feasts and are passed on from one generation to the next (Salender 1996a). Children's play dolls are either homemade from bits of fur and fabric, without hands and faces, or mass-produced, with the faces and hands removed. Play dolls are not permitted to have faces or hands because evil spirits might enter them and harm the children. Decorative details on the dolls reflect those used in Nenets clothing and footwear.

Traditional Clothing

Herding and fishing Nenets make the same type of clothing, and children are generally dressed as miniature adults. In the past, Nenets usually wore reindeer skin clothing with a trim of seal or other skins added at the neck and hemline. Seal skin is rarely used today, although occasionally it is made into men's hats or boots with rubber soles. Sturgeon skins were also used for men's parkas long ago (Levin and Potapov 1956 [1964], Salender 1996b). Fabric as well as skin clothing is worn by contemporary Nenets (Oakes and Riewe 1996).

Today, Nenets wear either a pull-over parka or a parka with an open front (Hajdú 1968, Mitlyanskaya 1983). The ancient open-front style, which has a neck decorated with arctic hare, is worn by both men and women. The pull-over, a more recent style used by Nenets men, is almost identical to the parka worn by Khanty (Oakes and Riewe 1996).

Contemporary Nenets herders continue to wear two layers of reindeer skin clothing throughout the winter. Sometimes a

FIGURE 21
Sewing supplies are stored by Nenets in reindeer skin bags, such as the one shown here. Brightly coloured items like these bags are turned upside down during mourning so that the designs cannot be seen. REM 8223.22

FIGURE 22
Nenets herders are mobile, living in chums made of skin or fabric.

22

23

24

FIGURE 23 & 24

Women use the best-quality reindeer skins for their festive apparel.
This traditional coat features several
horizontal panels of zigzag designs.
The many rows of light-coloured
skins are typical for Nenets. A large
brass belt buckle and narrow woven
tie are worn over this coat outdoors. REM 693.17 (coat), REM 8223.2
(hat), REM 8762.20274 (belt)

third parka is pulled over the other two. Parkas are worn with skin pants which have a distinct cut (Hatt 1914 [1969], Mytnie 1992).

Each year reindeer are killed for new winter clothing. If there are sufficient animals, everyone gets a new ensemble. If not, people with parkas and boots still in good condition wear them for another year. Winter clothing is worn for about four or five winters, then used for another ten to fifteen years as summer wear (Salender 1996a, Vanynto 1996). Well-worn parkas and footwear are suitable for cool summer days, and very old clothing is worn in hot summer weather. Older parkas and footwear are also passed on to younger Nenets or kept as spare clothing in case someone gets wet.

A woman's parka is often decorated on the lower panel, centre front, sleeves, and shoulders with narrow strips of light- and dark-haired skins, pieces of fabric (red and yellow are preferred), and complex geometric figures. The lower panel is always dark brown; the upper section can be dark brown or white. Bells are sewn to children's parka sleeves so that they can be easily found and to ward off evil spirits. Milya Salender (1996c), a seamstress and herder who travels with the herd year-round, explained:

> It depends on what skins you have to work with, whether or not someone makes a dressy parka with lots of decoration. If the parka is only going to be used for sleeping then there is no need to decorate it. Parkas are used like a blanket. People sleep out on the snow wearing skin clothing. You pull your hands inside the parka, wrap them around your body and pull the second parka over top as it has a hood with fur to the inside. Small ribbons are sewn to the parka so snow does not stick to the sides and back. The sleeves are left without ribbons because it is less likely snow will stick to one's arms as they are almost always moving.

Women and men wear hats for warmth in winter and to protect themselves from biting insects in summer. Elena Susoi (1996) was a Nenets herder and is now an author and historian. She explained that the whole tundra is depicted symbolically in Nenets hats.

> The rounded crown shape depicts man as the owner and protector of animals. The zigzag decoration around the hem represents

many chums. We believe that by placing multiple chum symbols on our clothing many Nenets families will be able to thrive. It is expected that each chum will have a Nenets family to care for the fire and family.

Hats are made from the reindeer forehead skins and trimmed with long fox tails. The reindeer eyes are sewn shut with a piece of red fabric placed in the seam. This prevents the reindeer spirit from finding its way home and leading the person wearing the hat into harm. It also symbolizes that the true "host" of the land is Nenets; animals can only communicate non-verbally. Reindeer communicate with their eyes; they express fear, need for protection, need for company and other concepts. Herders read the eyes of reindeer in order to better meet their needs . . .

Only women use hats with tassels. The copper pieces are usually purchased from Nalinsk and help keep the hat from blowing off. I have seen these pieces on illustrations of Enets hats dated 1725. Salekhard had large fairs so Nenets and Enets probably came here to trade for the copper. The tassels serve a decorative and medicinal function. When they touch each other they make a pleasant sound similar to wind chimes. When Nenets women feel depressed or alone, and the wolves are howling in all directions, the sounds of copper clinking are comforting and lift up our spirits.

Footwear

Footwear is designed to provide warmth and protection; as Larrisa Salender (1996a) emphasized: "Without legs, you can't do anything; if your feet are freezing, you can't work." In addition, the materials and decorative details used in footwear symbolize gender, economic status, marital status, special events, and other cultural identifiers used by Nenets. Some of these features are also seen in boots made by Khanty and other neighbouring groups.

Boots made from white-haired reindeer skins are considered more valuable than boots made from brown-haired skins, and they communicate one's economic status. Only individuals with large herds of reindeer can afford to kill enough animals to allow a seamstress to select the skins she wishes to use. Seamstresses prefer dark brown skins for everyday winter boots unless they have lots of white skins. Fancy, elaborately decorated footwear is also more quickly converted into daily wear by families with larger herds (Lapsoy 1996).

25

FIGURE 25
Throughout western Siberia,
women's leg skin boots
(*at right*) have a triangular piece of
skin placed at the front of the leg
near the ankle. Men's boots (*at left*)
have a horizontal bar of decoration
placed just below the knee. *Left:*
BSM P96.0172.a *Right:* BSM P96.0218.a

The economic status of a deceased person, as well as
respect for the spirits of the underworld, is shown by burying
the person in a pair of beautifully made boots. All the boots of
the deceased are packed into a boot bag and placed with the
corpse. It is desirable to have lots of boots in mint condition
to show one's economic success as a herder (Laposoy, 1996).

Leg Skin Boots

Winter boots are made from the leg skins of reindeer killed in
early fall, because the fur is thicker then. Summer leg skin
boots are made from reindeer killed in early summer, when
the hair is short and fine. These thigh-high boots continue to
be worn by males and females of all ages. The colour and
combination of skins, the number of side strips and gussets,
and the amount of decoration vary, as leg skin boots are created for different purposes.

Boots worn in summer were often made originally for winter. Skin boots are warmer, lighter, and feel better than store-
bought boots all year round (Lapsoy 1996). Nenets women
along the Yenisey River and in the forested regions also wear
an Evenki boot style made from dehaired reindeer skin
(Vasilevich 1963a).

The leg sections of leg skin boots are cut slanted at the top,
to allow extra ease for walking. A skin thong sewn to the top
of the leg at centre front is tied directly to a waist belt or
looped around a belt and tied to a thong attached to the top
of a stocking. The leg section may have four, five, six, or seven
panels of leg skins. Men's and boys' boots are made with an
even number of panels; women's and girls' have an odd number, because an extra panel tapering to a triangular point is
added to the centre front. Boots made with four or five panels
are cut from reindeer leg skins larger than those used for six-
or seven-panelled boots.

Leg sections are sewn to the sole either directly, with a side
strip, or with a side strip and gusset. Narrow red, yellow, and
green fabric welts are sewn into the seams of the front panels,
side strip, gusset, and soles (Vasilevich 1963a). Soles are cut
with a rounded toe that comes to a slight point on some
boots and a straight centre back seam. Many boots have an
extra piece sewn at the back (Oakes and Riewe 1996). Men's
boot soles are cut either from forehead skins, a combination
of leg and toe skins, or leg skins alone. Women's boot soles

are cut only from leg or toe skins; because women spend most of their time near the hearth, their boots do not require the extra insulation provided by forehead skin (Karapetova 1997b).

Leg skin boots are decorated in different ways for men and women. Boots worn by females have an inverted triangular inset at the base of the front of the leg. The triangle represents a chum, and a long straight strip of white fur at the apex of the triangle represents smoke rising from the chum (Lapsoy 1996, Salender 1996a, Susoi 1994, Vanynto 1996). The design symbolizes women's important role in caring for the chum, fire, and family. The front and side panel seams on women's boots are often decorated with long, narrow, straight strips of light- and dark-coloured skins, which represent chum poles and other household items that women cannot step over, nonverbally communicating unwritten rules that are reinforced repeatedly. Another explanation for these shapes is presented in a forest Nenets riddle: "The old man has a flat nose [horizontal stripes]; the old woman has a sharp nose [triangular inset]" (Karapetova 1997b).

Boots worn by males have a series of narrow, straight strips placed horizontally just below the knee. This horizontal band may be made from fabric welts, skins of contrasting colours, or a combination of skins and fabric. A red fabric welt is inserted into the centre front seam extending from the toes up to the lower shin. The shin-high vamp resembles a Nenets man's ladle-shaped snow beater (Lapsoy 1996, Salender 1996a, Susoi 1994, Vanynto 1996). The long narrow strips of contrasting coloured lines on each side of the centre front panel represent reindeer-harness reins and sled runners, bringing to mind the two most important aspects of a Nenets man's life: reindeer and travelling (Susoi 1994, 1996).

Slight differences between leg skin boot decorations identify specific groups of Nenets. For example, Nenets living along the Taz River use broader strips set parallel to each other on the centre front panel of women's boots, while neighbouring groups use narrower strips tapering slightly from the shin to the ankle (BSM P88.0083, NMF 4899.19/20). Differences and similarities in decorative designs also indicate interaction between Nenets and Enets, Khanty, Dolgan, Evenki, and other neighbouring groups (Vasilevich 1963a). For example, according to Ludmilla Alexandra (1996):

Khanty place the triangular decorative piece higher on women's boots than Nenets do; they also put more fabric or skin strips in the seams and fabric strips are often wider …

Khanty add more geometric ornamentation while Nenets use narrower and greater numbers of linear strips … Khanty have a narrower wedge-shaped piece placed above the side strip. The side strip placed between the sole and leg section of boots is always white on Khanty boots … Both groups use reindeer toes for the sole or part of the sole.

Everyday and Special Occasion Boots

Boots worn for everyday purposes are made from light- and dark-haired reindeer skins. Women's boots usually have a dark-haired skin for the centre front panel, which ends in a triangle at the lower edge. Light-haired skins are placed on each side to create the full front panel. Dark- and light-haired skins are alternated for the side and back panels. Occasionally just dark-haired skins are used (BSM P96.0215.ab, P96.0218.ab; REM 6630.3/1,2). Leg sections for men's and boys' boots are generally cut from dark-haired leg skins. Occasionally alternating light- and dark-haired panels (BSM P96.0235.ab, P96.0187.ab; MVB IVA 2150, IVA 310) or just light-haired panels (EMO 12.440, 45.031; REM 8223.11/1,2) are used. The latter practice is especially common for one group of Nenets, whose name reflects their preference for light-haired boots (Karapetova 1997b). The leg section on both male and female everyday boots, as well as that on festive occasion footwear, is sewn to a gusset extending back to the side or back panel and to a side strip encircling the foot. Side strips are cut from light-haired skins. Soles are made with or without reindeer toe skins. Red fabric welts are placed in many of the boot seams. These boots are used for light work, visiting, and other daily activities (BSM P96.0216.ab, P96.0222.ab, P96.0204.ab; DL 3169; EMO 2580).

Elaborately decorated footwear is worn to spring and fall reindeer festivals, fairs, and other special occasions (Karapetova 1997b). Once these boots begin to look worn, they are used for everyday wear. The main differences between footwear designed specifically for festive wear and styles used primarily for every day are the number of decorative strips and the skin quality. Festive footwear is made from the best skins, which have been carefully selected for richness in colour, lustre, hair density, and length. Festive women's

FIGURE 26
One distinct decorative style of Nenets men's leg skin boots has several extra rows of thin straight lines inserted above the knee. These boots are used for special occasions or for everyday wear by herders. *Left:* BSM P96.0205.ab *Right:* BSM P96.0217.a-d

FIGURE 27
These boots, made by a Nenets seamstress, use interlocking designs introduced by Khanty. Symbols representing "Nenets heads" and "women's paddle handles" appear on the side panels. REM 7469.1/1,2

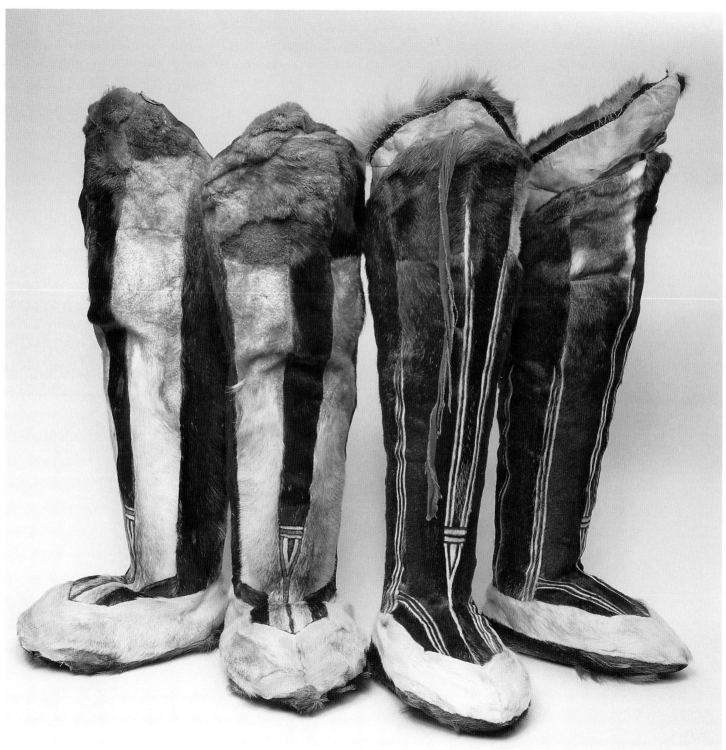

28

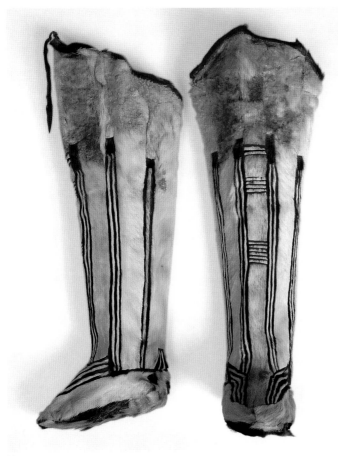

29

FIGURE 28
Women add thin, straight strips of light- or dark-haired skins and strips of fabric to their special-occasion boots (*right*). Less decorated boots are for everyday wear (*left*). *Left:* BSM P96.0218.a-d *Right:* BSM P96.222.ab

FIGURE 29
The skill of a seamstress is demonstrated by the number of thin, straight decorative lines she is able to fit on the footwear she makes. These boots have up to seven lines of contrasting skins. REM 8223.11/1,2

FIGURE 30
In one style of Nenets summer boots, the vamp and lower portion of the leg are stained with powdered ochre; red or orange is preferred. The boot is smoked so that it can be used in wet conditions. *Left:* BSM P96.0213.a *Right:* BSM P96.0223.a

30

boots are decorated with between two and seven straight, narrow strips of dark- and light-haired skins sewn on each side of the front panel, triangle, and side gussets (BSM P88.0083, P84.0143; EMO 5916, 45.023; MVB IVA 319). Festive male boots are decorated with straight, narrow strips of dark- and light-haired skins sewn to each side of the front panel, the side panel, and the gusset, and at the knee. Light- and dark-haired skins are inserted above the standard horizontal bar used on men's boots, creating additional vertical (BSM P96.0235.ab, P96.0205.ab, P96.0217.a-d, P96.0212.ab, P96.0187.ab, P96.0172.ab; EMO 5915, 45.025, 45.027; MVB IVA 2150, IVA 329; REM 1503.11/1,2), inverted V (EMO 45.030; MVB IVA 310, IVA 3075), and horizontal designs (EMO 45.031, 2581; MVB IVA 2274, 4673, 4674). Occasionally, the back panel of men's boots is also decorated with an oval inset placed just below the calf. Another square-shaped inset is placed above the heel. Both are accented with red fabric welts (BSM P96.0217.a-d).

Another style of festive footwear for men and women is made by following the pattern described above and decorating it with complex geometric or zigzag designs (BSM P96.0173.ab, P88.0084, P84.0142; MVB IVA 2193, 3075; REM 7469.1/1,2). This technique was borrowed from the Khanty and is relatively new to Nenets.

Work Boots and Over Boots

Plain skins are used to make functional but undecorated footwear for everyday tasks. Work boots and over boots have leg sections composed of two (for children), four (five for women), or six (seven for women) panels cut from dark brown or grey-brown leg skins. Men's, boys', and girls' work boots are occasionally made without side strips, but most work boots have a broad side strip cut from dark-haired skins, or from white-haired skins when available. When gussets are included, these strips extend to either the side panel or the back panel. Work boots are usually sewn with a red fabric welt in the following seams: centre front, gusset front panel, side strip gusset, and centre back side strip (BSM P96.0234.ab, P96.0224.ab).

Some men's and boys' work boots are decorated just below the knee with three horizontal strips of skin, alternating dark- and light-haired skins with a red fabric welt in each seam (BSM P96.0202.ab, P96.0219.ab, P96.0236a-d; NMF VK4899.19,

VK4934.160), or a band of colour created by several rows of fabric (DL 6.90.44). Women's and girls' work boots are decorated with a triangular inset placed lower on the leg (BSM P96.0215.ab).

Leg skin over boots are cut slightly wider than work boots. White-haired skins are generally not used to make these boots, which are left undecorated save for a single strip of red fabric sewn just below the knee on some men's over boots. Over boots are worn by children on top of their work boots in extremely cold weather (BSM P96.0225.a-d). They are also used by herders sleeping outside with their herds in cold weather.

A second over boot style is made from fall reindeer body skins with the fur to the outside (EMO 45.033). The sole is unpleated and the knee-high leg section has a front, side left, and side right panel with a centre back seam. The upper edge is cut straight across and is finished with a narrow strip of skin. The leg section is sewn directly to the sole without a side strip or gusset. This warm footwear is worn over winter boots in extremely cold weather (Lapsoy 1996).

A third style is made with a sole, double vamp, and leg section (NMF VK4934.11). The unpleated sole and vamp are cut from fall leg skins. The vamp encircles the foot and extends up the leg past the ankle. Sometimes a second, triangular-shaped vamp is placed at the centre front of this vamp. A thigh-high tubular leg section is then sewn to the upper edge. The second vamp and leg section are cut from wool fabric. Neighbouring groups use a similar style, usually made with only one vamp.

Dehaired Skin Summer Boots

One waterproof summer boot style is made with a pleated sole, a triangular vamp, and a leg section (BSM P96.0188.ab, P96.0213.ab, P96.0223.ab; MVB IVA 3455; NMF VK4899.17). The sole is cut from reindeer body or forehead skin with the fur to the outside. The hair around the seam allowance and around the area of the sole to be pleated is shaved. The sole is then pleated using accordion pleats secured with three rows of stitches. Historically, several holes were made in the sole to allow water to run out easily. The vamp is made from smoked dehaired or haired skins. Haired skins are used with the hair to the inside (BSM P96.0186.abc). The extremely long, pointed seam extends past the shin almost to the knee.

Sometimes the vamp seam is accented with a fabric welt, a stain of another colour traced around the seam, or a few skin tassels at the peak. Thigh-high leg sections, cut from the same material as that used for the vamp, have a centre back seam. The upper edge is cut on a slant and trimmed with a narrow piece of skin stained with ochre or a narrow strip of fabric (Lapsoy 1996). The use of a slanted cut was passed down to Nenets by early ancestors from the Sayan Plateau who rode horses before moving north to herd reindeer. The slant cut is actually more useful on horseback than when riding sleds on the tundra (Vasilevich 1963a).

Powdered ochre is rubbed into the vamp and lower leg of the boot to improve the waterproof qualities of the smoked skins. Ochre also symbolizes blood and acts to communicate with animal spirits in such a way that they offer their support to hunters (Lapsoy 1996). Two or three loops are sewn into the vamp-sole seam. A strip of dehaired, ochre-stained skin is used for a thong which is threaded through these loops (Karapetova 1997b). A variation of this style is made by soaking the boot in pine pitch to produce an even more water-repellent skin, similar to that used by Khanty.

Today, these waterproof boots are rarely used. Rubber boots are worn even though they are uncomfortable and difficult to keep dry. Rubber boots are sometimes made a little more comfortable by buying them extra large and wearing them with reindeer fur stockings (Salender 1996b).

Seal Skin Boots

In the past, seal skin was used for summer footwear (Hatt 1914 [1969]). Seal skin boots are made with a leg section (centre back seam), a pointed vamp, and a sole that is either flat and unpleated or coarsely pleated. Enets used an identical seal skin boot style (Vasilevich 1963a). Today, seal skin footwear is rarely used by Nenets, except in commercial rubber-soled boots known as "boorky." Felt is used to stiffen the leg section of these boots.

Shamans' Boots

A rare example of a Nenets shaman's footwear, in the collection of the Russian Museum of Ethnography, has a dehaired, smoked reindeer skin foot decorated with metal pieces and red fabric. The red cloth, symbolizing veins, and the metal, placed at the kneecap, shin, and foot, provide the shaman with protection from evil spirits (Karapetova 1997b).

Boot Ties

Ties or thongs are sewn to the upper edge of thigh-high Nenets footwear and used to attach the boot leg to a belt, a stocking, or loops sewn onto pants.

Today, almost all Nenets men and boys also keep their boots in position by wearing a hand-woven tie just below the knee. This tradition was acquired from Komi and non-Indigenous Russians. Traditionally, tundra Nenets did not use ties below the knee; forest Nenets used skin thongs. Boot ties are secured so that the tassels are even and symmetrical. Ties last for years, but they are easily lost. Because seamstresses have limited supplies of wool—and replacement ties are time-consuming to weave—they take extra precautions to prevent men from losing their boot ties. Ludmilla Alexandra (1996) shared the following riddle commonly spoken among Nenets: "She counts it in the morning and she counts it in the evening. What is it? Boot ties!" Once or twice a year, ties are washed in cold soapy water, rinsed, then dried. The tassels are combed when they are almost dry to make them fluffy. Dry boot ties are pressed flat and straight with a damp cloth and iron. Wearing the ties also flattens and straightens them out.

Slippers

An ankle-high outer slipper is made from leg skins or seal skins (NMF VK2631.10). Sometimes the slipper is soaked in pitch and then worn over a leg skin boot during damp weather. The leg and vamp are cut in one piece, with a casing and drawstring sewn to the upper edge on some slippers. The sole can be either pleated or unpleated. Side strips are omitted (Karapetova 1997b, Vasilevich 1963a).

Stockings

Reindeer body skin stockings are worn with winter boots. Stockings feature a slightly pleated sole, a vamp covering the toes or encircling the foot, and a leg section with a centre back seam. The seams are erratic, as skins are pieced together. The top of the leg is cut on a slant, and one skin thong is sewn to each stocking (BSM 11; MVB IVA 103; NMF VK4899.18, VK4899.23, VK4816.75). Ties are looped over a waist belt and tied to boot thongs. Once stockings are sewn, they are hung inside a chum until they are smoked. Some stockings are cut from smoked, haired skins.

Summary

Nenets wear mainly reindeer leg skin boots with flat, unpleated soles cut with a slight point at centre front. Reindeer toe skins are often used for part of the sole. Leg skin boots are usually made with a side strip that extends around the foot, plus a gusset that extends back to the side or back panel. The leg section is thigh-high and usually made with four, five, or six leg skin panels. Women's boots have an extra panel inserted at centre front. The leg is cut on a slant across the top and tied to a waistband or belt with straps. Ankle straps are not used on leg skin boots. Leg skin boots are worn with grass insoles and skin stockings. They are decorated with light- and dark-haired strips of skin, as well as with red, yellow, and green fabric welts in the seams. Women's boots are decorated with a triangular shape at the lower shin, men's boots with horizontal bands sewn just below the knee. Some boots are made with alternating panels of light- and dark-haired skins, and white-haired side strips. Nenets who are fishing and hunting sea mammals very occasionally use seal skin footwear with a pleated or unpleated sole. The vamp either encircles the foot or is cut with a triangular upper seam. Boots made from dehaired reindeer skin are used by Nenets living near the Yenisey River. The sole is pleated, the vamp extends up to the upper shin, and the leg section extends up to the thigh. This boot style has an ankle strap and a waistband strap. Nenets designs are similar to Khanty, Selkup, Komi, Ket, Mansi, and Enets designs; however, subtle differences are evident in distinct decorative details, sole design, leg section design, and gender-specific decoration.

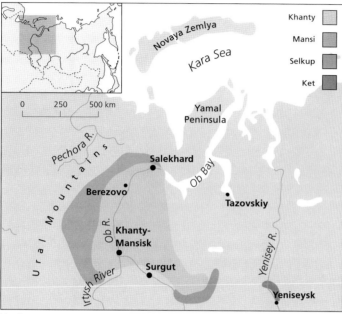

CHAPTER 2

Map 3

MANSI, KHANTY, SELKUP, and Ket occupy the taiga of western Siberia. The Mansi range extends from the Ural Mountains eastward towards the Ob River. Khanty live east of the Mansi along the Ob River, and Selkup and Ket occupy the region east of that. Although the Mansi, Khanty, Selkup, and Ket languages differ to such a degree that it is difficult for people to communicate, their economy, culture, and clothing are very similar (Prokofyeva 1964).

Today, there are roughly 22,000 Khanty, 8,000 Mansi, 3,500 Selkup, and 1,000 Ket (Vakhtin 1992). The majority of these people live sedentary agricultural lifestyles in small towns and villages, although there are still a few hundred people in the northern and eastern region living as hunters, fishers, and semi-nomadic herders with small bands of reindeer (Lukena 1979b, Muldanova n.d.).

Historically, Khanty and Mansi families inhabited neighbouring river valleys. Blood vengeance and plundering created conflicts that resulted in sporadic warfare, so both groups developed elaborate protective ensembles, including longbows, arrows, spears, coats of mail, and hand-forged iron helmets. Chiefs demonstrated their power and wealth with silver ornaments and lavish use of sable, fox, and other furs (Forsyth 1992).

Despite this long-standing animosity, tradition requires the Khanty and Mansi to intermarry. In the past, a bride price was paid in furs, clothing, utensils, and livestock, often anywhere from ten to two hundred head of reindeer or horses (Hajdú 1968). It was culturally acceptable for a man to take as many wives as he could pay for (Bakhrushin 1935).

Traditionally, Khanty, Mansi, and Selkup were seminomadic, living in log cabins covered with earth in winter and in birch bark chums in summer. Skis were the primary means of transportation in winter, and canoes (dugout or birch bark) were used after the ice broke up (Forsyth 1992, Prokofyeva 1964). These modes of transportation are still used today, along with snowmobiles, motor boats, and occasionally helicopters. Contemporary log cabins are insulated with moss, and chum covers are made of canvas and plastic tarps. Relatively small herds of reindeer (ten to one hundred animals) are kept close to camp. Log barns contain smudge fires in the summer, protect reindeer from mosquitoes, and

FIGURE 31
Overleaf: Michael Sartagov, a Khanty herder, still travels by dugout canoe while fishing, hunting, and trapping.

MAP 3
Khanty, Mansi, Selkup, and Ket homelands

FIGURE 32
Three layers of birch bark are used to make a waterproof cover for sleds. Layers are crisscrossed and then basted together with sinew or strips of roots.

keep reindeer from wandering away (Oakes and Riewe 1996).

Traditional Beliefs

Fish, birds, and mammals are the mainstay of Khanty, Mansi, Selkup, and Ket diets. These animals have spirits that willingly give themselves up to hunters if respect is shown. Fish is boiled, dried, or smoked; dried fish is also used to lure reindeer back to camp during the fall mating season. The kidneys, liver, marrow, eyes, and other tender parts of animals are still eaten raw, following ancient traditions. Berries, mushrooms, and wild onions are collected and supplemented with bread baked in outdoor ovens (Levin and Potapov 1956 [1964], Oakes and Riewe 1996). Tatyana Seraskovoi (1996), a Khanty seamstress from Katawoosh, a small village on the Ob River, remembered:

Seventeen barrels of berries were stored each year when I was growing up. We stored fish in barrels of fish oil. Collected cedar seeds, ate them dry, and got oil from the seeds. The seeds were eaten when someone felt down in the winter. We also soaked empty pine cones in vodka and put it on sore joints and used it for a cold. A medicinal tea used for liver and intestine ailments is made from hardened birch sap collected from a wound of the birch tree.

Bears often enter camps in the taiga, ransacking food caches and dwellings. The bear is an animal of great significance for the peoples of this region, and feasts and games are held when a bear is killed. Plays are staged, stories are told, and many bear songs are sung. Following the ancient custom of associating the number four with females and five with males, a bear feast lasts four days for a female bear, five days

32

33

for a male bear, and two or three days for a cub of either sex. The head of a dead bear is placed in a position of prominence inside the cabin of the person who killed it. Bones are stored safely outside on top of a tall, sacred cache (Forsyth 1992, Golovnev 1994, Hallowell 1926, Levin and Potapov 1956 [1964], Oakes and Riewe 1996).

In the past, some Selkup kept trained bear cubs in captivity for use in hunting. While a wild bear was occupied fighting a tame bear, it would be killed by the hunter (Prokofyeva 1964).

Khanty and Mansi spiritual values and beliefs are often embodied in the form of dolls. Dolls are decorated with multicoloured strips sewn to the hem. Like Nenets, Khanty and Mansi have play dolls, spiritual dolls, remembering-the-dead dolls, and guardian dolls to keep the chum safe. Dolls used for child's play are made without a face, hands, or feet;

this protects children from being hurt by evil spirits. Olga Khudyakova (1996), now chief curator of the Khanty-Mansisk Museum of Regional Studies, remembers her father breaking off the hands and feet of Russian dolls she got as a girl.

Dolls created to commemorate the dead are made by shamans or other spiritual leaders from willow branches, which symbolize the tree of life and have mystical powers. Hair from the deceased is bound to the doll, and arms and a face are added. When the official mourner wants to remember the deceased, the appropriate doll is brought out and nothing is eaten by the mourner until it is put away again. The correct use of dolls is critical for effective communication with under-world spirits that protect individuals and families from starvation and harm (Balzer 1980, Oakes and Riewe 1996).

In the past, Khanty erected effigy poles around their vil-lages to protect themselves from evil spirits. Otherwise these

34

FIGURE 33

The Khanty man on the left wears a birch bark mask at a bear ceremony, while the man on the right plays a stringed instrument. The number of songs performed at a bear feast is recorded by notching a special counting stick; as many as seven hundred songs have been counted at one feast. REM 1705.104

FIGURE 34

Khanty herder Vaselie Pokaychev has travelled by reindeer-drawn sleds for his whole life. During the summer, sleds must cross over shallow lakes, bogs, and muskeg.

35

bone was used to puncture the skin, and geometric designs were created by placing soot in the punctures (Forsyth 1992). Braids are another method of ensuring that the spirits are appeased; women continue to wear their hair in two long braids, with beads and strips of colourful fabric woven into and between the plaits. Hair is left unbraided for four days (for a female) or five days (for a male) after a family member dies. Then it is braided but worn on the chest rather than down the back for an additional four or five months (Golovnev 1994, Oakes and Riewe 1996).

To show respect for each other and themselves, men and women turn away from each other when getting dressed, even when pulling clothing over other layers of clothing. It is considered immodest for women to reveal their bare feet to men. Boot straps on thigh-high boots are tied to an inner belt worn around the waist as a sign of modesty and tidiness (Pokaychev 1996).

Burial Practices

For Khanty and Mansi, footwear is an important medium for communicating with and protecting themselves from the spirits of the underworld. Khanty and some other Siberian Indigenous peoples believe that if a person enters the afterworld wearing his or her old footwear, that person will be recognized and welcomed by those who have died before (Seraskovoi 1996).

The number of boots a man possesses is an indication of the love he has received from his mother and his wife; the more boots he has, the better he was loved. If a person is interred with only a few pairs of boots, people say that the person was poor and struggled all his or her life.

Some people construct a pair of boots for burial purposes. If these boots are made in advance, they are designed to be wider than normal, in case the corpse is bloated. The deceased's best clothing is tied around his or her arms and legs using a special "knot of the dead." A white cloth or best shawl is sometimes decorated with beads in the form of eyes, nose, mouth, and ears before it is placed over the body (Balzer 1980). This tradition has evolved from the use of reindeer skin masks with buttons and disks placed by the eyes, ears, and nose (Chernetsov 1963).

The deceased is also buried with a set of twelve leg skins,

spirits, which were sometimes thought to emanate from a recently deceased clan member, might follow mourners from the grave site back to the village.

Bracket fungi from birch trees are burned in a smudge to purge an area of illness and evil spirits. A piece of otter penis bone is added to this smudge when it is used to cleanse an area after a woman menstruates or gives birth. Women stay on the "female" side of the chum, and men protect themselves from harm by avoiding women's clothing and footwear stored in the chum. Hunters cleanse their tools and clothing by holding them over a boiling pot of moss. These traditions prevent animals from being offended by the spiritual powers of women and consequently refusing to give up their own spirits to hunters (Balzer 1981, Oakes and Riewe 1996).

In the past, tattoos were employed both to cure illness and as a form of decoration by Khanty and Mansi. A pike's jaw-

FIGURE 35
Khanty families wear intricately decorated reindeer skin winter clothing. This woman's festive fur coat was worn during the 1960s in the Yamal-Nenets region. It is made with a thick inner and outer layer of reindeer skin, and decorated with a rabbit ear design on the sleeves. REM 7358.31

FIGURE 36
Khanty and Mansi seamstresses decorate dresses, footwear, stockings, and chest ornaments with intricate geometric shapes. This cross-stitched nettle dress, along with these crocheted stockings and beaded slippers, was worn by Khanty from the Tobolsk Province in the late nineteenth or early twentieth century. REM 1711.416 (*slippers*), REM 7358.26 (*stockings*), REM 8762-17570 (*dress*), REM 3944.150 (*necklace*), REM 3950-63 (*kerchief*)

37

two sole skins, and sinew placed in a bag positioned under the head, so that he or she can make new boots in the afterworld. Male bodies are placed on five reindeer skins, females on four skins (Salender 1996a). Friends and relatives watch to make sure that all of the deceased person's possessions are placed in the grave (Oakes and Riewe 1996).

Traditional Clothing

Clothing styles traditionally varied slightly depending on available materials, location, and the occasion for which they were intended. Vaselie Pokaychev (1996), a traditional Khanty herder, explained:

> I sleep on top of the snow on branches wearing skin clothing. I have special clothes for skiing and different clothes for sleeping in.

In the north, Khanty and Mansi used primarily reindeer and moose skin for clothing; burbot, hare, squirrel, and bird skin was also employed in some areas. Clothing was made from fabric, too, once it became available. In the southern region, where Khanty live in small agricultural villages, clothing was traditionally made from hemp and nettles pounded, spun, and woven into cloth. Berries, grass, and tree roots were used for dyeing embroidery thread and other yarn. Nettle dresses were elaborately embroidered, using ancient designs that still appear on contemporary clothing, and decorated with glass beads and tin pieces. The nettle-weaving tradition was likely introduced by the Tatars. Khanty lost the art of weaving in the early twentieth century (Levin and Potapov 1956 [1964], Oakes and Riewe 1996).

Wraparound coats, with an apron underneath, were worn by Khanty and Mansi in the south. Pull-over hooded parkas were common in the north (Forsyth 1992, Mitlyanskaya 1983). Traditionally, coats were sewn with reindeer hair caught into each of the main seams (Forsyth 1992). It is believed that hair, blood, and blood's representative, ochre, are life-giving elements; imbedding hair into seams animated the reindeer spirits. Reindeer hair embroidery is rarely done today (Oakes and Riewe 1996).

Historically, inner parkas were hoodless, with a narrow neck opening and a reindeer or otter skin collar (Georgi 1799).

38

39

FIGURE 37
It is important for Tatyana Serasnova and other Khanty elders to have more than one pair of boots when they are buried, as this is one way those who died before them will recognize the recently deceased when they enter the afterworld.

FIGURE 38
Birch bark cradles are lined with reindeer skin, wood shavings, and moss. The back of this cradle is decorated with a bird design that provides additional protection for the baby. REM 7812.11/a-c

FIGURE 39
Khanty-style designs depict a wide variety of animals and familiar objects. Shown here, top to bottom, are "moose," "paddle handles," "rabbit ears," "duck necks," and "reindeer antlers." "Bear heads" are shown at left.

40

For the past hundred years or so, inner parkas have sometimes
been made with hoods attached; a ring or collar is added
between the neckline and the hood (Hatt 1914 [1969]). Today,
both hooded and hoodless parkas are used, especially in the
northern region. Reindeer skin coats lined with swan skins are
still worn by semi-nomadic Khanty and Mansi herders (Oakes
and Riewe 1996).

The traditional male herder continues to wear a belt over
his parka, to which his knife, bullet pouch, and other essential
tools are attached. In the past, everyone wore a pair of skin
pants under their coats; women added a pair of skin underwear under these (Hatt 1914 [1969]).

Many women and girls today wear handmade fabric
dresses with distinctive Khanty-style beaded patterns and
appliqué on the yoke, waist, cuffs, and hemline. These dresses
have dropped waistlines and gathered skirts, and a belt worn
around the waist creates a fitted look. Regional differences are
observed in the number of pleats, the height of the dropped
waistline, and the amount of decoration.

Parkas and footwear are decorated with geometric designs
created with hair embroidery, beading, stick painting, and skin
piecework. Animals are stylized in the ancient decorative patterns used by Khanty. Recently, Nenets and other neighbouring groups have adopted these patterns; however, experienced
seamstresses can identify the work of seamstresses from various groups. Each pattern is named after an animal or other
element of Khanty life. Some of the most common are
human heads, fox elbows, reindeer antlers, bear heads, rabbit
ears, and half persons (Lukena 1979a, 1992; Muldanova 1979,
1992a-i, 1993, 1994).

The meanings associated with decorative symbols are
part of the traditional knowledge passed from one generation to the next. For example, Selkup believe that their
ancestors were birds; one group were nutcrackers and
another eagles (Gachilov 1996, Prokofyeva 1964). Khanty and
Mansi believe that spirits live in all parts of nature and that
families are descendants of specific animals, which they continue to use as totems. Representations of totem animals,
including geese, beavers, moose, and rabbits, are placed on
clothing to protect the wearer from disease (Forsyth 1992).
Multiple use of a single design element such as rabbit ears
symbolically multiplies the population of the animal, thereby

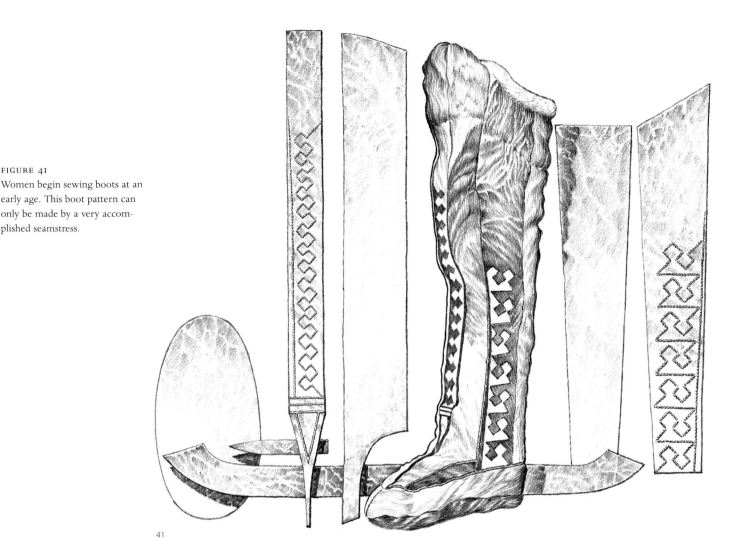

FIGURE 41
Women begin sewing boots at an early age. This boot pattern can only be made by a very accomplished seamstress.

41

increasing hunting success. Baskets, cradles, bags, and utensils are also decorated with these patterns (Oakes and Riewe 1996).

Two distinct styles of patterns exist. One is completely geometric, with the light and dark portions being mirror images; the other combines curved and straight lines to create geometric patterns from light and dark materials that are not mirror images (Oakes and Riewe 1996). Both styles symbolize marriage and elements of ancient relationships with deities or the environment, and provide an accurate means of tribal identification (Schuster 1951, 1964).

Patterns are made by cutting complex interlocking geometric strips from light- and dark-coloured skins. A light and a dark piece of skin are basted together to keep them from shifting; a geometric pattern is then cut through both layers, producing four matching strips, two of each colour. Dark-haired pieces are matched with light-haired pieces, and once these pieces are sewn together they can be attached to footwear, parkas, or other clothing. This system of creating identically shaped interlocking pieces, thus avoiding any

leftover material, was used by Indigenous people from many parts of the world. Today, the technique is especially common among herders and hunters living in close contact with the animal world (Chernetsov 1948, Schuster 1964, Sirelius 1904). Nganasan follow an identical process (Popov 1966 [1948]).

Skin clothing styles favoured by Selkup herders in the past were similar to those of Nenets. Reindeer skin coats had a centre-front opening; pull-over skin parkas were added in extremely cold weather (Hajdú 1968). Selkup also used loon and fish skin clothing, and their footwear resembled that of Khanty and Mansi. Today, most Selkup wear Russian-style clothing (Gachilov 1996).

Footwear

Protective footwear is extremely important for families who continue to be semi-nomadic, especially during late fall and winter. The quality of a pair of skin boots depends upon the health of the reindeer that provided the skin, as well as how that skin was prepared, stored, and sewn. Finely sewn foot-

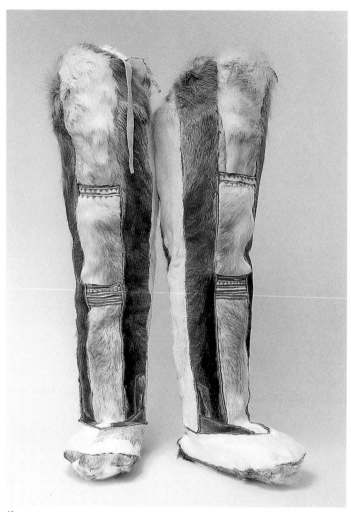

42

FIGURE 42
Men's boots are brightly decorated
with red, blue, yellow, and other
colours of fabric welts cut straight
or in a zigzag design. Northern
Khanty typically use an extra
curved line of decoration just
below the knee. BSM P96.0171.a-d

wear is also a sign of a woman's worth. Tatyana Seraskovoi
(1996) is an internationally renowned Khanty seamstress. She
explained:

> When a woman gets married she needs to make a pair of boots
> to show what she is capable of doing. At least a pair of working
> boots, because the life of her husband depends on her ability to
> sew. Her looks don't matter as much.

Khanty and Mansi footwear is made primarily from reindeer leg or body skins; moose and horse skins are also used by
people living farther south. Special occasions, weather conditions, and available materials are a few of the factors that
influence the different styles used by Khanty, Mansi, Selkup,
and Ket. Timothy Muldanova (1996), a Khanty cinematographer and former herder, explained:

> We have lots of snow, up to nine metres in the valleys, and snow
> stays until mid-August or September, so I wear extra-tall leg skin
> boots.

In the past, people wore thigh-high boots cut at a slant,
a style originally used by horseback riders (Vasilevich 1963a);
today, they also use shorter boot styles borrowed from Komi.

Every spring women take all of their skin boots out of
their boot bags and air them outside on nails or lines. White
fur is turned inside out or upside down so it will not yellow in
the sunlight. It is critical that women's boots are not lifted too
high above the ground when airing. If they are hung above
other people or other people's possessions, it can create serious problems, because the power of the woman, especially a
menstruating woman, is too strong to be put in that position
(Seraskovoi 1996).

Khanty turn their wet boots and skin socks inside out and
keep wringing and rubbing them with their hands until they
are dry. Wet smoked boots are dried by putting dried rotten
birch wood inside the boots, then rubbing them so that the
wood absorbs the moisture (Sopochina 1996). A good house-
keeper turns her husband's boots inside out and replaces the
grass lining each day (Muldanova 1996).

Today, some herders continue to wear skin boots throughout
the year. In summer, some wear mass-produced footwear pur-

chased in the villages. Villagers may use skin boots for special occasions, but many now own only mass-produced footwear.

Leg Skin Boots

Leg skin footwear is made from reindeer or moose leg skins and is the preferred style to wear with skis. Leg skins are used for the side strip and leg portion of the boot. Skin from between the reindeer toes is commonly used for soles, because it is warm, wears extremely well, and provides traction on slippery surfaces. Pieces of toe skin, sometimes nine or more, are sewn together in rows until a piece the size of a sole is created. This panel is then trimmed into an oval shape. For special occasions or for boots that are not expected to get extensive wear, the sole is cut from a leg skin. This takes less time to prepare and produces a neater finish (Oakes and Riewe 1996; Solovieva 1997a, 1997b).

This boot style usually has a side strip with a centre front seam and a short piece added at the centre back. Western Khanty around Kazhim use a wider side strip than do Khanty farther east (Sopochina 1996). Southern Khanty and Komi boots usually have a white-haired side strip. The seam that connects the vamp and side strip is rounded at the toe for everyday wear and for boots used by southern Khanty; it is more angular for special occasion boots and boots worn by northern Khanty (Seraskovoi 1996). The side strip is cut and positioned in a manner that creates a flat silhouette similar to that of Nenets footwear, reflecting the close relationship between northern Khanty and southern Nenets (Vasilevich 1963a). The side strip is sewn to the leg section before it is attached to the sole. A gusset tapers to a point on each side of centre front and extends back to the front, side, or back panel seam on Khanty, Mansi, Selkup, and Komi footwear. Ket sew the leg skin seams from the outside (Pelikh 1972, Vasilevich 1963a).

The leg section usually has six panels on men's boots; a seventh panel is inserted at centre front on women's boots. When skins are taken from bigger animals, four or five panels may be enough. A seam about one handspan long is made at the centre of the front panel. This seam is longer for southern Khanty and Komi than for northern Khanty. Light- and dark-haired panels are often alternated to create a decorative pattern. Boots for older eastern Khanty women have panels cut from skins of the same colour and fewer decorative strips. Younger women's boots have both light- and dark-haired panels and lots of decoration (Sopochina 1996).

The upper edge of the leg section is cut at an angle, covering the knees and part of the thighs in front, and tapering back to about knee height behind. A skin thong sewn to the top edge at centre front is used to tie the boot to a belt around the waist. These thongs are also used to tie boots together so they can be hung from a chum pole to dry. Women tie their boots at the knees with a skin thong sewn to the side of the leg section. In the past, men also tied their boots at the knees with skin ties, but more recently they have adopted the Komi practice of tying up their boots with handwoven bands with tassels (Pelikh 1972, Vandimova 1996, Vokueva 1996).

Boys' and men's leg skin boots are distinguished by a series of short, horizontal stripes placed just below the knee, similar to those described for Nenets (BSM P96.0171.a-d, P96.0221.ab; NMF SU5937.2, SU5967.2). Slight differences exist; for example, Komi omit the centre front seam, referred to by some people as depicting "the handle of a snow beater," on the lower edge of the front leg panel. Komi also add many small strips at mid-calf. Since the 1960s, the lower front leg panel is more closely fitted to the ankle on many of the leg skin boots used throughout northwestern Siberia, following Komi tradition (Vandimova 1996, Vokueva 1996). Girls' and women's leg skin boots have a small inverted triangle set into the front of the boot at the ankle, as described for Nenets (Hatt 1916; Vasilevich 1963a; BSM P96.0211.a-d; KM 5566, 439, 4586, 2124, 7420; NMF SU3904.32).

Khanty and Mansi decorate leg sections with a series of complex stylized animal or geometric designs and with narrow strips and zigzags of light- and dark-haired skins (REM 1711.412/1,2). Beads added to each point of the zigzag provide protection to the wearer of the boots, like the beads used on Nenets toddlers' footwear. Formerly, eastern Khanty decorated their boots only with narrow strips, but they started using zigzag designs about fifteen years ago when they began attending meetings with other Khanty, where they had an opportunity to compare designs and learn new ones. Prior to that, eastern and western groups rarely saw one another (Sopochina 1996).

Strips of woollen fabric are sewn into the seams. Red, blue, and yellow are the preferred colours; other colours are also used when the preferred colours are unavailable or scarce (Vokueva 1996; BSM S92.0030.2, P90.0359; KM 4763, 7420). Sometimes eastern Khanty use three strips of light and dark cloth for decoration. Western Khanty from the Kazhim area use less cloth in the seams (Sopochina 1996). Traditionally, Selkup used even less decorative material in their leg skin footwear (Gachilov 1996). Today, the more elaborate decorative style has been adopted by people throughout northwestern Siberia, including Nenets and Enets (Oakes and Riewe 1996).

Another variation of men's leg skin boots is created by decorating the front panel above the knee with narrow strips of light- and dark-haired skin and strips of fabric (BSM P90.0358, P90.0359, P96.0221.ab; MVB IVA 221; NMF SU5756.95). These strips are usually parallel to one another; in contrast, Komi position their strips so that they converge at the top. Sometimes the back panel is decorated with a lenticular-shaped piece sewn at the centre back near the calf (BSM P96.0221.ab).

Moose Skin Boots

Boots made from moose skin are similar to the reindeer leg skin boots; however, usually only two panels are needed per boot because moose leg skins are much wider than those of reindeer. Sometimes moose skin footwear is made with a flat, unpleated sole and a vamp that encircles the foot. Most men use only one pair of moose skin boots per hunting season.

Over Boots and Sleeping Boots

When the weather is extremely cold, a pair of extra-wide thigh-high reindeer or moose leg skin boots are pulled over everyday footwear. These are especially useful to herders sleeping out with their reindeer in winter. This boot style is made from either two moose leg skins or four reindeer leg skins. Side strips and gussets are usually omitted. A skin thong is sewn to the top of the leg, which is cut on a slant and decorated with a small strip of fabric or skin at the knee (BSM P96.0220.ab). Komi make a version of this style that extends up to the middle of the shin; skin ties are sewn to the boot top and wrapped around the shin (NMF SU5756.16, SU4810.232).

Over boots are also made from fall-killed reindeer body skins, especially by Komi. This style, which extends up to the middle of the shin, has a sole, pointed vamp, and leg section. The upper edge is cut straight across and finished with a casing and drawstring. Over boots are worn with the fur to the outside (NMF SU4899.26).

Selkup traditionally wore another over boot style with an unpleated moose skin sole, placed with the hair to the outside. The deep, triangular-shaped vamp and knee-high leg section were cut from two layers of sacking or canvas material, with moose or reindeer hair quilted between the layers. Ankle straps were sewn onto the boot just above the ankle at the back (Karapetova 1997d). Pieces of dried birch bark were used as insoles, both for extra insulation and to make a squeaking sound when the person walked, which served purposes similar to the use of bells to force evil spirits away (Gachilov 1996). This boot style was worn over leg skin footwear in extremely cold weather when travelling across the tundra (Karapetova 1997d).

Trappers' Boots

Khanty, Mansi, Selkup, and Ket make a style of footwear with a combination of moose or reindeer skin and fabric. This style is made from skins with the hair left on for winter wear and with dehaired or smoked skins for summer. Occasionally the fur is turned to the inside on the vamp and the sole. Unpleated soles are cut from reindeer toe, forehead, or dehaired skins. The vamp encircles the foot and is cut a bit higher on Ket boots than on Khanty or Mansi boots. Ket place the seam on their vamp at the side, while others place it at centre back.

Before fabric became available, the leg section was cut from alder-stained dehaired reindeer or moose skin. Initially, the front and back panels were cut from different-coloured fabric, but today the same piece of fabric is used. The leg section reaches to mid-shin, knee, or thigh and is cut straight across the top. A small triangular piece is sewn at centre front just above the vamp-leg seam. For short boots, Mansi sew loops to the top vamp seam and thread an ankle strap through (Vasilevich 1963a; MVB IVA3504, IVA 3739; NMF SU5243.4, SU4866.12, SU5930.3). Selkup introduced these boots to Russian trappers who travelled by dog and snowshoe. They were worn with a thick, sack-shaped sock. Trappers carried along an extra pair of boots and a piece of skin for repairs (Bychkov 1994).

Winter Version   The winter version of this style is decorated by Ket with a single strip sewn to the front or two strips sewn to the back and sides (Vasilevich 1963a). Khanty and Mansi sew on a few strips of handmade zigzag trim created by folding a long strip of fabric into many mitred corners (Oakes and Riewe 1996). Selkup add beads and several decorative strips (Karapetova 1997d, Pelikh 1972).

Summer Version   The summer variation on this boot style is made from dehaired reindeer skins; catfish skins were used by Selkup in the past (Gachilov 1996). The boot has a flat, unpleated sole, a vamp that encircles the foot, and a vamp extension that encircles the ankle. Khanty and others in this region also occasionally use a triangular-shaped vamp for this boot style. The leg, thigh-high and cut straight across, has been made from fabric since it became available. A triangular piece, made today from red fabric, is inset at centre front. A thong is sewn to the upper edge of the leg. The leg and vamp sections are cut with a tighter fit than in the winter style, and seams are sewn on the outside because these boots are worn without stockings. Grass insoles absorb moisture and provide insulation (Hajdú 1968).

Vamps and vamp extensions are stick-painted with classic Khanty and Mansi designs. Dye from pine or larch bark (sometimes boiled with ashes), or red or orange-coloured ochre mixed with fish glue, is used for traditional paint. Stick-painted designs are outlined with reindeer hair embroidery or skin appliquéd to the stained skin (BSM P95.0182.AB, P95.0181.ab, P96.0181.A-D; KM 5673; NMF SU4866.13, SU3904.31; REM 3950.79/1,2).

A slight variation on this summer boot style is made by omitting the vamp extension. This style has a sole, a vamp encircling the foot, and a leg section. Sometimes an extra triangular vamp is inserted at the top centre front of the other vamp (MVB IVA 3415). The leg section is often cut in two pieces, with the front piece made from dark smoked or stained skins and the back piece made from bleached skins. Selkup once decorated this boot style with circles and stripes representing the elements of the universe (Karapetova 1997d, MVB IVA 3415, NMF SU5930.4, REM 302.3/1,2). This style is rarely used today, although the Selkup world view remains unchanged.

43

FIGURE 43
When herders have to sleep outside with their reindeer in extremely cold weather, they slip a pair of undecorated, extra-large boots over their everyday wear. Stockings and straw insoles provide extra insulation. BSM P96.0220.ab

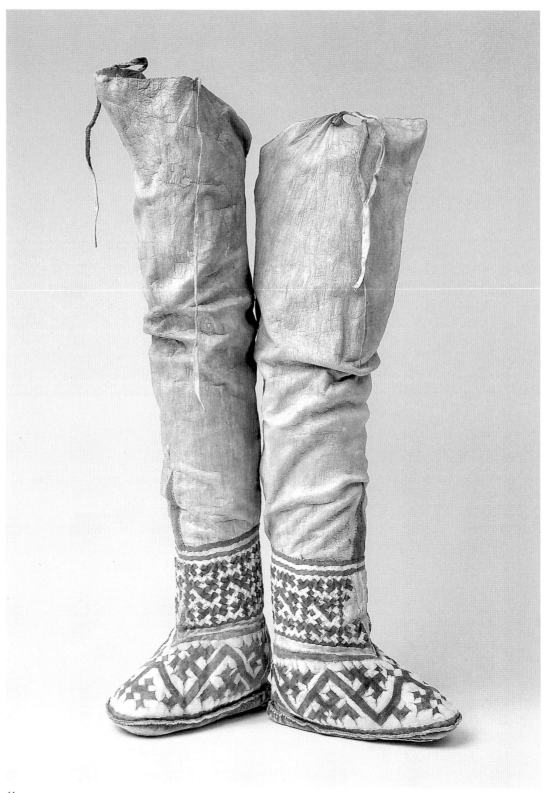

44

FIGURE 44
Traditionally, people throughout the Khanty region decorated dehaired boots with interlocking geometric shapes. These were created by appliquéing alder- or ochre-dyed skins onto the vamp and lower leg. BSM P96.0181.a-d

FIGURE 45
During warm summer weather, some women herders continue to wear this boot style, made with pleated soles. They are rarely decorated with stick-painting today. An ankle strap is threaded through loops on each side of the vamp and laced up tightly to keep the boots in position. Nenets use a similar boot style. REM 8762.17587/1,2

46

FIGURE 46
Selkup decorate their footwear with
stripes and circles that represent the
universe. REM 302.3/1,2

Tarred Work Boots

In the past, water-repellent footwear was made by applying pine pitch to canvas and dehaired skin boots. The narrow, fitted, unpleated sole of these boots has an extra layer of skin at the heel. The sole and the vamp that encircles the foot are cut from dehaired bull reindeer, moose, or horse skins. The leg section is made from dehaired reindeer skin or heavy canvas; it usually has a centre back seam and is cut straight across the top. Ties are sewn to the ankle seam or threaded through loops sewn into the seam. This boot style is rarely made today. A mid-shin wraparound variation was also made for damp conditions in the past.

Leg skin work boots cut from skins wide enough to require only a front and a back panel are also tarred with pine pitch. Extra height is created by sewing an upper section to the leg (Seraskovoi 1996). Forehead skin from a male reindeer is preferred for the sole of these work boots, because it is thick and very durable. The leg section is cut from large skins with a film of fascia still intact to prevent the tar from eating through the skin. The skin is sewn while still a little wet.

Work boots made from skin and canvas, or from leg skins, are tarred by placing one boot inside the other with the skin sides, rather than the hair sides, together. Tar is poured between the sides and worked back and forth. Boot legs are then sewn together (or occasionally tied) at mid-shin height to prevent the tar from pouring out the top. The tar is allowed to soak in for about twenty-four hours.

Excess tar is poured back into a bowl and recycled, even though it is not sticky any more. The tarred portions of boots are a dark blackish-brown colour. If the boots get wet, they are turned inside out to dry. Before World War II, some people made rubber-soled reindeer leg skin boots for work wear. Once the war began, traditional tarred waterproof boots were used until rubber rations were lifted. Today, rubber boots are commonly used in wet weather.

Dehaired Skin Summer Boots

Another dehaired skin boot style is rarely made today, even though elders observe that their legs do not ache if they wear these traditional water-repellent boots rather than rubber boots. Smoked dehaired skins dry easily and are ideal for warm, damp weather. Smoked haired body skins take a bit longer to dry but provide more insulation for damp conditions during colder weather. Seamstresses who no longer live in chums smoke skins and footwear in fish smokehouses (Sartagov 1996).

This water-repellent style once made by Khanty, Mansi, Selkup, Ket, Nenets, and other neighbouring groups has a pleated sole, a steeply pointed vamp, and a thigh-high boot leg. The sole is cut from haired reindeer calf or forehead skin, or from smoked moose skin with the seam allowance shaved and the rest of the hair left intact. Deep accordion pleats are formed by drawing a needle and thread through the skin to create three rows of stitches. The long, pointed vamp and thigh-high leg are cut from smoked body skin, either dehaired or haired. The leg section is cut straight across for Mansi and Selkup boots, and at an angle for Khanty and Nenets boots (BSM P96.0214.ab, KM 5558, MVB IVA 227, REM 7150.30/1,2). A tie is sewn to the upper edge. Loops are sewn to each side of the vamp along the vamp-sole seam; an ankle strap is threaded through these loops and wrapped around the lower leg several times. Men cross the ties while lacing up their summer boots, but women do not.

The vamp and the lower part of the leg section are painted one solid colour with an alder bark or ochre mixture (KM 6411, 4755) or stick-painted (KM 7.1, REM 8762.17587/1,2). Occasionally, the vamp is also decorated with hair embroidery and a few white and navy beads. Mansi decorate these boots with alder bark stain, while some Khanty use ochre, which is collected by reindeer herders in the northern part of the Ural Mountains. When herders migrate near villages they exchange ochre for grass and fish oil. Khanty living near Surgut do not use ochre at all, but others use it not only for its water-repellent properties but also to make moose skins—which they often must use instead of reindeer skins—look more beautiful (Sopochina 1996). Stains strengthen the water-repellent properties of this footwear.

Shamans' Footwear
Shamans wear boots made from alder bark–stained reindeer skins with the hair sheared and worn to the inside. They attach metal pendants in the shape of reindeer and bear legs to their footwear. Irena Karapatova (1997d), a curator at the Russian Museum of Ethnography, described a pair of boots in the museum's collection as having a metal pendant representing reindeer legs sewn to the front at mid-shin. Another metal pendant with five fingerlike horizontal prongs, representing a bear claw, is sewn to the foot. The bear pendant is a spirit helper needed for the shaman to communicate between the upper and lower worlds.

Infants' and Children's Boots and Stockings
Reindeer calf skins are used to make flexible, warm stockings for newborn babies. Seams are sewn on the outside, providing a smooth inside finish. Stockings have four beads sewn to the vamp of female stockings and five beads sewn to male stockings. These beads remain on the footwear until children get their baby teeth. They protect infants from ill health and evil spirits (REM 8694.20/1,2).

Children get their first pair of boots when they are about a year old, or once they start walking. Squirrel skins and reindeer calf skins are preferred for children's clothing because they are light, warm, and flexible. Children wear miniature versions of adult footwear cut from young reindeer skins. These boots often have a V-shaped inset at the centre front over the toes. This inset, which represents the split in reindeer hoofs, is not used in adult footwear. Sometimes the triangular piece is edged with red fabric. Its purpose is to attract the extra protection provided by spirit helpers associated with reindeer (Seraskovoi 1996). Bells are placed on children's footwear and clothing so that they do not get lost in the forest and to keep evil spirits away (Oakes and Riewe 1996).

Loon Skin Slippers
Until the 1950s, Selkup and Ket wore loon skin slippers over their dehaired summer footwear to provide extra protection in wet conditions. Once loon skins were pulled off the carcass, the fat was sucked out, feathers were brushed with willow, and the skin was rubbed against aspen bark (Gachilov 1996, Karapetova 1997d, Pelikh 1972, REM 249.7/1,2). Today, men put rubber galoshes over their skin boots to protect them from oil and gas stains and from having holes worn in them by driving snowmobiles. In some areas, twigs are placed inside boots to keep moths from eating them (Oakes and Riewe 1996).

Slipper and Stocking Combination

In summer, Khanty and Mansi women and girls wear short beaded slippers with hand-crocheted or -knit stockings that are thick enough to protect their legs from mosquitoes (REM 7358.26/1,2). The slippers are made from dehaired reindeer skin blackened with a mixture of fish eggs and soot or commercial paint. The sole is flat and sometimes has extra layers added to create a raised heel. The sole is stitched to the vamp, which either encircles the foot with a join at the centre back or has a side seam. The upper edge is finished by sewing a narrow strip of skin around the top and folding it to the inside. Slippers may also be finished by sewing a skin lining around the top and folding it to the inside (KM 5214, 5212, 916, 4994, 1697, 3711; NMF 4810.347; REM 1711.416/1,2).

Slippers are decorated primarily with blue and white beads, secondarily with beads of other assorted colours. The beads are couched on by stitches placed every two or three beads. Women prefer to have all surfaces except the sole covered with beads. This footwear is still used for dances, celebrations, and other special occasions.

Stockings and Grass Insoles

Footwear is worn with stockings and grass insoles. Grass is collected by the river after it turns yellow in the autumn. Medium-high grass is preferred, because it is not as sharp and abrasive as taller grass. Insoles for children and toddlers are made from shorter grass because it is even less abrasive and will not cut through the skins of their boots (Sopochina 1996).

Historically, thigh-high reindeer skin stockings were attached to a belt worn around the waist (Forsyth 1992). According to Evgeniya Vandimova (1996), an exceptional Khanty seamstress, stockings are usually sewn from leftover pieces of reindeer skin and worn with the fur to the inside. They are made with a few pleats at the toe and a U-shaped insert at the heel. The vamp is either triangular-shaped or encircles the foot. In wealthy families, each pair of boots has its own pair of stockings, and women's stockings are made from reindeer belly skins or calf leg skins. Dog skin is used only for men's and children's stockings (KM 4764, 32; NMF SU5243.5, SU5949.17).

Contemporary Footwear

Traditionally, skin boots were thigh-high and very supple. Since World War II, people have made short, stiff skin boots with mass-produced composite soles better suited to the abrasive surfaces in their villages. Soap or hot glue is applied to the leg skins to stiffen them. The vamps and upper sections of the boots are often made by village women, but the composite soles are attached at a boot factory (Seraskovoi 1996). Some modern footwear is made with skin soles (KM 3669, 4757), other styles entirely from wool fabric (KM 2100, 2099, 1491). Modern slippers are also worn in urban centres (BSM s92.0028.2).

Summary

Khanty, Mansi, Selkup, and Ket footwear reflects cultural values, traditions, and the environment. Khanty and Mansi typically use flat, uncrimped soles, shaped side strips, instep gussets, six panels of reindeer legs for the leg-vamp section, and complex zoomorphic totems for decoration on reindeer skin winter footwear. One style of summer footwear is made with an accordion-pleated sole, a deep inverted V-shaped vamp, and ochre-stained lower leg and vamp sections. Another classic Khanty and Mansi style uses a flat, uncrimped sole, a vamp that encircles the foot, and a leg section with a horizontal seam at the lower end. This boot style is generally decorated with stick-painting and a small triangular inset at the centre front. Tarred boots were also commonly used in the past. Each of these styles is thigh-high. In addition, Khanty and Mansi women wear beaded skin slippers with wool stockings in the summer. Today, the elaborately decorated reindeer leg skin style is the most common form of handmade footwear. The leg skin and dehaired skin boots used by Khanty, Mansi, Ket, Komi, and Selkup are similar to those used by Nenets and other neighbouring groups. Subtle differences occur in colour choice, cut, and decorative techniques. A triangular inset for women's boots and horizontal bars for men's boots are used throughout this region.

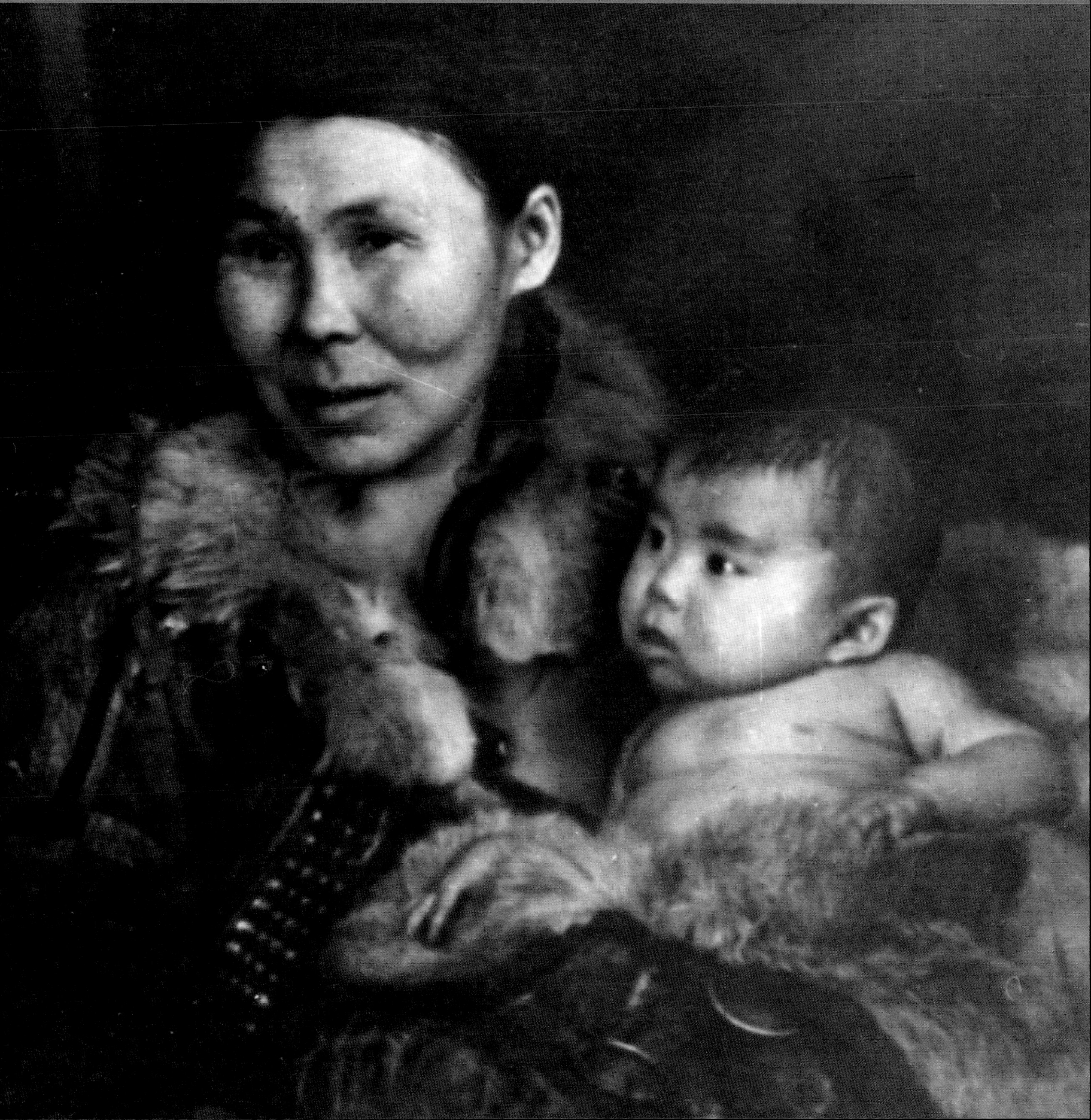

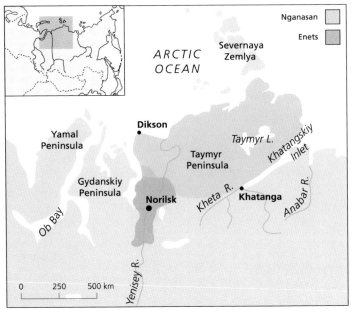

CHAPTER 3

Map 4

FIGURE 47
Overleaf: Nganasan woman and child. REM 199.1

MAP 4
Nganasan and Enets homelands

FIGURE 48
These Nganasan people are wearing traditional inner parkas, which are made from two layers of skin sewn together; the innermost layer is longer than the outer one. The hemline of the inner layer is trimmed with dog fur; the outer layer is ornately decorated with narrow strips of red and black fabric or skin. REM 1099.61

N'GANASAN WERE AMONG the last Indigenous groups in Siberia to be influenced by non-Natives. On the remote Taymyr Peninsula, the approximately 1,300 Nganasan and 200 Enets continue to live a traditional life of hunting wild reindeer and waterfowl, herding reindeer, and travelling by reindeer-drawn sleds (Hajdú 1968, Vakhtin 1992). According to an ancient legend, "Nganasan were born from the skin hairs of the wild deer" (Dolgikh 1957:286). Nganasan, Enets, and Dolgan herders now live in mobile frame huts rather than their traditional skin tents. They transport these huts by mounting them on sled runners; huts are insulated with reindeer skins and wrapped with canvas (Gracheva 1987). Today, Enets and Nganasan are indistinguishable from one another in terms of material culture and lifeways.

The Annual Cycle

Nganasan, like all nomadic peoples, live according to an annual cycle. Many of their activities are influenced by the wild reindeer upon which they are so dependant. Reindeer spend summers on the tundra to gain some respite from the heat and hordes of biting insects, then migrate south to the forest-tundra in search of food and shelter from winter blizzards. During these annual migrations, reindeer herders drive their tame herds away from the wild reindeer; otherwise, domesticated reindeer will join their wild relatives (Popov 1966 [1948]).

According to Popov (1966 [1948]), the Nganasan year is counted as two years: a winter year and a summer year. The winter year is divided into eight months, the summer into four.

The first winter month, known as the Big Month, corresponds to the second half of September and the first half of October. This is reindeer mating season, when bulls gather large numbers of cows around them. The herd instinct is so strong at this time of year that if a dominant bull is killed, cows will return several times to the site of his death. During this month, Nganasan follow their reindeer herds southward and hunt wild reindeer. After the snow flies and the lakes freeze over, the men trap arctic fox, ice-fish, and make sled runners. Women prepare reindeer skins and sew winter clothing.

The second month, the Autumn Month, runs from mid-October to mid-November. By this time, the lush grasses and creeping willows that fattened the reindeer over the summer no longer provide the necessary nutrition. Nganasan herders follow their herds farther south towards the forest-tundra, hunting wild reindeer, trapping arctic fox, and fishing along the way. Due to the lack of sunlight, women stop sewing unless they have another light source.

The third month, from mid-November to mid-December, is known as the Hornless Reindeer Month, because the bulls begin to shed their antlers at this time. Traditional Nganasan continue to hunt wild reindeer herds en route to the forests, but intensive hunting wanes. Men trap the arctic fox feeding on blood left at reindeer kill sites and stop fishing once it is too difficult to set their nets under the thickening ice.

The fourth month, known as the Dark Month, extends from mid-December to mid-January. Nganasan herders camp at the edge of the forests as twenty-four-hour darkness and frigid temperatures restrict most activities. Men gather firewood, trap arctic fox, occasionally hunt wild reindeer, and tend their tame herds. Camps are moved only when the supply of reindeer fodder is exhausted. Women maintain the household.

The fifth month, mid-January to mid-February, is called the Sunrise Month. Due to the limited light and the intense cold, people carry on with sedentary activities.

The sixth month, the Frosted Trees Month, extends from mid-February to mid-March. During this time, as hoarfrost appears on the trees, reindeer often begin to leave the forest-tundra. With the increasing sunlight, hunters are able to more

48

actively hunt wild reindeer, trap arctic fox, and set nets in the willows for ptarmigan.

The seventh month, from mid-March to mid-April, is called the Blackening of Trees Month. Nganasan move their herds northward, following the natural migration of wild reindeer to the tundra. Occasionally a sudden cold spell forces the reindeer back to the shelter of the forests; reindeer are rarely hunted then, because the animals are usually very thin.

The eighth month, mid-April to mid-May, is called the Cold Month, because the barren female reindeer, which are in poor condition, shiver in the cold. Men hunt wild reindeer, net ptarmigan, and trap arctic fox until this season ends. Women continue their household chores.

The summer year consists of four months. The first month, from mid-May to mid-June, is known as the First Fawns Month. Wild reindeer are hunted and ptarmigan netted.

The second month, called either the Fish Appearance Month or the Last Fawns Month, extends from mid-June to mid-July. Men hunt ducks, ptarmigan, and geese; gather eggs; and seine fish. Sleds are repaired in preparation for the summer migration onto the tundra. Women cache winter clothing and make waterproof clothing needed for the summer. Boys and girls tend the domesticated herd as the group waits for their tame reindeer to finish calving.

The third summer month, mid-July to mid-August, is the Goose Moulting Month. As the month passes, men hunt wild reindeer in earnest and continue to do so through to the Autumn Month. Sudden cold spells with torrential rainstorms often occur on the Taymyr Peninsula at this time of year. Under such conditions, reindeer move to the lowlands. Because the animals have become very fat over the summer, they cannot run fast and therefore can fall prey to wolves. Consequently, reindeer feed close to lakes and deep rivers, which they enter when threatened. Adult geese, moulting and flightless at this time, are driven into nets. Women butcher the game, dry goose and reindeer meat, and render fat to prevent spoilage, as well as prepare skins and sew winter clothing for their families. Youth tend the tame reindeer and participate in some goose and reindeer hunts.

The final month of summer, the Gosling Moulting Month, is from mid-August to mid-September. At the beginning of the month, some men hunt goslings with dogs, but wild reindeer are the primary focus for hunters. Towards the end of the month some men forge tools. When the moon becomes "the size of a fingernail," men build their winter sleds, and women jerk wild reindeer meat, render fat, prepare reindeer skins, and sew winter clothing. As the cycle begins again, Nganasan prepare to follow the reindeer herds south towards the forest.

According to Dolgikh (1965), the meat and fat of the wild reindeer are all-important to the Nganasan. The wild animal is highly respected. Domesticated reindeer are slaughtered only in exceptional cases, such as in the spring before waterfowl and fish arrive. In the past, Nganasan usually led a life of near-starvation. Only in the autumn, with the intensive hunting of wild reindeer and the netting of fish under the ice, was there a plentiful food supply.

Traditional Beliefs

Nganasan attribute spirits to all objects (including sleds, clothing, and tools), to environmental features, and to conditions such as storms, starvation, and illness. For example, smallpox is considered by Nganasan to be a Russian spirit. Ceremonies and rituals mark the changing seasons and enable Nganasan to speak to all aspects of their surroundings. In late winter, when the sun returns, a new chum is made and then cleansed by a shaman. Festive clothing, which celebrates the spirits, is worn at this "clean tent" ceremony, as well as at weddings. During the clean tent ceremony, chum poles are covered with the blood of a sacrificed dog (Dolgikh 1957; Popov 1966 [1948], 1984a). For both festive occasions and daily life, Nganasan women and men wear their hair long and braided, with buttons, strips of skin, and other ornaments woven in. Both men and women wear skin clothing as well as red, black, and white fabric clothing for festive occasions (Popov 1966 [1948], 1984a). Similar garments are worn by the deceased at funerals.

Traditional Clothing

Contemporary Nganasan consider their clothing styles to have been borrowed from Enets (Dolgikh 1957, Hatt 1914 [1969]). For example, both groups historically wore a sacklike boot style. Ancient connections with Evenki from the Yenisey River area are seen in Enets footwear. The silhouette and lack of instep are features acquired from ancient arctic Aboriginal peoples assimilating with Sayan Samoyed groups (Vasilevich 1963a).

Nganasan and Enets wear an inner parka made of two layers sewn together. Both layers are constructed from reindeer skins with very short hair or from skins that have been dehaired. Men now wear hooded pull-over inner parkas, which in ancient times opened down the centre front. Women wear a hoodless inner parka with a centre front opening over a sleeveless skin shirt. The hemline of men and women's inner parkas is trimmed with red- and black-stained skins and two rows of white dog fur. Ochre or lead is used to stain skins red, graphite to paint skins black. Fine lines are created with a stick-painting tool. Reindeer hair is also embedded in the seams as they are sewn (Dolgikh 1957, Hajdú 1968, Hatt 1914 [1969], Levin and Potapov 1956 [1964], Mitlyanskaya 1983, Popov 1966 [1948], Prytkova 1970, Smolyak 1988).

In extremely cold conditions, such as when riding on sleds, people also wear an outer reindeer skin parka made from fall skins, which have much longer and warmer fur. Children wear miniature versions of adult parkas. Nganasan also used to wear dehaired combination suits decorated with metal pendants (Dolgikh 1957, Hajdú 1968, Hatt 1914 [1969], Levin and Potapov 1956 [1964], Mitlyanskaya 1983, Popov 1966 [1948], Prytkova 1970, Smolyak 1988).

To make one adult parka takes approximately two reindeer skins: one white-haired and one black-haired skin or a combination. Special occasion parkas have extra strips of skins stained black, gussets stained red, pieces of white belly fur, and other forms of decoration. White-haired skins are preferred for clothing and footwear (Dolgikh 1957). During the summer months Nganasan wear old inner parkas that have grown thin from use.

Nganasan geometric designs are similar to those of Khanty. There is also a special category of decorative patterns used to protect the wearer from evil spirits (Popov 1966 [1948]). Stylized zigzag-shaped human figures, seen as spirit helpers by numerous groups, including Nganasan, Evenki, and Khanty, decorate everyday clothing as well as shamans' clothing. A more simplified Y-shaped human figure is also used by Ket for protection (Schuster 1964). Indigenous peoples around the world create designs that are similar in form and usage

49

FIGURE 49
White-haired skins are preferred for men's clothing, and men wear thigh-high footwear also cut from white-haired skins. The straight silhouette of these reindeer leg skin boots was traditionally used by Enets. The silhouette and the decoration of the vamp represent a reindeer hoof. REM 11703.7 (*parka*), REM 11703.2/1,2 (*boots*)

(Issenman 1985; Ivanov 1963, 1970; Ivanov and Stukalov 1975; Schuster 1964).

Parkas are worn with pants, footwear, and mittens made from skin; women also wear caps or bonnets with their hoodless parkas. The bonnets are often trimmed with black dog hair; festive caps are trimmed with white arctic fox fur (Dolgikh 1957, Popov 1966 [1948], Prytkova 1970). Pants are usually short. Outer pants are worn with the fur to the outside and inner pants with the fur removed. Inner and outer pants are adorned with fringes of dehaired reindeer skin tassels. Fine lines made with black and red stain and reindeer hair embroidery are also used for decoration. Tufts of white reindeer neck fur with red lines on one side and black on the other are placed on pants used for festive occasions. A skin belt worn around the top of men's pants carries a hunting knife, pipe, tobacco pouch, and other items. Boot ties are also attached to this belt. Copper plates, needles, tubes, chains, needle cases, and flint bags are all sewn to women's skin underwear (Dolgikh 1957, Hatt 1914 [1969], Popov 1966 [1948]).

Footwear

The remoteness of Nganasan territory has allowed the people to preserve their traditional clothing and footwear designs. They are the only Aboriginal group in Eurasia or North America to still use a unique boot design made without a fitted ankle (Hajdú 1968, Hatt 1914 [1969], Levin and Potapov 1956 [1964], Vasilevich 1963a). This design is believed to have been given to Nganasan by the master spirits, and it carries its own spirit which is critical for people's survival. The same pattern is used for summer and winter adult and children's boots and stockings. Children's snowsuits have sacklike Nganasan footwear attached directly to the bottom of each leg.

Leg Skin Boots

Nganasan boots have a sole, side strips, gussets, and leg panels cut and assembled in a specific order. The broad circular soles are cut from reindeer foreheads, leg skins, or toe skins sewn together. Soles constructed from reindeer toe skins are considered the best, as they last for an entire year. Dehaired skins are also used, sometimes crosshatched to add more traction. The hexangular front piece and the long wedge-shaped piece adjacent to it are cut out and then sewn together, first for the

right boot and then for the left. Then the side strips—which encircle the foot—and the gussets are cut and sewn. The piece cut for one side is used as a pattern to cut an identical piece for the other side, and pieces are sewn into position as they are cut. In this manner, identical left and right boots are produced (Popov 1966 [1948]). The rest of the leg is made from a centre front panel; two (rarely), four, six, and occasionally eight side panels; and a centre back panel. Leg sections are occasionally cut straight across the top, and no straps are attached to the ankle. Red or yellow and black fabric welts are often sewn into seams for decoration (Vasilevich 1963a; MVB IVA 3487; REM 11703.2/1,2, 11703.4/1,2).

Winter Boots

Nganasan prefer white-haired reindeer leg skins for their footwear, especially for winter. Soles are cut from forehead, toe, or leg skins. When leg skins are used, the hair is cropped in rows to provide more traction. Nganasan footwear includes one or two narrow side strips and two gussets, above the side strip and on each side of the hexagon-shaped vamp. The leg section is cut from six to eight panels of leg skins and has the top edge cut on an angle. A skin strap is sewn to the top of each leg and used to tie the boot to a belt. Two more skin straps sewn just below the knee are tied around the knee to hold the boots in position (Karapetova 1997a, Vasilevich 1963a).

Women's boots are usually shorter than men's, extending to just above the knee. The tops of women's boots are tucked under pant legs and laced tightly in position, creating a distinctive bent-knee gait. Women's footwear is easily distinguished from men's by broad strips of dark-haired skin sewn up the sides and a rectangular piece of dark-haired skin sewn at centre back just above the heel (Dolgikh 1957, Karapetova 1997a, Popov 1966 [1948], REM 11703.4/1,2). Similar dark strips are used on white-haired skin boots made by some groups of Yakut, Dolgan, and Yukagir (Dolgikh 1957).

To keep men's legs warm while they are hunting from a kneeling position, their boots extend up over the knees and are worn with reindeer skin stockings that have an extra layer of skin sewn to the knees. It takes approximately one entire reindeer skin to make a pair of stockings, which follow the same pattern as the boots (Karapetova 1997a, Vasilevich 1963a).

50

FIGURE 50
In extremely cold weather,
Nganasan wear a long over parka
on top of their double-layered inner
parkas. This over parka is made
from the skin of reindeer killed in
the fall and is decorated with light-
and dark-haired strips of reindeer
skin. REM 199.85

52

51

FIGURE 51
Nganasan shamans wear the same footwear styles as other Nganasan, but shamans' boots are decorated with metal pendants and other spirit helper symbols created with ochre, reindeer hair, and blackened skins. REM 146.30/1,2

FIGURE 52
Nganasan women wear knee-high footwear cut from white-haired skins. Dark-haired skin is used for one of the side strips, a side leg panel, and a small piece at the heel. REM 11703.4/1,2

FIGURE 53
Nganasan cut and assemble their footwear in a standard way to ensure that left and right boots are identical. Each pattern is slightly different; for example, the exact placement of the straight lines on the leg panels is not duplicated from one pair of boots to the next.

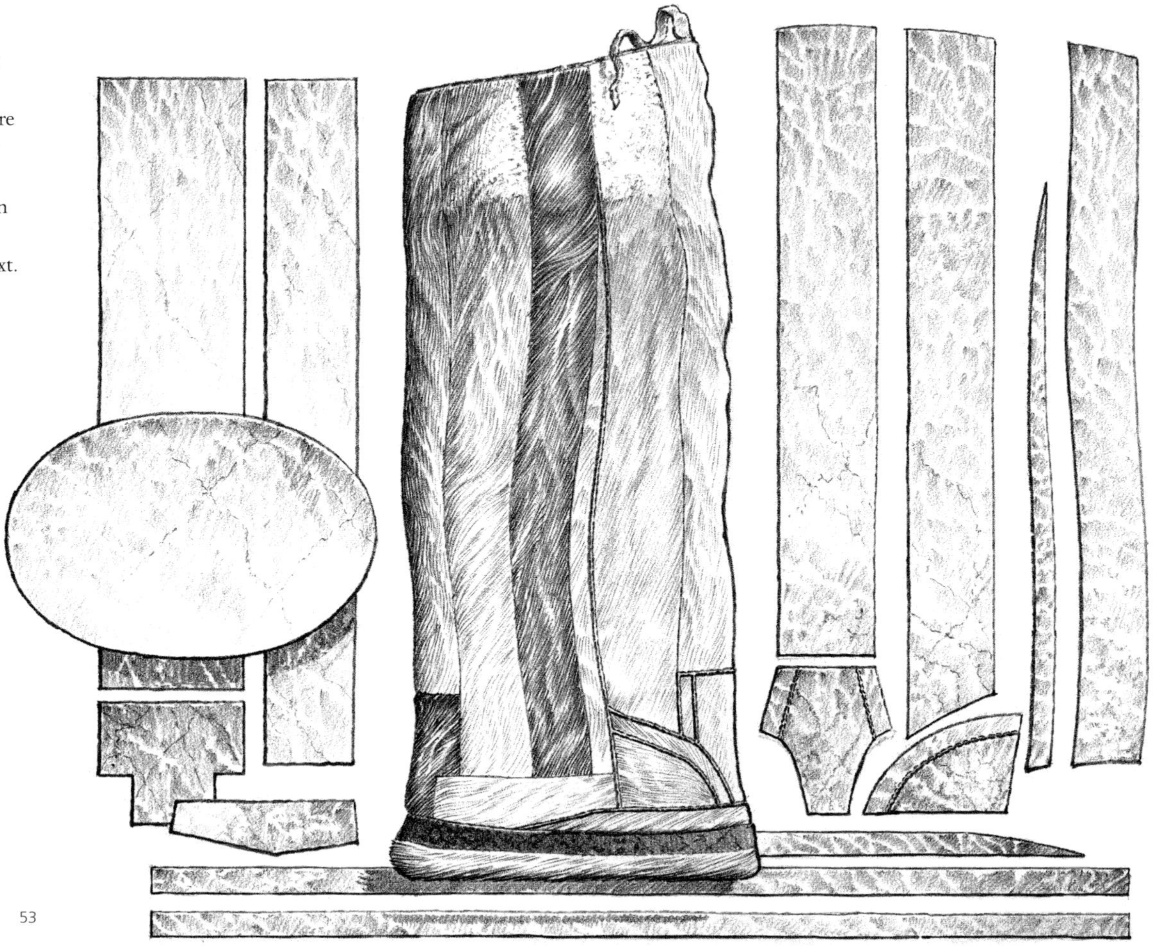

53

Men also use a reindeer skin foot bag to keep their feet and legs warm on long sled trips. These foot bags, made from two reindeer skins, are decorated with reindeer hair embroidery; with stars and crosses created by wooden stamps dipped into ochre or graphite mixtures (Popov 1966 [1948], REM 1360.14/1,2); and with narrow strips of either red and black or yellow and black cloth, which are inserted in the front seams of the boot leg (Vasilevich 1963a).

Dehaired Summer Boots

Summer boots for men and women are made from dehaired reindeer skin. Soles are cut from forehead or leg skins and placed with the fur outside. Summer boots are worn with bare feet, and the soles have holes in them to let out any

water that might soak inside (Popov 1966 [1948], Vasilevich 1963a).

Shamans' Boots

Boots used by shamans are cut following the typical sacklike Nganasan design; however, they are constructed and decorated differently. A pair of shaman's boots in the Russian Museum of Ethnography collection illustrates this well (REM 146.30/1,2). The boots are sewn from reindeer skins stained with ochre and placed with the hair to the inside. Black graphite mixed with egg, oil, or fish glue has been used to paint vein- or skeletal-shaped broad lines that converge in a circle placed just below the knee on each boot. Reindeer hair embroidery traces these lines, which represent the veins and arteries of a reindeer and of a shaman who successfully performs the ritual of becoming a reindeer. Metal amulets placed over the knees, shins, and feet act as spirit helpers and provide protection from evil spirits. For example, the metal pieces over the feet symbolize reindeer hoofs, endowing a shaman journeying to the underworld with the reindeer's ability to travel through difficult conditions. Engraving on a metal piece placed at each knee represents bone marrow, another important source of life and energy (Karapetova 1997a).

Summary

The key distinguishing feature of Nganasan and traditional Enets leg skin and dehaired reindeer skin footwear is the lack of a fitted ankle. Women's boots are knee-high, cut straight across the top or at an angle, and have a dark-haired side strip; they are held in position with a strap sewn to the bottom of women's pant legs and wrapped around the top of their boots. Men's boots are thigh-high, cut at a slant across the top, and tied to the waistband with a strip sewn to the upper edge. Leg skin boots are made with two side strips plus one or two gussets. The leg section has two (rarely), four, six, or sometimes eight panels. Winter boots are usually made with six or eight side panels. Ankle straps are not used. Light-haired leg skins are preferred, and seams are decorated with narrow strips of red or yellow and black welts.

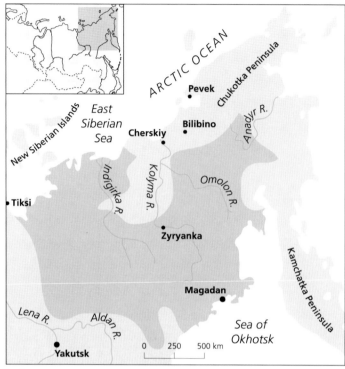

Map 5

FIGURE 54
Overleaf: Even people wear coats with a fully pleated back. The extra fullness allows for easier movement when riding reindeer. REM 10100.1

MAP 5
Even homelands

FIGURE 55
Even herders and their dogs tend reindeer twenty-four hours a day all year round, working on eight-hour shifts.

THE EVEN, APPROXIMATELY 17,000 people, are widely scattered between the Ob River and the Chukotka Peninsula, with the highest population concentrations occurring on the Okhotsk coast and in the Indigirka and Kolyma river basins. Even, formerly known as Lamuts, are closely related to Evenki, who were formerly known as Tungus (Federal Service of Geodesy and Cartography of Russia 1995, Forsyth 1992, Krupnik 1995a, Popova 1981).

As can be seen in their ceremonies, clothing, dwellings, and way of life, Even have both borrowed and influenced the ideas and material cultures of their neighbours. Traditionally, Even used chums similar to those of Nganasan, Khanty, and Nenets, as well as a dome-shaped tent similar in shape to the yurangas used by Chukchi and Koryak (Clark and Finlay 1977, Levin and Vasil'yev 1956 [1964], Popova 1981). Depending upon the season and the available materials, fish skin, larch bark, and reindeer skin coverings were used. Bark tents were preferred in milder weather. Some Even built flat-roofed dugouts, which they entered and exited through the dugout's smoke outlet, for their winter dwellings. Today, cloth tents are often used, along with fabric sleeping bags.

Even, the reindeer herders and hunters of the taiga, are primarily nomadic. In the past, they raised fewer reindeer than their Chukchi and Koryak neighbours, but their animals were considerably larger and stronger, and Even were able to trade one of their reindeer for two Chukchi or Koryak reindeer (Arutiunov 1988a). Reindeer for the Even were primarily riding and pack animals, rather than draft animals. In fact, the use of sleds is a recent innovation for Even; they adopted the practice from Chukchi and Koryak, or Yakut. Historically, when a family of Even lost their riding reindeer they either starved or became vassals to a wealthier herder (Levin and Vasil'yev 1956 [1964]).

Some Even living in southwestern Siberia began milking their reindeer after being introduced to the practice by Yakut, who milked cows (Arutiunov 1988a, Okladnikov 1970). It was not until about the beginning of the twentieth century that Even began to breed reindeer on a large scale. Before that time, they rarely slaughtered their reindeer, considering them too valuable an asset. The Even subsisted primarily by hunting wild reindeer (using their tame reindeer as lures), fox, and mountain sheep. After contact with the Russians in the 1600s, they also trapped squirrels for the fur trade.

Fishing was of secondary importance to the nomadic inland herders in the past. Coastal Even living along the Sea of Okhotsk, however, fished with nets, spears, and hooks for migrating humpback salmon and Siberian salmon. Hunting marine mammals was also an important activity. Coastal Even drove their dog teams to the floe edge and harpooned or shot seals in the fall. In spring, they approached basking seals silently, wearing white cloth gowns as camouflage (Levin and Potapov 1964). Today, herding and fishing are the main occupations of the coastal Even (Arutiunov 1988a). On the Okhotsk coast, reindeer are herded by Even on horseback (Levin and Vasil'yev 1956 [1964]).

In the past, some fishing Even had a few reindeer that were looked after by herding Even. Currently, inland Even use dogs to assist them in herding their reindeer. Dogs are usually tied up so that they will not attack the reindeer. They are used to control the herds during mushroom season, however, when reindeer scatter in all directions in search of the delicacies; barking dogs on long leashes scare the reindeer into quickly moving together.

Until recently, hunting and trapping were the most important economic endeavours of herding Even, bringing in almost 90 per cent of their income. Squirrel was one of the most commonly traded skins; wild reindeer, moose, mountain sheep, and bear were also hunted, but traditionally it was considered taboo to hunt wolves (Levin and Vasil'yev 1956 [1964]). During the 1990s, demand from the Orient created a lucrative market for reindeer antler velvet used for medicinal purposes.

55

56

FIGURE 56
Even women wear hats or scarves
with coats featuring a centre-front
opening. Mittens are attached to
coat sleeves, and elaborately decorated aprons are worn underneath.
REM 3962.15

Breeding bulls usually shed their antlers after the mating season in November, cows after the calving season in late May or June. Now, in July, when bulls' antlers are about half-grown and covered with velvet, they are sawed off by herders and sold to buyers who fly around the tundra in helicopters, purchasing the antlers for a pittance. The buyers resell the antlers for outrageous profits, and herders are upset about this economic imbalance. However, they are pleased to have access to helicopter services for a couple of weeks each summer (Oakes and Riewe 1990, Yudin et al. 1979).

Traditional Clothing

Even and Evenki wear similar clothing styles. The distinguishing characteristic of Even coats is the fur trim along the side and hem. Even wear a lavishly beaded apron under a hoodless coat with a beaded centre front opening. Men's aprons have either a curved or a pointed lower edge. Horse and goat hair are used for trim on aprons and coats. Pleats are added across the back of the coat to make it easier to wear while riding, an ancient style passed down from Even ancestors (Anonymous n.d., Arutiunov 1988a, Forsyth 1992, Levin and Vasil'yev 1956 [1964], Okladnikov 1970). Men wear inner and outer skin pants. Inner pants are made from young reindeer skin with the fur worn inside; for outer pants, the fur is turned to the outside. Those Even living in the eastern part of the region have pants with footwear sewn to the bottom, a style worn over inner pants during the winter. Sometimes inner pants also are made with footwear sewn to the bottom edge. The lower portion of this pant style is made from reindeer leg skins, the upper portion from body skins. Soles are cut from seal skin (Semeonovna 1997).

Extensive trade dating back more than a thousand years has provided Even with access to trade beads (Forsyth 1992). Today, beads from the nineteenth century are often combined with contemporary beads on Even aprons, boots, and coats. The Even living in taiga areas commonly wear Yakut clothing styles, and those living on the tundra commonly use Chukchi clothing rather than their own traditional styles (Levin and Potapov 1956 [1964]).

Some Even children wear a one-piece reindeer skin suit similar to the Chukchi style. The suit is hoodless, with the fur to the inside. Sleeves have slits on the side rather than open ends for the hand. These slits are cut by a talented seamstress or hunter, so that the child will inherit these skills.

Shamans' clothing among the Even is less complicated and less highly decorated than that of Evenki or Yakut, and Even use fewer iron figurines and much smaller drums. Traditionally, Even interred their dead by placing them in wooden boxes on platforms. A wooden bird image was placed above and behind the grave, and broken goods owned by the deceased were scattered around the grave (Levin and Potapov 1956 [1964]).

Footwear

Even make ankle-, knee-, and thigh-high boots. Shorter boots are for everyday wear. In winter, knee-high boots are worn with leggings or have an extension sewn to the upper leg. Thigh-high boots are worn by men, and sometimes women, for hunting and long trips. Even men living near Chukchi and Koryak wear leg skin boots cut just below the knee when hunting on skis (Zakharova 1974). The upper edge is cut at a slant on thigh-high boots, straight across for boots reaching to the knee. Even make boots from reindeer or moose leg skins, dehaired reindeer skins, sheared sheep skin, or seal skin. Although white leg skins symbolize high economic status, dark brown skins are most commonly used, even in boots for festive occasions. Summer footwear is made from dehaired reindeer or moose hides, or from summer reindeer leg skins with the hair left intact; winter footwear always has the hair left on for extra insulation. Even living near Koryak and Chukchi stain dehaired skins with ochre and willow bark, using techniques similar to those of Chukchi. Casings on short boots, straps, and drawstrings are usually made from dehaired and smoked or stained skins (Hatt 1916, Levin and Vasil'yev 1956 [1964], Sem 1997, Semeonovna 1997, Vasilevich 1963a).

Leg Skin Boots

Leg skin boots are designed for work wear, everyday wear, and festive occasions. Two different patterns are used to make both knee-high and thigh-high boots.

Work, Everyday and Special Occasion Boots

The first leg skin boot pattern has a sole with slight pleating at the toe and heel, a narrow side strip that encircles the foot,

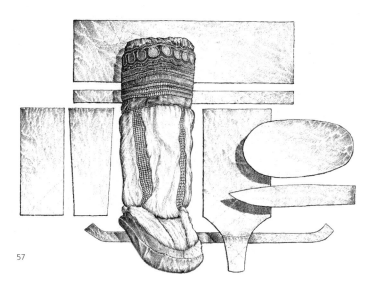

57

and a gusset that tapers to a point on each side of the centre front and extends back to the back panel or to a centre back seam. The leg section, made from one continuous leg skin, consists of four panels (front, back, side left, and side right), with several pieces added at the sides when needed. The upper edge is finished with a strip of skin. Drawstrings are used on knee-high versions of this style, and a thong sewn to the top of thigh-high boots is tied to a waistband or a stocking thong. This boot is used mainly for work wear. It may either be left undecorated or have red fabric welts sewn into the front seams. A few lines of beads and possibly a strip of skin are placed at the knee and across the toes (EMO 27.602B, 27.602A). This pattern may also be made with smoked reindeer body skin for the leg section. Fishers sometimes use commercially produced cowhide for boots made in a similar manner (Semeonovna 1997).

The second leg skin boot style, which has an upper and a lower leg section with a horizontal band around the knee, is used for everyday and festive wear. Skin soles are gathered slightly at the toe and heel, and some heels are made with a T-seam. Soles are cut from reindeer forehead, toe, or leg skins; moose is also used by Even living in the taiga, and seal by Even living near Koryak and Chukchi. Small pieces of toe skin are sewn into a panel, then the panel is cut into the shape of a sole with the hair, which is placed to the outside, flowing towards the toe. Careful positioning of the hair direction

makes boots easier to wear on skis. Hair on other types of skins used for soles is also usually worn to the outside, although sometimes it is turned to the inside or dehaired and stained with ochre or alder bark (Oakes and Riewe 1990, Semeonovna 1997).

Leg skin boots made by Even living in the Far East have a side strip with a centre front seam and a gusset that tapers to a point on each side of the centre front and extends around to a centre back seam. In this variation, the side strips are generally narrower than those used by Nenets, and the gussets are wider. A long, relatively wide gusset is used without a side strip by Even living in the western areas. Gussets are placed with the hair going towards the front (Oakes and Riewe 1990, Semeonovna 1997).

The leg in this second boot style is cut with a front, back, side left, and side right panel for men's and women's boots. (Four rather than six panels are most commonly used by Evenki, Chukchi, Koryak, and Yupik.) On women's boots, the front panel has a seam across the vamp above the toes. On some boots, a small piece of light-haired skin is inserted, with a red felt welt appearing at the tip of the front panel, near the spot where the reindeer's metatarsal gland was before the legs were skinned. A narrow strip of skin is often added to the leg side panel for extra width, rather than as a design feature. The shape and width of this strip varies depending on the width of the reindeer leg skins used for the main panels and the size of the finished boot. This section extends to below the knee. A broad skin panel is sewn horizontally around the top, making the finished boot rise to just below the knee. The upper edge is finished with a casing and drawstring (Semeonovna 1997, Vasilevich 1963a).

Thigh-high boots in this style are made by sewing vertical leg skin panels to the tops of knee-high boots. The upper edge is finished with a straight strip of skin or with a casing. A thong is sewn to the top at centre front and tied directly to a waist belt or looped over the belt and tied to a stocking thong. These tall boots are also worn with the top section folded down over the lower portion (Semeonovna 1997, Vasilevich 1963a).

Both of these boot styles are decorated with narrow, vertical bands of beading along the front panel seams. Lines of alternating black (or dark blue) and white beads, two beads of

FIGURE 57
The Even knee-high boot pattern has a slightly pleated sole, side strip, gusset, and broad-beaded band sewn around the top. The centre-front vamp and side strip of women's boots are often cut from skins of contrasting colours.

FIGURE 58
Even women wear dark-haired leg skin boots with an extra band of beadwork placed across the vamp.
BSM P90.0281.ab

58

59

FIGURE 59
Even thigh-high boots are often decorated with extensive beading below the knee and worn for special occasions. REM 5589.23

FIGURE 60
Unbeaded leg skin boots are used for everyday wear by Even reindeer herders. A few pieces of white-haired skin from the belly of a reindeer are added for decoration. BSM P90.0298.ab

FIGURE 61
Even men's and women's boot styles are similar, but in men's footwear the strip of beading across the vamp is omitted. These men's boots are elaborately beaded for festive occasions. REM 2027.1/1,2

60

61

62

FIGURE 62
Even and Koryak make similar boot styles with unpleated soles, one-piece vamps, and triangular skin mosaics decorating the leg sections. REM 7112-78/1,2

FIGURE 63
This boot was made first as a knee-high boot with a drawstring around the upper edge; the thigh-high extension was added later. The vamp with a small insert; blue, white, and black beads; and semicircular bead pattern are typically Even. REM 1186.9/1,2

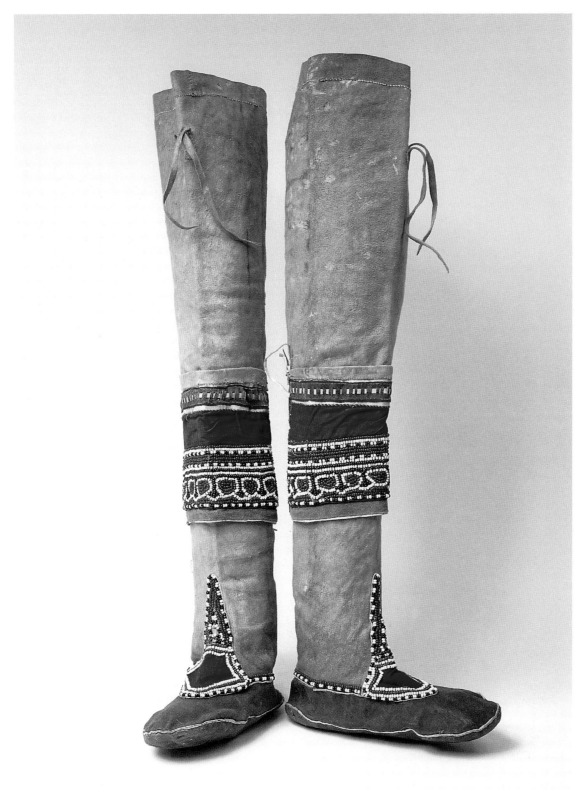

63

FIGURE 64
On these shamans' boots, hair embroidery, beads, and ochre create skeletal formations that protect shamans' knees and legs while they journey to the under and upper worlds. REM 1636.6/1,2

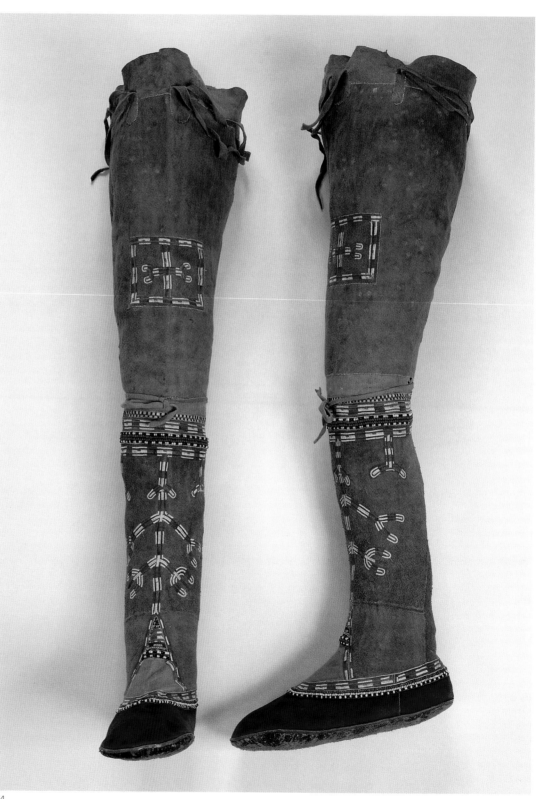

64

each colour, are commonly used along with solid-coloured lines of beads. Similar beading patterns decorate the seam across the vamp above the toes on women's boots. Narrow strips of fabric and fur are also commonly added to this seam (BSM P90.0279.a-d, P90.0281.ab; NMF VK1826.2). A broad, horizontal, beaded band of red fabric placed just below the knee is covered with a series of linear strings of beads that are intermixed often with a chain of semicircular, archlike motifs (Hatt 1916, Vasilevich 1963a, NMF VK1826.2). Some of the more common designs are known as sun, face, spider, fingernail, claw, horns, cross, teepee, bird, and bird's footprint. Red, white, blue, and black are the colours used most by traditional Even. Light blue is also seen, and even occasionally yellow and green.

Traditional Even designs depict elements of the environment, and decorative patterns are passed from mother to daughter. Everyday footwear often has less elaborate beading and only straight lines of decoration. Beaded designs tell who made the footwear and who wears it, as well as the cultural group of the seamstress. When one seamstress likes a design used by someone else, she pays the other seamstress to make her a set of beaded panels, which she then sews into the seams of her own boots (Oakes and Riewe 1990, Semeonovna 1997).

Festive footwear is made with dark-haired leg skins from reindeer killed in the early summer when the hair is still short, fine, and very dark. It is lavishly beaded using traditional Even colours and other colours (Semeonovna 1997). Straps are usually omitted; if they are included, they are camouflaged by being attached to a base made of black fabric that is beaded and then appliquéd with a strip of red fabric. Another strip of red fabric is used to make the ankle strap, so that it appears to be part of the decoration (Oakes and Riewe 1990, Semeonovna 1997).

Funeral Boots

Footwear used for funeral clothing by Even living near Yakut is similar to that worn for weddings and festive occasions. Ancient designs are used for decoration, including a circular chain, rows of figure eights, zigzags, and rhomboid shapes made by combining chum-shaped triangles. Seams are accented with red fabric welts (Sem 1997).

Dehaired Skin Summer Boots

Dehaired skin boots used by many Even are worn with dry grass insoles and no stockings. They are made with a flat, unpleated sole, a vamp, and a leg section with a centre back or centre front seam. Soles are cut from seal skin, dehaired moose hide, or cropped reindeer skins. The vamp and leg sections are made from dehaired reindeer or moose skin or early summer reindeer leg skins. The vamp seam may either be sharply pointed or have a truncated point; alternatively, the vamp encircles the foot. Even living north of Yakut wear similar footwear with a pleated sole; those living near Koryak and Chukchi use an unpleated sole and a vamp that encircles the foot. Bleached skin welts are placed in the seams. A few lines of beads are sewn to the vamp seam on some boots made in this style (Oakes and Riewe 1990; Semeonovna 1997; Vasilevich 1963a, REM 7112.78/1,2).

A second dehaired boot style is made with a flat sole, a vamp that encircles the foot, a pointed second vamp, and a thigh-high leg section with a centre back seam. The top side of a broad, horizontally beaded band is sewn to the boot at the knee, creating a beaded flap, and the top edge of the boot is often worn folded down. Beaded figures are added to some boots, as are combinations of beaded panels and beaded outlining (Sem 1997, REM 1186.9/1,2).

In addition to beading, Even from the Far East decorate boots with skin and fur mosaics. Light and dark skins are cut in identical geometric shapes and sewn next to each other, creating a repetitive design of contrasting colours. Often, light and dark chum-shaped pieces are sewn together to create distinctive patterns. Checkerboard, flower, and claw designs are also common. Combinations of beading, hair embroidery, thread embroidery, and fur mosaics appear occasionally. Dyed baby seal fur, squirrel tails, and other light and dark skins are also used to trim some beaded panels; these are most often placed in the seam that crosses the front panel just above the toes and in the seam that encircles the broad upper panel (Oakes and Riewe 1990, Sem 1997, Semeonovna 1997).

Seal Skin Summer Boots

In damp weather, coastal Even use seal skin footwear constructed with a flat sole. The vamp is either pointed, truncated, or encircles the foot, and the leg section is cut in one piece with a centre back seam. A casing is usually sewn to the upper edge, with a drawstring threaded through. This boot style is made either ankle-high or knee-high (Oakes and Riewe 1990, Semeonovna 1997).

Shamans' Boots

Symbolic designs are especially important in the clothing and footwear worn by shamans. Contrasting colours are used throughout an ensemble. For example, the right stocking may be made from red, dyed reindeer skin and the left stocking from white, bleached skin; the right boot may be made from dark-haired leg skins and the left from light-haired leg skins (Sem 1993).

The colour red and beads are both used by shamans as spirit helpers. For example, seal fur dyed red may be cut into pendants in the shape of people and attached to boots to help a shaman bring life back to an ill person. Alternating white and black beads at the boots' upper edge, knee, and mid-shin and a strip of beads just below the knee provide additional assistance. During a healing ceremony, footwear is switched from one foot to the other to confuse evil spirits (Sem 1993).

Additional powers may also be channelled through the use of significant symbols and numbers. A circle of dehaired, red-dyed skin bearing a human figure outlined with white reindeer hair embroidery is attached to a shaman's right boot near the knee to represent the shaman's ancestors. On a shaman's left boot, two concentric circles with crosses in the middle are stitched using red-dyed hair embroidery on a white background, symbolizing a vital force. A tree embroidered on the instep of a pair of shaman's boots using white reindeer hair has four pairs of branches pointing downwards on the left boot, three on the right. Some Even shamans decorate their boots with a series of seven beaded anthropomorphic figures in a horizontal row (Sem 1993). These skeletal designs also help shamans draw on ancestral support and wisdom.

Leggings and Stockings

Knee-high and thigh-high stockings are worn with winter footwear, with women wearing thigh-high stockings most often. Both styles are constructed in a similar way. Short stockings are made from late fall reindeer skins with the hair left on or lightly cropped, or from wild mountain sheep skins with the fur left on; the sole and leg are cut from one piece. Thigh-high stockings have a much longer leg that widens at the top. A piece of dehaired skin or red fabric is sewn to the top of both stocking styles, along with a skin thong. These thongs are used to tie two stockings together, for drying or storage, and to tie long stockings to a specially designed waistband worn by older women. The waistband has two straps with metal rings on the end; stocking ties are slipped through these rings and tied in position (Oakes and Riewe 1990, Semeonovna 1997, EMO 27.601).

Leggings are cut from one piece of reindeer or sheep skin with the fur to the inside. The upper edge, wider than that of thigh-high stockings, is finished with a strip of dehaired skin and ties that attach the leggings to a waistband. Sometimes ties from a stocking or legging are looped over a belt and attached directly to the ties at the top of thigh-high boots. Leggings are worn with short stockings. Boots are lined with grass and then stocking-covered legs are slipped inside (Semeonovna 1997).

Coastal Even women's leggings and stockings are often decorated with a strip of red cloth and a few beads sewn to the centre front at the knee. Even living farther inland near Yakut embroider a symbolic pattern using reindeer hair, coloured thread, and beads to the knees of leggings and pants worn by a bride at her wedding (Oakes and Riewe 1990, Sem 1997).

Summary

Leg skin boots worn by Even are knee-high, with a thigh-high extension added if needed. The tops of knee-high boots are cut straight across and finished with a casing and drawstring. Thigh-high versions often have the top portion folded down. Straps are sewn to the ankle, knee, and top. Blue, white, and black beads are traditional. Beaded panels are sewn horizontally around the knee, vertically down each side of the front panel, and across the top of the foot on women's boots. Men's boots are decorated in a similar manner, omitting the band across the top of the foot. Dehaired skin boots are made with a flat sole, pointed or truncated vamp, and leg section with a centre back seam. The Even also use styles influenced by Yakut, Koryak, Chukchi, and Evenki.

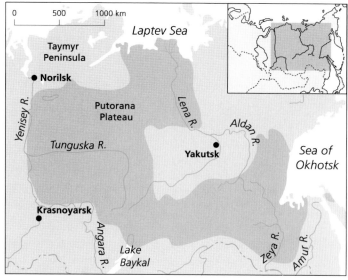

CHAPTER 5

Map 6

FIGURE 65
Overleaf: Evenki hunters spear bears
as they emerge from their dens
after hibernation. This hunter is
wearing a kerchief on his head, as
do most Evenki. REM 5659.30

MAP 6
Evenki homelands

FIGURE 66
In winter, Evenki hunt and trap
on skis hand-carved from pine.
Short-haired summer reindeer skins
line the bottom of skis for extra
traction when climbing uphill.

THE EVENKI, WHO number about 30,000, occupy a huge territory from the mixed forest of the Amur region westward across the taiga and tundra to the Yenisey River (Federal Service of Geodesy and Cartography of Russia 1995, Levin 1963, Vakhtin 1992, Vasilevich and Smolyak 1964). The word "Evenki" means "he who runs swifter than a reindeer." The informal economy of the Evenki is based on hunting wild reindeer and moose, herding reindeer, fishing, trapping sable and fox, and, in the south, herding cattle. Milk is the most highly prized product derived from cattle and reindeer herds. Evenki use reindeer as pack and riding animals, since the animals are well suited to travelling over rocky and boggy terrain (Anderson 1991, Forsyth 1992, Vasilevich and Smolyak 1964).

The national BAM railway (Anderson 1991), mining, hydroelectric projects, and other industrial developments across Evenki territory have radically influenced the traditional way of life. Most people, including the families of nomadic herders, are now settled in Russian villages and belong to collective or state farms.

Shamans

At one time, Evenki and Yakut shamans were known to be particularly powerful. Today, shamanism is experiencing a revival in remote parts of Evenki territory.

Traditionally shamans either inherited their powers or were selected by the spirits. They identified metaphysically with all things—trees, rocks, plants, water, fire—including the animals that provided food, shelter, and clothing, and they communicated with spirits in the lower, middle, and upper worlds. While in a trance, a shaman would journey into the upper world to persuade the master or mistress of game to release animals for the hunters. The spirits of deceased animals were pacified by the shaman to protect a hunter's family from revenge (Okladnikov 1970).

Moose play a central role in the beliefs and rituals of Evenki. Various rites traditionally performed before a moose and wild reindeer hunt involved everyone in the group. The shaman first walked into the forest, to the group's sacred tree, to find the woman spirit who protected their lands and ask for her help in the hunt. She in turn sent the shaman to a zoomorphic spirit which took the form of a giant cow moose or reindeer. Through the help of this spirit, the shaman was able to picture himself lassoing animals. This vision would help to bring animals closer to the hunters. If insufficient animals had been caught by the time the shaman returned home, a symbolic hunt would begin. The shaman once again visited the spirit woman, stealing from her some magical strands of wool that turned into animals as soon as he got back to camp and shook them. Following this, hunters dressed in ceremonial costumes with caps made from the skulls of reindeer or moose enacted animal movements in order to bring moose and wild reindeer to their hunting grounds. Using willow and larch branches, they created a thick bush in which they placed figurines representing herds of animals. Elders would tell stories and legends while small "calf" figurines were placed next to the figurine representing the cow moose, symbolically

multiplying the population and ensuring a successful hunt. Finally, hunters searched for animal "tracks," ritually stalking and shooting arrows at the wooden cow and calf figurines. Several reindeer were also sacrificed and eaten so that they could be resurrected as moose. Red ochre representing the suffering, dying, and resurrection of the moose was used to create moose images in cliff drawings (Okladnikov 1970).

Shamans were skilled at mediating conflicts between humans and the spirits. They protected people from enemies, evil spirits, illness, bad luck, and starvation. Drums, songs, dance, sacrifice, ritual, and discussions with spirits were their tools. They also acted as vehicles for communication with deceased ancestors, especially at the moment someone died (Anisimov 1963a, Vasilevich 1963b).

Traditionally, in addition to shamans who mediated with

66

good and evil spirits, there were also orators, humorous story-tellers, singers, and wise individuals (Okladnikov 1970). Both men and women could be shamans. Shamans learned from more experienced shamans; they also studied oral traditions, natural history, and the behavioural psychology of their group in order to better understand the social-historical fabric of their community. A strong knowledge base was needed in order to make sound predictions (Anisimov 1963a). Depending on cultural affiliation, experienced shamans protected either individuals, a group, or a territory. When a shaman died, all the spiritual defence built by that person around a group was removed (Czaplicka 1914).

Shamans were shown respect by being given a place of honour, the best food, and conversations with the eldest family or group member. The group tended a shaman's reindeer and always gave a shaman the best fishing place on a stream. For each ritual performed, shamans were paid one to four reindeer, depending on how wealthy the family was (Anisimov 1963a).

Some rites, such as looking for lost reindeer or foretelling the future, were performed in an ordinary chum. More complicated rites were conducted in a special shaman's tent, which had strong connections with the lower, middle, and upper worlds through the hearth, a larch tree, and effigies. The hearth was used after the fire had cooled. Symbolically, it was seen as the beginning of life, the lower world, and the home of the fire mistress, who was the spirit of fire, hearth, chum, and rebirth. Historically, women were thought to be shamans as they were the guardians of the hearth and all it represents (Anisimov 1963a).

A larch was placed in the centre of the shaman's tent to help connect the three worlds. Its roots were in the hearth, or lower world, and its branches extended out through the top of the tent, into the upper world. When a shaman was symbolically in one of the other worlds, he or she rested by the larch's roots to gather strength and knowledge from ancestor spirits. Shamans also used the larch as a ladder to climb into the upper world, and spirit helpers rested on the tree's branches.

The welfare and fates of individuals, the group, and the shaman were connected with the larch. The shaman's external animal soul and the souls of each member of the group resided in the tree (Anisimov 1963a, 1963b). By hitting a drum that has a larch rim, the shaman allowed the animal soul to enter his or her body and sent spirit helpers to the underworld to check conditions before making the journey (Anisimov 1963b; Dioszegi 1968; Dioszegi and Hoppal 1978; Michael 1963; Prokofyeva 1963, 1971; Serov 1988). This external soul was also critical for the shaman's journeys in the middle world, the world of humans. "If the tree dies, the shaman dies" (Anisimov 1963a).

The shaman's tent was carefully protected from evil spirits and hostile shamans. Two wooden figures representing the shaman's ancestor spirits were placed at the tent's entrance, and two large blocks of wood symbolizing eels were placed within sight of the tent to scare away or swallow harmful underworld spirits entering the middle world. Inside the shaman's tent, wooden figurines of moose, reindeer, salmon, and other animal spirit helpers were placed at strategic places to trap any evil spirit that managed to pass through the other protective barriers. Additional spirit helpers with spears were placed inside the tent to prevent the spirits of hostile shamans from entering through the shaman's spirit river (Anisimov 1963a).

Evenki believed that illness and death were spirits sent by another group's shaman. Spirit helpers were called upon to swallow the disease spirit and carry it to the lower world, where it was released through the shaman's anus. A barricade or fence of larch saplings placed around an ill person or around an entire camp provided further protection (Anisimov 1963a).

Traditional Clothing

Traditional Evenki clothing was designed to accommodate the cold dry climate, the nomadic way of life, and travel on foot or skis. Winter clothing was made from reindeer and moose skins, spring and summer clothing from dehaired, smoked reindeer skin and fabric. Loincloths sewn from newborn reindeer skin, worn with reindeer skin leggings and thigh-high boots, provided ideal protection in deep snow. Parkas were open at the front and had several pleats at the back for extra ease when sitting on a reindeer. Today, a pull-over parka is used by Evenki living on the tundra.

Parkas were worn with an apron elaborately decorated with fur, embroidery, beads, and painted trim. In winter,

Evenki added close-fitting reindeer skin caps, often with the reindeer ears left in place. A hunter's belt carried his gunpowder, bullet pouch, and knife (Vasilevich and Smolyak 1956 [1964]).

Shamans' Clothing

Traditionally and in contemporary times, the skills and responsibilities of a shaman are communicated through clothing and accessories (Caseburg 1993). According to Hajdú (1968), shamans who have received their footwear are almost at the highest rank; footwear is received only after the shaman has earned his or her drum, apron, and cape. The highest rank is symbolized by a cap and staff.

Shamans' garments—parkas, gloves, aprons, headgear, and footwear—are believed to be both powerful animal totems and armour against evil spirits sent by shamans from other groups (Anisimov 1963a). The copper trim placed along the hem of a shaman's clothing symbolizes death.

Among some groups, such as Enets, shamans never make their own garments. These are made by the shaman's wife or another woman, using skin from reindeer killed by the shaman. New garments are hidden near the shaman's tent, and shamans are not allowed to practise if they are unable to find them (Prokofyeva 1963). Evenki shamans' garments are painted or embroidered with images of their helping spirits, which take the form of various animals, such as birds, fish, snakes, and lizards. Coloured strips of skin, ribbon, and cloth are attached for added protection (Anisimov 1963a; Prokofyeva 1963, 1971). Wooden and metal images of spirit protectors, including tigers, fish, and humanoid figures, are used, and the universe is represented by a metal lattice worn around the shaman's neck (Okladnikov 1970). Male shamans usually wear a second jacket bearing painted symbols of lizards, snakes, and frogs. Multiple images of spirit protectors hang from the back of the belt, and smaller images appear on the shaman's headpiece (Dioszegi and Hoppal 1978, Okladnikov 1970, Serov 1988).

Each cultural group has its own typical costumes and tools for shamans. The Evenki shaman wears a parka, a hat, an apron with iron trimmings, and footwear also often trimmed with iron. A mask is thought to transform the shaman into an animal. A shaman's costume and drum are sacred and can

67

FIGURE 67
An Evenki shaman's clothing carries many symbolic references to flight, such as metal pendants and tassels made with bird wings and tails. Metal and skin spirit helpers are also important elements.
REM 4871.216a-c (*coat*), REM 4871.212 (*hat*), REM 4871.217 (*apron*)

68

never be used by anyone else; otherwise, the spirits will be unable to hear the shaman (Prokofyeva 1963, 1971; Serov 1988).

Footwear

Some Evenki have footwear typical for unmounted hunters on the taiga: dehaired skin boots with slightly pleated soles and a vamp, and leg skin boots with a single set of gussets, which reflects the Evenkis' long association with their unmounted neighbours. Throughout the Yenisey Basin in the west and along the Amur River in the east, these footwear styles are used for both working and hunting. Other Evenki, who have intermarried with eastern reindeer hunters such as Even, prefer boots with a leg section sewn to a vamp and attached to a flat, unpleated sole. This style may have been adopted from ancient herdsmen in Central Asia and passed on to Even and Evenki reindeer herders, who eventually settled on the taiga and introduced it to Evenki living in the north, northwest, and southeast (Vasilevich 1963a).

Generally, Evenki have shin-high footwear for hunting, knee-high footwear for everyday wear, and thigh-high footwear for travelling. Short boots are lengthened by sewing an upper section to them or by wearing them with leggings. The upper edge is cut straight across, and Evenki east of the Lena River fold their boot tops over. Materials used in Evenki footwear include skins from reindeer, wild goats, moose, fish, and cows, in addition to fabrics acquired through trade (Sem 1997).

Leg Skin Boots

Leg skin footwear is usually made with an unpleated sole, although Evenki living east of Lake Baykal or near the Sea of Okhotsk use pleated soles. The sole shape varies from oval in the west to pointed in the Amur region. Evenki living close to Yakut use a Yakut-style sole that narrows into a long point which wraps over the toes and is sewn into a long, slashed dart cut into the vamp at centre front. Some of these Yakut-Evenki moved to the Amur River region and introduced this sole design to Negidal, Nanai, and Orochi. Soles for boots to be used by hunters travelling on foot are made from reindeer toe skins. Soles with the fur placed on the inside are used for skiing. Evenki from Tunguska River make a special sole with nubs sewn to the bottom for added traction when descending steep mountains (Vasilevich 1963a).

FIGURE 68
Evenki women wear coats decorated with long tassels of fabric and horse and goat hair to spring festivals and hunting ceremonies. REM 5589.17

FIGURE 69
Like the Even, Evenki ride reindeer. Their clothing has been adapted to riding by adding more fullness across the back. Seven pleats are used; seven is a sacred number for several Siberian groups. REM 5659.4

69

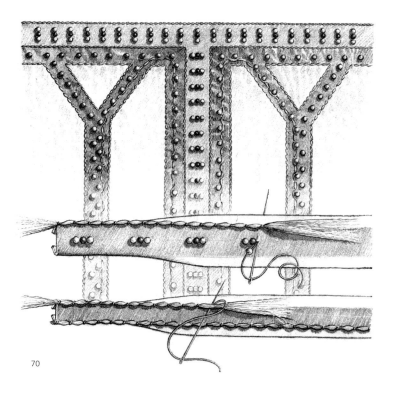

70

Soles are sewn to the leg section using different techniques. A few Evenki make leg skin boots without gussets or side strips, sewing the leg section directly to the sole. Evenki living west of the Yenisey River, along part of the Lena River, and along the Sea of Okhotsk are a few of the people who use one side strip. This strip is narrower than that used by Nenets, and the centre front seam is cut on less of an angle. A side strip plus a gusset tapering to a point on each side of centre front, and extending back to the side or back panel or ending with a centre back seam, is used by Evenki living north of the Tunguska River, who adopted this feature from their Nenets neighbours.

Leg sections on knee-high boots are usually made from reindeer or moose leg skins with a front, back, side left, and side right panel. Boots made from extra-large taiga mountain reindeer or moose leg skins have only a front and a back panel, because these skins are much wider. The front section of Evenki boots has a tongue-shaped seam, unlike the more angular seam line used by Nenets and Khanty. Women's boots have an extra seam across the vamp just above the toes, and a square inset is often placed at the top of the front panel. A

wide band of skin is sewn around the upper portion of the leg. Knee-high boots are finished with a casing sewn to the upper edge and threaded with a drawstring. One style of thigh-high boots is made by sewing an upper panel of leg skins to the top of knee-high leg skin boots. Thigh-high boots are finished with a narrow strip of skin sewn to the upper edge and skin thongs sewn to the ankle, knee, and top (Sem 1997).

Knee-high and thigh-high leg skin boots are decorated with beaded panels by most Evenki, including those living west of the Lena River and Lake Baykal. The vertical seams on each side of the front leg panel and sometimes the seam across the top of the foot above the toes are decorated with a few strings of beads sewn to red fabric. Some strings are made with beads of the same colour, but strings which alternate two white beads with two black or dark blue beads are common. A broad upper band placed near the front knee area and extending around to each side is decorated with horizontal rows of beads. These strings may have beads of the same colour or alternate two black and two white beads. A variety of linear, zigzag, arch, rhombic, circle chain, floral, and other designs used by Even are also commonly used on this band (Sem 1997; MVB IVA 3924; NMF VK5275.2; REM 6805.1/1,2, 2027.1/1,2). East of the Yenisey River, some Evenki boots have a much narrower and shorter horizontal band of beading placed at the front near the knee. Strips of fabric or skin are used instead of vertical strips of beads on each side of the front panel (PRM 1914a).

Beading colour schemes vary from one region to the next. For example, Evenki living near the Sea of Okhotsk use red with dark blue and white with black. Evenki near the Tunguska River use either red, black, white, dark blue, and pink beads or black, two black and two white, yellow, and dark blue bead combinations. West of the Lena River navy, green, and white are preferred, and east of the Lena River navy, blue, white, yellow, red, and pink are common (Vasilevich 1963a).

Some Evenki add strips of different-coloured skin and hair next to beads. Evenki near the Sea of Okhotsk add red piping and natural-coloured dehaired skin mosaics to beaded panels. Neighbouring Evenki use patterns composed of red zigzags on a black background and narrow red and

FIGURE 70
Evenki clothing and footwear is
decorated with parallel lines of
colour created by combining ochre,
appliquéd fabric, hair embroidery,
and beading.

FIGURE 71
Reindeer body skins are sewn with
the hair to the inside on these knee-
high boots, which are worn during
the coldest part of winter. Vamps
are decorated with the winglike
beaded appliqué typically made by
Evenki. REM 1763.24/1,2

dark blue strips. Near the Amur River, Evenki use multicoloured embroidered flower and plant designs (Sem
1997).

Evenki from the eastern coast and the Amur River region
decorate the upper band of their boots with checkerboard-
style fur mosaics: squares or rectangles of light- and dark-
haired skins are alternated on a vertical or a horizontal plane.
Vertical seams are finished with red or black folded welts.
Evenki living to the northwest of Yakut decorate their
footwear with fur mosaics in the form of stylized reindeer,
birds, and dancing people. Decorative boots are worn by reindeer herders with ceremonial clothing during the spring
solstice (Sem 1997).

Work Boots

Thigh-high work boots have a front, back, two left-side, and
two right-side panels that extend along the full length of the
leg in one continuous strip. It takes approximately eight pairs
of reindeer leg skins to make one pair of thigh-high boots
(Sem 1997). This boot style is usually left undecorated (MVB IVA
3324), although one or two strings of beads may appear in the
front panel seam (PRM 1914b).

Leg skin work boots are also made with a leg skin lower
section and a reindeer body skin upper section. Evenki across
Siberia sew strips of white- and brown-haired skins into each
side of the front panel and in vertical seams (MVB IVA 3897).
Evenki near the Tunguska River use strips cut from two

72

FIGURE 72
Embroidered panels are often
added to dehaired summer boots.
REM 809.8/1,2

FIGURE 73
Evenki hunters wear boots
covered with decorations to
appease the animal spirits.
REM 8762.19180/1,2

73

distinct shades of brown hair and white hair for their vertical insets (Sem 1997).

Knee-high boots are made from reindeer skin stained with bark and worn with the fur to the inside. This style, which has a slightly gathered sole, a pointed vamp, and a leg section with a centre front or centre back seam, is left undecorated (MVB IVA 3907) or covered with beaded fabric. One common technique is to sew strips of different-coloured fabric to the vamp's top seam, creating a broad, horizontal bar. Beads are clustered in groups of two and sewn along each of the fabric strips (MVB IVA 3898; REM 1763.23/1,2, 1763.24/1,2).

Hunters' Boots

Thigh-high hunters' boots are made with a slightly gathered sole, a pointed vamp, and an upper and lower leg section. Ties are placed at the ankle, knee, and top edge. The lower part of the boot is made from smoked reindeer skin with the hair removed or worn to the inside; the upper part from smoked skin, reindeer leg skins, or a combination of reindeer leg skins in the front and smoked skin in the back. Knee-high boots may also be made using this pattern and the decorative technique described below (BM 1913.11.45.52).

This boot style is decorated with a series of parallel lines created with stain, fabric, hair embroidery, beads, and skin. The lines follow a standard pattern, although each woman's design is distinct. Before the back seam is sewn, the vamp is decorated with one line that encircles it, followed by several other shorter lines that fill in the centre. The leg section is divided by decorative lines into three symmetrical sections: a side section, an upper front section, and a lower front section. Lines in a rectangular shape outline the side section, which extends back to the centre back seam. The centre of the side section is often left without decoration. The front section is divided into two parts by a horizontal line just above the top of the vamp-leg seam. The upper front section is decorated with a series of vertical lines running parallel to the centre front fold, and the lower front section has slanted lines running parallel to the vamp-leg seam. Lines of contrasting colours are sewn on with space between them so the natural skin colour forms part of the design (MM AS1913.11.14.52; NMF VK1898-1900, VK3904.1322a and

1322b, VK4934.174; MVB IVA 300; REM 5589.23/1,2, 8762 19180/1,2).

Blue and red or blue and yellow fabric or paint is used with white reindeer hair embroidery in the east. Strings of beads outline strips of skin, fabric, or stained skin, symbolizing the tree of life. The materials used to produce the tree (red dye, reindeer hair) symbolize the elements of nature needed for fertility and success (Sem 1997). These features reinforce the hunter's pre- and post-hunt ceremonies and strengthen the seamstress' ability to communicate with spirit helpers while absent from the hunt.

Dehaired Skin Summer Boots

Evenki from different regions have slightly different types of knee-high dehaired skin boots for the summer. Near the Amur River and east of Lake Baykal, boots are made with a front and a back leg panel; the vamp is omitted and there is a seam on each side of the leg (Vasilevich 1963a). In many areas pointed, truncated, rounded, or squared vamps are used. The height and width of vamps vary regionally and from seamstress to seamstress. Dehaired skin boots are also made with a pleated sole, a vamp, and a short leg section with a centre back seam (Sem 1997, REM 809.8/1,2).

Evenki from the east coast and the upper Amur River region decorate this boot style with coloured embroidery thread in running, chain, and satin stitches. Pink, violet, red, light blue, and dark blue, used with shades of yellow, or with yellow, red, black, and green, are common colour combinations. In addition, coloured thread and reindeer hair are overcast to seams, and coloured fabric welts (red and sometimes black) are folded into seams for extra decoration (Sem 1997).

Yukagir-Evenki Style Boots

A variation of the above style is made from haired skins for winter and dehaired skins for summer. It is decorated following Yukagir tradition by adding a contrasting coloured welt in the seam. This style has an unpleated sole and a vamp with a truncated point that extends either to the base of the shin or partway up. The leg section has a narrow front panel and a broad back panel that extends around to the front, a style adopted from Yukagir by Evenki living near the Lena River. Evenki who moved from this area eastward to the Sea of

Okhotsk brought this design with them (Vasilevich 1963a).

Another variation is created by sewing a slightly pleated Evenki sole to a leg section cut from haired reindeer body skins. This style, worn in cold winter weather, has the side strip and vamp seam painted with ochre (BM 98.7.2.3).

Beaded Sole Boots

One boot style used by Evenki living in the southern region has a leg section sewn directly to the sole. It is influenced by people living in the Altai Mountains, whose footwear is tied only at the ankle. The leg is either knee-high or thigh-high with a centre back seam and white felt sewn in the seam. The sole is narrow, short, and oval-shaped, and the vamp covers the toes. The upper edge is decorated with a 10-cm-wide band of red felt appliquéd with brown, green, and white felt cut into animal and plant images.

In the past, wealthy women wore elaborately decorated shin-high boots. Even the soles of these boots were decorated with embroidery, rows of black beads, and crystals, decoration that was visible only when one sat straight-legged with one's toes together and heels turned out. This was a common position for the steppe peoples of Asia and for Altai Mountain nobility, as they had soft-carpeted floors. This style of boot was worn with two pairs of elaborately decorated thin socks (Rudenko 1970).

Pointed Toed Boots

East of Lake Baykal and in the Amur region, Evenki use boots with a pleated sole gathered to a round, upward-curving point at centre front. The leg section is made with a centre back seam and sewn either directly to the sole or to a vamp. The upper edge of the leg section is often cut on a slant, which is unusual for Evenki footwear. According to Vasilevich (1963a), the gradual increase in the curvature and degree of rise in this distinct toe design reflects the eastern movement of Even and Evenki.

Evenki-Buryat Style Boots

Evenki living east of Lake Baykal have adopted a boot style from their southern neighbours, the Buryat. The sole is very thick, made of numerous layers of skin, and turns up at the front. The vamp encircles the foot and is sewn to a short,

wide leg section with a centre back seam (Forsyth 1992, Vasilevich 1963a).

Shamans' Boots

Evenki shamans' boots are made from reindeer skin with closely cropped hair turned to the inside. Skin thongs used to tie the boots in position are sewn to the top and ankle. Each boot has a different purpose; for example, Enets shamans wear "the boot of the sun" on the right foot while "the boot of the forest spirit monster" is worn on the left (Prokofyeva 1963:143). On the shaman's right boot, animal leg bones are often represented by vertical black strips decorated with reindeer hair embroidery. Circular lines at the knee symbolize the animal's kneecap, and the hoof is indicated in a similar manner. On the left boot, one vertical black line begins with a black circle covered with several layers of metal. These decorative details, and their variations, depict the bright world and the dark world; this distinction is often reinforced by the use of white reindeer hair and black bear hair to trace decorative markings. Bears are seen as animals of the lower, or dark, world.

Shamans' footwear carries anthropomorphic symbols, ancestral symbols, spirit helpers, and protective symbols to help shamans journey safely between worlds. Metal bear-shaped pendants, symbols of Mother Earth, the universe, and ancestors, are sewn to shamans' boots (Sem 1997, Anisimov 1958, Vasilevich 1963a). Red and white stains outlined with black are painted in a zigzag formation on the skin, along with human figures. Red stains stand for blood, symbolizing life in the middle world. Black is associated with the ground and the underworld. White or yellow represents the upper world and the sun. The zigzag motif symbolizes the transition between the human world and the world of spirits and ancestors. The human figures are a shaman's spirit helpers in the underworld (Sem 1997).

Evenki living east of Lake Baykal use iron pendants on their footwear to represent the underworld as well as the shaman's skills. An iron pendant of a reindeer leg represents the entire universe of the reindeer; a bear paw represents the bear's universe and Evenki ancestors. Several iron pendants are attached to a female shaman's boots in the collection of the Russian Museum of Ethnography (Anisimov 1958). A circular piece representing the sun or solar system and the upper world appears above the other pendants. A moose with antlers is positioned under the sun, symbolizing the entire universe of the moose and the middle world. Below this pendant is an ancestral mask in the shape of a bear, representing the underworld. The overall composition reinforces rites performed by shamans to maintain necessary harmony among people, nature, and spirits. Boots worn by shamans during healing ceremonies have figures symbolizing snakes, frogs, and figure eights, which have the power to receive the life-giving forces of fertility (Sem 1997).

Fish Skin Boots

Evenki living in the east wear fish skin footwear sometimes decorated with blue-dyed fish skin that is attached to the boot with fish glue and overcast with sinew. Black skin welts are put into the leg seams (Sem 1997, Vasilevich 1963a).

Boot Ties and Straps

A drawstring inserted into a casing sewn around the upper edge of short boots is used to tie boots on the leg. Thigh-high boots are also tied on the leg, with ties sewn to the knee and ankle. Ties sewn to the top of thigh-high boots are tied directly to a waistband or looped over a waistband and knotted to similar ties sewn to the top of stockings. Evenki from the Tunguska River area use straps sewn to the inside of their boots, several centimetres down from the top. This method of tying on boots, also employed by Koryak, Chukchi, and Yupik, reflects previous interaction between this group of Evenki and Indigenous peoples from the northern Far East (Vasilevich 1963a).

Leggings, Stockings, and Grass Insoles

Short winter boots are worn with leggings, or an extension is sewn to the top of the boot (Vasilevich 1963a, REM 1763.20/1,2). Leggings are made from reindeer body or leg skins. Light- and dark-haired panels are sewn together to create a vertical design on the front, and the back is often undecorated. Lines of beads are sewn around the lower edge, and thongs are sewn to both the upper and lower edges. The lower edge is tucked into the boot top and tied tightly; then the upper thong is either tied to the waist belt or looped over the belt and then tied to an inner stocking.

Stockings are made with the fur worn to the inside or outside. They have an unpleated sole, a pointed vamp or a vamp that encircles the foot, and a leg section with a centre back or centre front seam (EMO 4972, NMF VK4934.177). Skin boots are lined with grass and then slipped over stockings. In extremely cold weather, children wear two pairs of boots for extra insulation (Sem 1997).

Evenki use grass insoles to keep feet warm and dry. Wet grass is replaced with dry grass as necessary. Some people also put holes in boot soles to allow water to drain when they are walking in marshy conditions (Sem 1997).

Summary

Evenki use a wide variety of footwear styles as a result of their regional and cultural diversity. The top of the leg is usually cut straight across on boots of all heights. Knee-high boots may be combined with leggings when thigh-high protection is required. Thigh-high boots are often folded over. A variety of different-coloured beads are used for decorative panels placed in a manner similar to that described for Even. Knee-high leg skin boots are often cut from four leg panels. The length of gussets and side strips varies considerably.

Dehaired skin boots are made with pleated or unpleated soles, vamps cut in several different shapes—with the elongated pointed and truncated versions most common—and slim-cut leg sections. Loops are sewn around the ankle for ankle straps, or ankle straps may be sewn to the back. Straps are also sewn at the knee and to the top of thigh-high boots, where they are tied to a waistband.

Style features, decorative details, and materials used by Yakut, Yukagir, Even, Nenets, Buryat, and Altai Mountain groups, and by people from the Far East, are incorporated into boot styles used by Evenki.

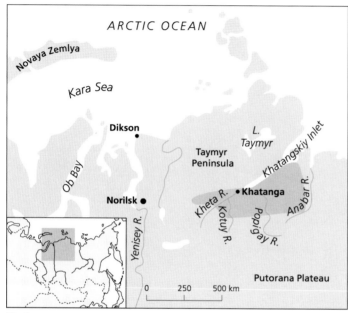

CHAPTER 6

ARCTIC OCEAN

Map 7

FIGURE 74
Overleaf: Dolgan soften reindeer and other skins for clothing. REM 1085.52

MAP 7
Dolgan homelands

FIGURE 75
During the summer, Dolgan reindeer are herded to areas where patches of snow linger well into July, providing relief from biting insects.

THE DOLGAN ARE descendants of Yakut who moved north and intermarried with Evenki during the nineteenth century. Dolgan have combined the Evenkis' milking of reindeer and use of reindeer as packing and riding animals with Nenets techniques of harnessing reindeer to sleds and using herd dogs. Traditionally, Dolgan lived in chums that originated from Evenki, earth-covered lodges introduced by Yakut, or log cabins brought to Siberia by Russians (Forsyth 1992, Levin and Potapov 1956 [1964], Sem 1997).

Today, Dolgan inhabit the Taymyr Peninsula. Eighty-four per cent of them have retained their native language and continue their traditional way of life: herding and hunting reindeer, trapping arctic fox, and fishing. In the 1989 census, 6,932 persons were registered as Dolgan (Vakhtin 1992).

Traditionally, on their western territory on the Taymyr Peninsula, Dolgan pastured their reindeer herds and hunted on the treeless alpine tundra in summer and wintered in the wooded river valleys. In their eastern range, they moved from the forest-tundra to the tundra in summer and returned to the shelter of the forest-tundra for the winter months (Sem 1997).

In the past, Dolgan hunted wild reindeer using a variety of techniques, including ambushing the animals at river crossings with javelins and slings, stalking them from behind wooden blinds attached to skis or while camouflaged in white dog skin parkas, and employing tame reindeer as decoys (Sem 1997). Wild bull reindeer snared in the rut were used to strengthen the genetic lines of domesticated reindeer herds (Levin and Potapov 1956 [1964]).

Traditional Beliefs

Dolgan cultural taboos are passed on from one generation to the next. For example, to protect infants from being born with a variety of ailments, pregnant women do not eat certain foods. Neither do they associate with other pregnant women, thereby protecting themselves from difficult or premature births. When women are about to deliver, a special chum is constructed and shamans perform rituals there. A young larch tree is placed on each side of the chum entrance, enabling the woman's soul to rise up and then return after the infant is born (Popov 1984b).

Women give birth standing up, holding onto a bar that has

a wooden carving of a fox or a rabbit hung above it. This amulet protects women from harm and is used by shamans to relieve pain during childbirth. It is kept near the woman throughout her labour and is reused during each new pregnancy. Women symbolically feed their amulets regularly to ensure their survival (Popov 1984b).

Clothing, skins, and accessories are gifts that show respect for a midwife. A large copper ring symbolizing the female reproductive system is given to the midwife after each birth. Mothers who can afford to also pay the midwife one female reindeer for delivering their first-born. Enough fabric or reindeer skin to make a dress, plus scented soap, is given after she delivers successive infants. These are normal payments, but women who are poor give whatever they can afford.

A new cradle is built prior to an infant's birth. Before the cradle is used for the newborn, a dog is placed in it and rocked to sleep, so that evil spirits will enter the dog rather than the sleeping child. Boys' cradles have a wooden or iron bow and arrow and a knife in a scabbard attached to them, whereas girls are protected by a wooden knife hanging from their cradles. Additional protection is gained by hanging wooden spirit figures inside boys' and girls' cradles (Popov 1984b).

Children's ears are pierced when they are about six years old to thwart evil spirits, who are believed to cut off young people's ears otherwise and use them as spoons (Popov 1984b).

Children play a variety of games involving sticks, lassos, and string. Complex string games can depict complicated skin piecework, animals, and tools. Once children are about ten to twelve years old, boys begin to hunt wild reindeer and girls become responsible for housework, food preparation, and sewing. Children often begin smoking at this age (Popov 1984b).

75

FIGURE 76
Dolgan men wear reindeer skin coats with a slight flare across the back. Beaded chevron designs easily distinguish this style from that of Even and Evenki. Men wear thigh-high leg skin boots for extra protection in deep snow. REM 1283.2 (*coat*), REM 1283.9/1,2 (*boots*)

FIGURE 77
For special occasions, women wear boots with extra beaded panels and beautifully coloured leg skins. REM 1283.11/1,2

76

77

78

Young people meet at dances and family celebrations. Couples who are interested in each other exchange gifts of increasing value, thereby securing permission for the man to visit the woman during the night. His first visit is made in daylight hours so that he can memorize the placement of the chum poles near the woman's sleeping quarters. After dark, he sneaks up to her chum wearing his boots with the fur on the outside to silence his footfalls. If the parents approve of the man, they pretend to sleep while he lies with their daughter. If they do not, they draw attention to the fact that he did not fulfill his needs in secrecy (Popov 1984b).

Traditional Clothing

Dolgan clothing styles combine the hood of the Nenets parka with the beaded centre front opening of the Evenki parka (Levin and Potapov 1956 [1964]). Dolgan also use the long fur coats introduced by Yakut. The most characteristic features of Dolgan clothing and footwear are the colourful stripes, geometric designs (especially chevron shapes), and extensive beadwork used to decorate them. The beadwork designs and their method of application express Dolgans' distinct cultural identity and complex relationships with Yakut, Evenki, and Nenets. Beading designs are passed down from one generation to the next. Archaeological digs in central Siberia indicate that beads were part of Siberian culture 33,000 years ago (Dubin 1987). Large blue beads, often referred to as "Siberian beads," were most likely acquired in trade with China, as Russia did not manufacture them (Mark 1988). Beaded items are included with grave goods to enable the spirits in the other world to

recognize the deceased and to help prevent the corpse's spirit from returning to camp.

Footwear

Dolgan footwear design has clearly been influenced by that of several other groups, which supports the theory that Dolgan descended from Tungus-speaking reindeer hunters. For example, Dolgan leg skin boots are similar in cut and beaded decoration to Evenki boots.

Dolgan women make elaborately decorated boots for the spring and fall reindeer festivals. Once they become worn, these beautiful boots are relegated to everyday wear alongside the plainer boots made for that purpose.

Over boots made from reindeer skin, which have extra room around the sole and ankle, are worn over regular skin boots during extremely cold weather (Vasilevich 1963a).

Leg Skin Boots

Male and female boots are generally made from dark-haired reindeer leg skins. Men's boots are thigh-high; women's, which are knee-high, can be made to reach to the thigh by adding a reindeer skin to the top. Leg skin boots are made with pleated or unpleated soles sewn with the hair either to the inside of the skin—stained with ochre or bark—or to the outside. A side strip encircles the foot. A gusset tapers to a point on each side of the centre front panel and extends around to a centre back seam, and leg sections are made with a front, back, side left, and side right panel. Some Dolgan insert a light-haired centre front panel below the knee. Occasionally, the upper portion of the leg is made from dog skins. The upper edge of thigh-high boots is cut on a slant, and knee-high boots are cut straight across. A thong is sewn to the top of tall boots, a casing and drawstring to knee-high boots.

Occasionally this boot style is made from white-haired skins and either left undecorated (MVB IVA 3521, IVA 3925) or decorated with a few lines of beads along the vertical seams of the front panel (NMF VK4934.195). Generally, men's and women's boots have numerous rows of beading sewn vertically to the front panel seam. Men's boots are also decorated with a short, horizontal band of beading, strips of cloth, and bits of fur just below the knee (BSM P83.0369, P88.0082; MVB IVA 3156, IVA 3923, IVA 3376; NMF VK4934.175; REM 1283.9/1,2). A wide

FIGURE 78
Fancy beaded goggles protect the wearer from snow blindness by eliminating much of the light reflected off the snow's surface.
REM 1876.5

FIGURE 79
Dolgan children are dressed in clothing similar to that of their parents.

FIGURE 80
Dolgan often use dog skins for boots and inner stockings; boots have dog skin inner and reindeer skin outer layers. The beading designs shown here are typically Dolgan. *Left:* BSM P83.0369 *Right:* BSM P88.0082

80

FIGURE 81
A key characteristic of Dolgan boots is chevron or zigzag designs created with multicoloured beads. Beads act like amulets to provide good luck and prosperity. REM 1283.9

band of beaded red fabric is sewn around the top of women's boots (MVB IVA 2564, IVA 3924; NMF VK4934.194; REM 1283.11/1,2).

Dolgan favour beads and small metal pieces similar to those used by Yakut, although Dolgan prefer yellow, red, pink, green, blue, black, and white beads (Vasilevich 1963a). Chevrons and arches are commonly used on male and female boots. Floral designs also appear on women's footwear. Boot styles are similar to those of the Yukagir and Yakut, reflecting the close interactions between these three groups in the past (Karapetova 1997c, Vasilevich 1963a).

Dehaired Skin Summer Boots

Dolgan make a thigh-high boot from dehaired skins for summer use. The sole is slightly pleated at the toe and heel, and the vamp is usually an extended pointed style similar to that of Yakut. Leg sections, cut in one piece with a centre back seam, are slanted at the top. A thong sewn to the top of the boot is tied to the waist belt (Vasilevich 1963a, NMF VK4934.197).

Stockings

Women's and men's winter boots are worn with reindeer stockings with the fur to the inside. Thin strips of cloth are sometimes sewn into the seams around the soles for decoration, insulation, and durability (MVB IVA 3926, NMF VK4934.196).

Summary

Dolgan typically make thigh-high leg skin boots for men and knee-high boots for women. The style is similar to that of Nenets and other groups in the west. The sole is flat and unpleated or slightly pleated. One side strip plus a gusset is commonly used. The leg section is cut from four or six panels, with an alternate-coloured panel inserted at centre front below the knee. The upper edge is cut straight across on short boots and on a slant on some tall boots. Straps are sewn to the knee and upper edge. Dolgan decorate their boots with multi-coloured beaded panels similar to those of Even and Evenki, but often with a chevron design. Like Yakut, Dolgan use metal decoration. For dehaired reindeer skin summer footwear, Dolgan use the same style as Evenki. The sole is pleated, the vamp cut in a variety of styles, and the leg often knee-high.

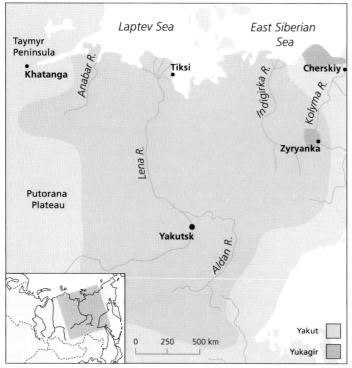

CHAPTER 7

Map 8

Yakut
Yukagir

0   250   500 km

FIGURE 82
Overleaf: Due to fierce winter weather and deep snow, Yakut travelling long distances traditionally wore layers of footwear, starting with a light skin stocking and ending with fur over boots. All layers had to be lightweight so that people could move easily on foot. In summer, dehaired boots were worn with light skin stockings. REM 1085.79

MAP 8
Yakut and Yukagir homelands

*I*N THE DISTANT past, Yakut moved northward from the Siberian steppes into the taiga and lived with Evenki in the region of the Lena River. The Yakut, who call themselves Sakha, are one of the largest groups of Indigenous peoples in Russia, numbering some 380,000 (Petrov 1997). They now inhabit much of central Asia, as far north as the arctic coast. They have formed an independent republic known as Yakutsia, 80 per cent of which lies north of 60°. In the winter their territory is one of the coldest places in the northern hemisphere.

Yukagir are descendants of Yakut and Evenki living in two small areas of northeastern Asia. Their population is about 1,100 (Vakhtin 1996).

Yakut

Traditionally, Yakut have been herders of cattle and horses. Their cows produce a very rich milk from which Yakut create a slightly sour condensed milk. Small horses with heavy coats are kept mainly for their tender meat, of which Yakut are extremely fond. Today Yakut have also adopted the Evenki style of reindeer herding. Reindeer provide meat, hides, and fur, and are used for transportation. Evenki techniques of hunting moose and wild reindeer, trapping furbearing animals, and fishing are now used as well (Armstrong 1968, Forsyth 1992, Okladnikov 1970). Yak herding has also been introduced (Luick 1978).

Over hundreds of years, Yakut have developed a complex metalworking culture. In addition to forging articles from iron as do Evenki, Khanty, and other groups, Yakut also have the skills to smelt iron directly from ore. In the past, metal was used to decorate clothing, as well as for household utensils and tools (Forsyth 1992, Okladnikov 1970).

In the Middle Ages, Yakut warriors were as heavily armed as European knights. They not only wore body armour and helmets, including helmets made from local gold deposits, but also put armour on their war horses. Special points attached to the breast of the horse armour penetrated the horses of the enemy or fallen enemy warriors during battle. The spurs used by Yakut riders ended in dagger points on both front and rear. The style of Yakut armour, fashioned from small plates laid end to end like fish scales, was common in the Orient between the tenth and fifteenth centuries. The metallurgical

83

FIGURE 83
Through smelting and smithing, Yakut continue to produce complex tools, weapons, pots, jewellery, pendants, and decorations. Neighbouring groups, who were unable to smelt iron from ore, perceived Yakut smelting skills to be gifts from the spirits. REM 2451.6.

84

FIGURE 84
Yakut shamans acquired additional powers from the metal ornamentation placed on their clothing.

FIGURE 85
For festive occasions, traditional Yakut women wear highly decorated long coats and tall hats. Heart-shaped designs are engraved on the metal pendants attached to this coat and on the broad metal necklaces. They are also embroidered on the hat with silver thread.
REM 7200.157 (coat), REM 7200.213 (hat), REM 8762.19976.ab (necklace)

skills of ancient Yakut surpassed the skills of northern Yakut smiths working today (Okladnikov 1970).

Yakut shamans were, and still are, regarded by neighbouring groups as the most powerful shamans in Siberia because of their ability to smith and smelt metal. One distinguishing feature of the Yakut is their use of both black and white shamans: white shamans cure illnesses and participate in weddings, spring festivals, and fertilization rites; black shamans deal with evil powers, foretell the future, journey into the other world, and call up spirits (Czaplicka 1914, Jonaitis 1978).

Sacrificial offerings were often made by Yakut in the north to propitiate various spirits, such as those of the "sacred cliffs" or the "sacred tree." Offerings were made by both men and women and included such items as arrows, arrowheads, spears, bow drills, and ornaments made with beads cut from river shells. More contemporary sacrificial gifts include bullets, matches, and glass beads (Okladnikov 1970).

Traditionally, Yakut had a custom of sharing the remains of their honoured dead. People would remove the flesh of the deceased and dry it for use as a talisman. Then they disarticulated the bones and sewed them into a reindeer skin, which was embroidered with beads and used as a fetish (Okladnikov 1970). Yukagir also honoured their dead by dissection and mummification (Alekseyev 1941).

In ancient times, wealthy Yakut owned slaves who performed such functions as cow keeper, servant, groom, driver, and butcher. One type of slave was responsible for cooking, entertaining, cutting firewood, and drying skin boots. Prior to the Russian rule of Siberia, a slave's service to his or her lord did not end even with the lord's death; wealthy Yakut men often had their most trusted slaves (or wives) buried alive with them so that they could be served in the afterlife (Okladnikov 1970).

Yukagir

In the past, Yukagir ruled vast lands and were considered fearsome by their Yakut and Koryak neighbours. Yukagir legends recall a time when Yukagir campfires were "as numerous as the stars in the sky on a clear winter night." According to these legends, when white birds flew over Yukagir lands they became yellow from the smoke of the many fires. However, once smallpox and other diseases had ravaged this group, neighbouring peoples began to trespass on Yukagir hunting territories, and the resulting wars exterminated almost the entire Yukagir population (Okladnikov 1970).

Yukagir people have adopted the Evenki way of life and material culture (Black 1979; Jochelson 1926b, 1928, 1933). One group live primarily by hunting and fishing; the other are primarily reindeer herders.

Fishing Yukagir had an annual cycle of hunting and gathering that utilized available species. They lived as a large group in permanent homes for four months during the winter. In early spring, they split into smaller groups to hunt moose and wild reindeer, and in early summer the groups reunited to go hunting and fishing. After the first snowfall, Yukagir families would head into the mountains and hunt squirrels until the heavy frosts came. Then they would complete the cycle, returning to their permanent homes (Kreynovich 1979).

Inland Yukagir had a different cycle. Those living in the taiga and forest-tundra were dependant on moose, whereas those living on the tundra relied on the migratory herds of wild reindeer they slaughtered at water crossings. Domesticated reindeer were set free in the taiga and forest-tundra in the early fall, and everyone went fishing. After the first snowfall, reindeer were gathered and moved every few days while the herders hunted and trapped. After spring calving, people and reindeer moved on to the summer camp, where they fished and hunted geese (Forsyth 1992).

Traditional Clothing

Traditional Yakut clothing reflects Yakut ancestral ties with the pastoralists of the southern steppes. During the eighteenth century, women and men both wore a coat made from reindeer and other kinds of fur with the fur to the outside; this coat extended down to their shins. Insets in the shape of eagle wings were sewn into the back of this garment. It also had a pleat extending from the lower back to the hem, which facilitated movement while horseback riding. The coat had narrow sleeves and was closed with ties along a centre front opening (Alekseyev 1941, Georgi 1799).

Women decorated their fur coats and hats with beads and metal chains, spangles, pendants, bells, and heart-shaped disks.

85

FIGURE 86
For Yakut festive occasion footwear, smoked moose hide is elaborately embroidered with heart-shaped symbols and trimmed with dark green or black velveteen. REM 1459,7/1,2

86

Such highly decorated garments took a good seamstress up to three years to sew. They were used for burials, weddings, and shaman ceremonies (Okladnikov 1970).

Yakut clothing styles are distinctly different from those of other Siberian peoples, except for some Even, Evenki, and Yukagir who adopted Yakut styles (Okladnikov 1970). By the nineteenth century the long fur coats were worn only by women. Men adopted shorter reindeer skin jackets (Okladnikov 1970) closed with a belt and worn with an apron, reindeer pants, and leg skin boots in the Evenki style (Sem 1997). With their coats, women wear metal chest ornaments made of intricate chains and heart-shaped disks linked together to form a large rectangle. A twisted metal ring hung around the neck supports these ornaments.

Prior to the nineteenth century, Yakut men and women wore a hat with a sharp point on top and long side flaps or wings, a style reminiscent of the fur, felt, or cloth hats worn by the steppe tribes. Yakut women also wore tall conical hats of fur and cloth, with richly decorated cowls around their necks (Okladnikov 1970).

Traditional Yakut clothing and footwear are still decorated with ancient designs and lavish metalwork. One distinct design, observed in cliff drawings made by Yakut in the Neolithic period and still seen today in beaded footwear (Okladnikov 1970), is a series of crisscrossing lines that represent corrals or fences, ensuring a successful hunt by symbolically trapping animals.

Another typical feature of Yakut design is the use of stylized heart-shaped patterns that have been passed from grandmother to granddaughter for generations. "Heart" designs symbolizing health, happiness, and success are used repeatedly by both Yakut and Yukagir (Petrov 1997, Vasilevich 1963a, REM 1459.7/1,2), although the shape and silhouette of these designs vary considerably. They are embroidered onto skin and fabric and engraved into metal pendants, panels, and jewellery. The beaded designs done by Yakut are similar to those of Even and Evenki.

Linear reindeer hair embroidery was used by all northern peoples, and this, according to Shternberg (1931), is a strong indication of ancient cultural and genetic ties. The Yakut embroidery now often done with silk thread is similar in colour, design, and width to hair embroidery. In fact, it is possible that the silk and cotton threads available from the Russians and other neighbours for hundreds of years actually replaced horse hair, sinew, and reindeer hair threads. Yukagir also introduced distinct embroidery styles now commonly used by Yakut (Okladnikov 1970).

In the past, Yukagir wore two parkas. The outer parka was used for hunting, gathering wood, hauling water, and other outdoor chores, and the inner parka was worn inside the chum. A man's outer parka was left under a smoke-tanned reindeer skin tarp by the entrance of the chum. Women's clothes were stored separately on a sled nearby. Men's outer parkas were fashioned from white-haired reindeer skins that acted as camouflage, allowing hunters to closely approach the game. Parkas worn for special occasions were trimmed with newborn seal skins dyed red with alder or larch. Hats were made from the skin of newborn white-haired reindeer (Kreynovich 1979).

Footwear

In the seventeenth and eighteenth centuries, Yakut winter footwear consisted of a light skin or cloth stocking, a second, heavier reindeer or rabbit skin stocking, and a winter boot with grass or horsehair insoles (Petrov 1997). Wealthy Yakut with access to reindeer herds made their outer boots from reindeer leg skins; less wealthy Yakut made them from horsehide. Over boots of reindeer, horse, moose, bear, or wolf skins were worn during long sled trips when walking was not required (Nosov 1955, Petrov 1997).

Leg Skin Boots

Yakut make three different styles of leg skin boots, using skins from reindeer and other animals. The first style, which lacks a separate vamp, shows Altaic influences. It has an unpleated sole, no side strip, and a leg section cut from four panels of leg skins (front, back, left side, and right side) that extends down to the sole. A band of fabric is sewn to the upper edge and folded to the outside. Ankle ties and a tie at the upper edge are used (MVB IVA 3966, Vasilevich 1963a).

The second style has a sole, a wide gusset on each side of the front panel, and a leg section cut from four panels as described above. The upper edge is finished with a broad band of fabric (dark green and black are preferred) which is folded over to the front. Ties are sewn at the ankle and upper edge (MVB IVA 227, IVA 2199). An extra seam is often sewn across the vamp, just above the toes, as in Even and Evenki boots (Vasilevich 1963a).

The third style was introduced by Yakut living in the northeast, who acquired the design from Nenets via Dolgan. It has a sole, a side strip, a wide gusset that extends back to the side or back panel, and a leg section cut from four or six panels (Vasilevich 1963a; MVB IVA 2228, IVA 757).

Two variations of leg skin boots are commonly worn by Yukagir. One style has a sole sewn directly to the leg section, which is cut with a broad front and back panel. Side panels are omitted. A side strip that encircles the foot sometimes appears in this boot style, along with a single gusset on each side of the foot. The use of one gusset is typical of the ancient hunters from the eastern taiga. The second style has a flat sole, two gussets sewn between the sole and the leg, and six panels forming the leg section. The top of the leg is cut either straight across or on a slant. Dolgan-style beaded panels are sewn vertically to each side of the front panel, horizontally just below the knee, and in the seam that crosses the foot above the toes. Boots may also be left undecorated (Vasilevich 1963a).

Yukagir typically use dark-haired leg skins for their footwear and add tiny strips of white-haired leg skins in seams. Leg skin boots are also decorated with beading, embroidery, and metalwork similar to that of Evenki and Yakut (Vasilevich 1963a).

Pointed Sole Yakut-Style Boots

One distinctive Yakut boot style has a sole that narrows to an extended flap, then wraps up over the top of the foot at centre front. The front leg panel is cut at centre front and spread apart to accommodate the flap extension from the sole. This affects the fit of the shoe much as slashed darts affect the fit of clothes. Footwear with these insets has a snugger fit around the ankle without the use of gussets and side strips (Nosov 1955).

The leg section of this style consists of a narrow front panel and a broad back panel cut from dehaired skins that have been blackened with caviar and soot (MVB IVA 3967, IVA 3968, IVA 3971), smoked (EMO 22.721, 9474; NME 1202.56, 1202.54), bleached white (MVB IVA 1847), or stained green (MVB IVA 2170,

IVA 3970). These knee-high boots are cut straight across and finished with a broad band of predominantly black or dark green velveteen or wool folded over the skin. The band may be left undecorated or decorated with metalwork and a few beads. Red or black fabric or skin welts are sewn in the seams for decoration and to protect seams from leaking. Multicoloured and metal threads are used to embroider the vamp and front section of smoked skins. Long, wide suede straps are attached at the ankles. On women's boots, the straps were sometimes ornamented with beadwork in the past. Longer straps that wrapped around the foot five or six times were considered especially chic (Petrov 1997).

Yakut living near Yukagir make a thigh-high version of this style with pleats at the front panel near the ankle. These pleats are held in position by a narrow strip of skin sewn to the inside of the boot (Vasilevich 1963a, MVB IVA 3298).

Pointed Vamp and Straight Vamp Boots

Smoked, alder-barked, or ochre-stained skins are fashioned into boots with slightly pleated round soles. In these boots, a long, pointed vamp extends well up the leg towards the top of the shin. The pointed vamp style may have evolved from ancient Turkish footwear (Hatt 1916). The leg section is thigh-high and closely fitted, with several distinct pieces along the centre back area, and the upper edge is finished with a fabric or skin casing. Vamp seams are decorated with reindeer hair embroidery, curvilinear appliquéd skin or fabric, painted designs, and occasionally white, blue, and black beads. Skin thongs are attached at the ankle, knee, and upper edge (DL 10999; MVB IVA 641, IVA 643, IVA 2224).

This style is also made with a less exaggerated pointed vamp (MVB IVA 742) and with a vamp that is truncated at midshin (MVB IVA 2198, IVA 2234, IVA 640, IVA 2225). Reindeer herders use a slight variation with a vamp cut on a slant across the top, a style similar to Evenki dehaired footwear. Evenki styles were acquired by Yakut interacting with Orochi in the Far East (Vasilevich 1963a).

Double Vamp Boots

Another style used by Yukagir is influenced by Chukchi and Koryak. It is made with an unpleated sole and two vamps; one vamp encircles the foot and a small second vamp (pointed or

FIGURE 87

Yakut boot soles are either flat, slightly pleated around the toe and heel, or made with a long tab that extends over the toes and is sewn to the vamp. This latter version represents a cloven hoof; the vamp is split at centre front to accommodate the long extension.

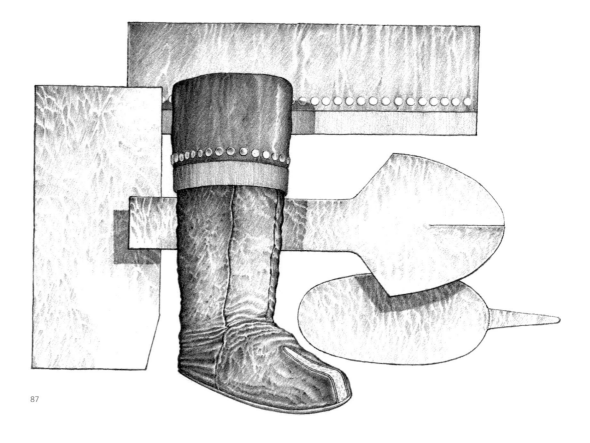

87

curved) is sewn to the top centre front of the first one. Bleached skin welts and loops are sewn into this seam. The leg section is cut from one piece with a centre back seam. The boot is cut straight across the top and either left undecorated or decorated with skin mosaics or a fabric panel (Vasilevich 1963a).

Yukagir Dehaired Skin Boots

Thigh-high and knee-high footwear made from dehaired reindeer skin and leg skins is commonly worn by Yukagir. One style has either a flat sole or a Yakut-style sole with a narrow strip that extends from the sole over the toes and is sewn into the vamp. The narrow vamp is actually the front panel, extending up to the top of the boot. This panel is pleated around the ankle, and the pleats are held in position by a strip of skin sewn on the inside. The leg section is completed with a broad back panel sewn to the front panel, and the top section of the leg is often finished with a panel of

fabric and folded over. Ties are sewn to the back near the ankle. The technique of sewing the leg section and sole together without a typical vamp, side strip, or gussets indicates ancient connections with Altai Mountain people. The broad back panel, narrow front panel, and pleats held in position with a strip of skin are distinctly Yukagir (Vasilevich 1963a).

Another dehaired reindeer skin style used by Yukagir is a soft-soled boot with a T-shaped heel seam and slight pleating at the heel and toe (Hatt 1916). The vamp, which extends to a point, is not as long as the extended vamp used by Yakut. Thigh-high leg sections are made with ankle, knee, and upper-edge ties (Kreynovich 1979). This style reflects the interactions Yukagir had with ancient Evenki hunters.

Slippers

Loon skin slippers were used by Yakut for extra insulation (REM 7200.23/1,2). This style of slipper is not made today.

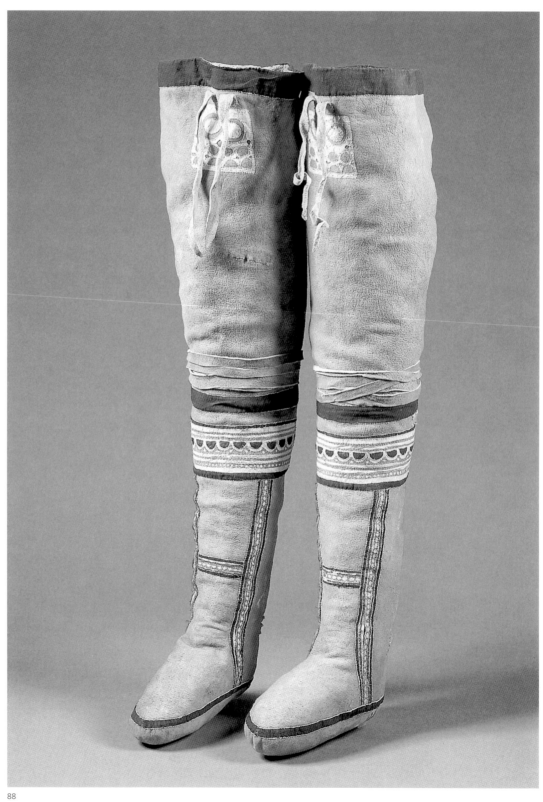

FIGURE 88
The lower portions of thigh-high
boots are decorated in a manner
similar to that of knee-high boots.
The boots depicted here are decorated with dehaired bleached skins,
ochre-stained skins, strips of green
and blue fabric, and reindeer hair
embroidery. MVB IVA 2225

88

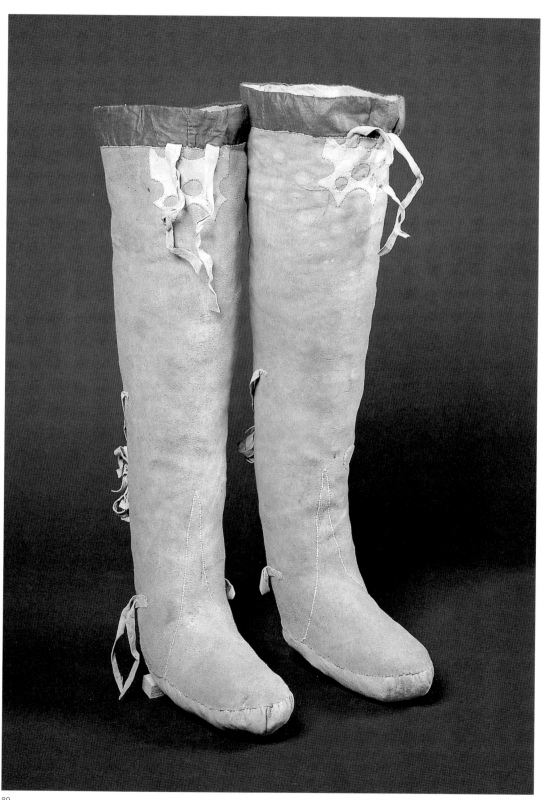

FIGURE 89
Yakut triangular vamp seams
are finished with reindeer hair
embroidery. Reindeer hair is
one of the life-giving elements
needed for successful hunts, and
linear reindeer hair embroidery
is linked directly to hunting and
herding customs. MVB IVA 643

90

91

FIGURE 90

Unlike Even and Evenki, Yakut
bead their boot vamps by tracing
around the outer vamp shape,
adding stylized branches at the top
and dividing the vamp into several
lobes. Black and white beads represent the black and white shamans
who manage evil and good. The
back of this pair of boots has
several pieces inserted lengthwise,
similar to footwear worn by Yakut
shamans. MVB IVA 640

FIGURE 91

Footwear made from the skins of
loons and other local birds provides
excellent insulation against the cold.
Unlike bird skin footwear made in
other regions, these loon skin boots
are made by cutting and sewing
pieces together. Bird skins are rarely
used today. REM 7200.232/1,2

Contemporary Footwear

Traditional footwear of the Yakut and Yukagir has not under-gone any drastic changes in modern times. Men's, women's, and children's winter boots made with reindeer leg skins and soles of reindeer toe pads are still very popular. The broad strip of cloth around the top of the boots is decorated with fur. Some people wear Evenki-style thigh-high boots; others wear short boots with white panels on the front and back, and side panels of black horse skin. Although traditional Yakut footwear is slowly being replaced by the manufactured variety, most Yakut and even visitors to their territory prefer to wear Yakut boots in winter, because they are so well adapted to cli-matic conditions (Petrov 1997).

Summary

The key feature identifying Yakut footwear is the use of a sole with a long pointed extension that wraps over the top of the toes and is sewn into the vamp. Yakut have knee-high summer boots and thigh-high winter boots. A style feature that evolved from Yukagir is the use of a narrow front panel and much wider back panel that extends around the sides to the front. This feature is used by Yakut, Evenki, and other neighbouring groups. The top of the leg is cut straight across and often folded over. The upper edge is finished with a band of fabric folded to the outside. Heart-shaped symbols, beading, embroi-dery, and metalwork are common decorative features.

CHAPTER 8

Chukchi
Sea

Bering Strait

Wrangel
Is.

East
Siberian
Sea

Chukotka
Peninsula

Anadyr R.

Bering
Sea

Omolon R.

Kolyma R.

Indigirka R.

Palana

Sea of
Okhotsk

Kamchatka Peninsula

Petropavlovsk
Kamchatskiy

Magadan

0   250   500 km

Map 9

FIGURE 92
Overleaf: The centre-front neckline
of the Koryak parka is finished with
a biblike extension elaborately decorated with inlaid skin work. This
extension is used to protect a person's face when travelling on a sled
or sleeping. REM 4952.2

MAP 9
Koryak homelands

*K*ORYAK INHABIT THE rugged northern section of the
Kamchatka Peninsula and adjacent mainland, biologi-
cally one of the richest regions in northern Siberia
and the Far East. Covered with tundra in the north and taiga
in the south, it supports reindeer, moose, Dall sheep, furbear-
ers, marine mammals, shellfish, and several species of Pacific
salmon. Itelmen, Indigenous neighbours of the Koryak, lived
in the past as fishers in the central and southern portions of
the Kamchatka Peninsula. Prior to Russian contact, Itelmen
were numerous and militant; after contact, they were deci-
mated by disease and acculturation, their population reduced
to 2,500 (Kos'ven 1962).

Koryak, who now number about 9,000, have been heavily
influenced by their neighbours, including Chukchi, Yupik,
Aleut, Itelmen, Nivkhi, Ainu, and Russians. Many Koryak
were moved by the Soviets into centralized villages and forced
to work on state farms. But despite these outside influences,
Koryak have managed to retain much of their traditional culture. As a result of the work of Koryak activists, the Koryak
Autonomous Area seceded from the Kamchatka Province in
1990 to become an independent member of the Russian
Federation (Kos'ven 1962, Krupnik 1995e).

Prehistorically, maritime Koryak gathered mollusks and
developed an intense marine hunting economy based on seals,
sea lions, and beluga whales (Vasil'evskii 1969). About half the
people evolved into inland nomadic reindeer herders; the
remainder became sedentary maritime hunters living in semi-
subterranean homes in coastal villages. Coastal and inland
groups spoke dialects that were incomprehensible to one
another (Krupnik 1995e).

Inland Koryak herded their reindeer on foot, moving herds
between winter and summer pastures in the mountains.
Herders set up nomadic camps beside bodies of water, relying
heavily upon fish to avoid depleting their herds (Antropova
1971, Forsyth 1992, Gurvich 1987, Jochelson 1928). Coastal
Koryak hunted seals from skin kayaks and umiaks, or with
dog teams on the sea ice (Zimmerly 1986). They also used
dugout canoes for travelling on inland waters; occasionally
they lashed two canoes together to make a catamaran for use
on the open sea. There was considerable trade between inland
and coastal Koryak. Reindeer meat and skins were exchanged
for muktuk, seal meat, seal skins, and thongs (Arutiunov

FIGURE 93
Like Chukchi, Koryak are marine mammal hunters and reindeer herders. Herders travel to the windy coastlines in summer to provide their reindeer with relief from biting insects; in winter, they remain inland. Marine hunters spend both winter and summer at the coast.

1988c, Levin and Potapov 1956 [1964]). Today some inland Koryak continue to herd, and coastal Koryak still rely on marine resources to sustain their way of life.

Koryak inhabiting the Kamchatka isthmus survived by combining fishing, marine mammal hunting, and the maintenance of small reindeer herds. During the summer salmon runs, most Koryak moved to the mouths of rivers, leaving their herds under the supervision of younger herders. Fish caught with nets, weirs, harpoons, and traps were dried and used for human and dog food. Fish formed the basic diet of coastal Koryak; the entire head and the cartilaginous parts were eaten raw. Seal meat and beluga muktuk and meat were favourite foods. People also consumed bird eggs as well as many varieties of plants, including such delicacies as fireweed, wild lily, crowberries, blueberries, and the roots and sprouts of sedges. Berries were often mixed with reindeer and seal meat, along with various wild roots, to make pemmican. Blueberries were also brewed into a mildly alcoholic beverage. The amanita mushroom, a hallucinogen, was used to induce shamanistic trances (Arutiunov 1988c, Levin and Potapov 1956 [1964]).

Traditional Beliefs

The most senior male in a Koryak family acts as the head. Traditionally, only men ate food served in the inner yuranga; women ate leftovers in the outer yuranga. Nonetheless, women were treated kindly and with respect. Specific taboos were followed in order to maintain the family organization. For example, a family's hearth, drum, and fire starter—which symbolized the roles of women, men, and spirit helpers respectively (Levin and Potapov 1956 [1964])—were never used by individuals outside of the family. Fire drill boards, made from dry aspen, were shaped with a headlike end. When a new board was consecrated to protect the hearth and herd, a reindeer was sacrificed to the Master on High. The fire board was covered with sacrificial blood and fat, following which an incantation enabled the board to come to life (Czaplicka 1914, Kraseninnikov 1755).

Shamans

In the past, Koryak employed both family shamans and professional shamans. Each Koryak family had its own drum, and each family member took a turn beating the drum while another member communicated with the spirits through dance. Both family and professional shamans used drums belonging to the family in whose home they were performing. Drums were covered with reindeer skin, and the thick whalebone beater was covered with a wolf tail skin (Serov 1988).

Koryak dances depict the key characteristics and mannerisms of animals and elements of the universe. The raven dance is especially important, because the raven is a powerful spirit and a masterful shaman who appears in Koryak origin stories. The raven plays an important role in protecting Koryak from evil or harmful spirits. Dances depicting the raven and other animals help individuals speak to the spirits, call on helping spirits for protection, and mediate conflicts with the spirits that cause illness, danger, or poor hunting (Krupnik 1995e, Wallen 1990). Clothing worn during raven dances, whale ceremonies, or other special ceremonies is decorated with animal and universe symbols used as spirit helpers by shamans (Czaplicka 1914, Jochelson 1905–1908, Kraseninnikov 1755, Siikala 1978).

Funeral Rites

According to Koryak tradition, when someone dies his or her body is transferred to the next world by either cremation, surface burial, subsurface burial, or burial at sea (Serov 1988). Historically, cremation was the most common process. The deceased was placed on a funeral pyre with his or her possessions and a bag of gifts for those who had died earlier. The dead person's possessions were broken, thereby ensuring that the deceased would not return; broken tools are used in the other world. Other precautions were also taken to prevent the person's spirit from returning, such as guarding the house where the corpse lay and painting relatives' faces with soot (Charrin 1984). The corpse was removed from the yuranga through a special hole cut in the wall; this hole was later mended, so that the corpse's soul could not reenter to take the souls of the living. Several false departures were made from the burial site, and all tracks were camouflaged to prevent the corpse's spirit from following the living back to their yurangas (Serov 1988).

Funeral clothing is made from white-haired reindeer fawn skins elaborately decorated with skin, hair, and oesophagus

FIGURE 94
This Koryak man's burial parka
from the Kamchatka region is
almost a hundred years old. The
long back tail is designed to act like
a bird's tail, helping to guide the
deceased spirit on its journey into
the other world. Women sew burial
parkas at night in privacy. Thin
strips of seal oesophagus are
embroidered on the strips of black
skin. REM 7113.51

FIGURE 95
Black and white checkerboard
designs on funeral boots help
Koryak deceased carry the powers
of evil and good into the underworld. REM 7113.52/1,2

95

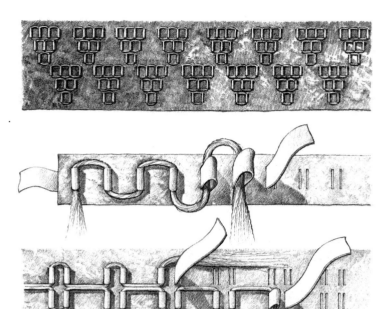

96

FIGURE 96
Combinations of reindeer hair and seal oesophagus create distinctive repeated designs on Koryak clothing and footwear.

FIGURE 97
Koryak women wear reindeer skin parkas stained red with alder bark. These pull-over parkas are also worn for dances and other special occasions today.

embroidery, and with dyed tufts of wool, hair, and newborn seal fur. Women sew these garments in secrecy, because the clothes are not to be seen before the funeral or finished before someone actually dies. They are usually made in a hurry during the nights between death and cremation. While the women sew, men play cards on the body of the deceased, who is wearing the right glove on the left hand, the right boot on the left foot, and vice versa. The deceased's boot soles are cut before the corpse is placed at the grave site, so that the spirit may escape from the body. Reindeer used to pull the sled carrying the corpse are harnessed in reverse order to that usually followed, with the lead animal harnessed last. An adult dog is sacrificed to take the place of the deceased during the funeral rites (Serov 1988).

Traditional Clothing

Koryak men and women wear loose-fitting, flared, knee-length, pull-over reindeer skin parkas with long sleeves. A large rectangular bib-shaped piece of skin is attached at centre front. Parkas are either hooded or worn with a skin bonnet, which has an inner and an outer layer of skin and occasionally a biblike extension (Antropova 1971, Iokelson 1990, Kalashnikova 1990, Kocheschov 1989, Levin and Potapov 1956 [1964], Mitlyanskaya 1983, Prytkova 1976).

Circles of fur trimmed with beads, depicting the sun, are sewn to the front and back of these parkas. Tassels and strings of beads are added in small clusters, and the skins are commonly stained red with alder bark (Chubarova 1985, Garena 1989, Smolyak 1988).

Koryak also decorate parka hemlines, bonnets, biblike extensions, and footwear with rows of triangle, checkerboard, and zigzag designs, as well as animal silhouettes (Anonymous n.d., Iokelson 1990, Klimova n.d., Levin and Potapov 1956 [1964], Mitlyanskaya 1983). Koryak men, women, and children wear basically the same styles of skin clothing as their Chukchi neighbours (Antropova 1971).

Footwear

Reindeer leg skins, reindeer body skins with the hair inside, dehaired reindeer skins, and seal skins are commonly used for Koryak footwear. Footwear styles and decorative techniques are similar to those of Chukchi and Yupik; however, Koryak

97

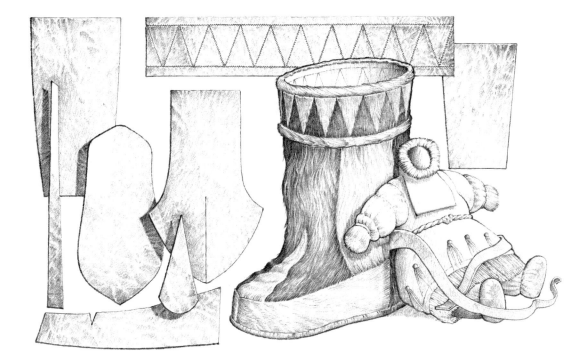

98

FIGURE 98
Koryak children wear miniature versions of adult boots. The inset over the vamp, broad side strip, silhouette, and triangular design shown here are common features.

FIGURE 99
Some Koryak boots are decorated with beaded panels placed in a manner similar to that of Even and Evenki. *Left:* BSM 92.0118.ab *Right:* BSM 92.0119.ab

usually use flat, unpleated soles rather than preformed, crimped soles. The leg section extends to mid-calf, the knee, or just above the knee and is cut straight across. Unlike Chukchi and Yupik, some Koryak add beaded panels to their boots.

Leg Skin Boots

Leg skin boots are usually made with unpleated soles cut from reindeer or seal skin. A welt extending around the entire foot or just the front area is usually placed in the sole seam. A side strip with a centre front seam extends around to the back panel or to a centre back seam. The side strip is narrower at the front than at the back. White-haired skins are used for some side strips. The leg section is made with front, back, left side, and right side panels. Generally, dark-haired skins are used for all panels; however, a few Koryak boots are made with alternating light- and dark-haired panels. The upper edge, cut straight across, is often finished by folding it over to form a casing, or by sewing a dehaired skin casing to the top. A drawstring threaded through the casing is used to tie the boot on the leg (Gorbacheva 1997, Vasilevich 1963a).

Leg skin boots are decorated with combinations of beaded panels, fur mosaics, hair embroidery, and fur sculpturing. Checkerboard, triangular, semicircular, and circular designs are sewn horizontally around the upper leg, vertically down each side of the front panel, and across the toes on some boots (BSM P92.0119, P92.0118; EMO 27.974; NME 1070.39; REM 8762.16425).

Shin-high leg skin boots are also made using the double vamp style, where the larger vamp encircles the foot and a small vamp is added at the top centre front. Vamps and leg sections are cut from alternating light- and dark-haired skins to create a decorative effect. Ankle ties are sewn to the back, and a casing and drawstring are added to the upper edge of the leg (Vasilevich 1963a).

Dehaired Skin Summer Boots

Several waterproof boot styles are made by Koryak from dehaired reindeer skin. One has an unpleated sole and a double vamp. The first vamp encircles the foot, and a smaller second vamp is sewn to the top centre of the first one. A welt

99

100

101

FIGURE 100
Boots made from reindeer skins
stained with alder bark, ochre, and
soot mixed with fish eggs are worn
by Koryak in damp summer
weather. BSM P92.0117.ab

FIGURE 101
Triangles and handmade rickrack are
commonly made from bleached
skins to decorate Koryak summer
boots. REM 3964.27/1,2

and loops are sewn into this seam, and straps are threaded through the loops. Dehaired boots are decorated using white and brown hair embroidery, thread embroidery, skin mosaics, and fur mosaics (Vasilevich 1963a; BSM P92.0117.ab, P92.0119.ab; REM 3964.27/1,2, 7113.78/1,2). Dehaired skin boots are always made with straps either sewn into the seam at the ankle towards the back or threaded through ankle loops. This style is also made with canvas leg sections (REM 7113.80/1,2).

Koryak living near the sea make a seal skin boot with a thick seal skin sole (unpleated), a pointed vamp, and a one-piece leg section with a centre front seam (Vasilevich 1963a). This boot style is also worn by Chukchi and Yupik. In the past, sea lion skins were used for the soles of footwear (Smolyak 1988).

Summary

Koryak footwear styles are similar to those of Chukchi and Yupik. Leg skin boots are usually made with unpleated soles, side strips, and leg sections of four or six panels that extend to mid-shin or are knee-high. They are cut straight across the top and finished with a casing and drawstring. Skin or fur mosaics, hair embroidery, and ochre or alder bark stain are commonly used for decoration. Koryak use more steep triangular shapes than do Chukchi and Yupik. Semicircular, tongue, and circular shapes are also common. Dehaired skin boots often have a vamp that extends around the foot, with a second vamp inserted at centre front. Ankle ties are either sewn into the ankle seam or threaded through loops sewn into the ankle seam.

CHAPTER 9

ALASKA

Chukchi
Sea

Bering Strait

St.
Lawrence
Is.

Lavrentiya

Wrangel
Is.

Mys Shmidta

Providenia

East
Siberian
Sea

Chukotka
Peninsula

Pevek

Anadyr R.

Anadyr

Bering
Sea

Cherskiy

Bilibino

Markovo

Kolyma R.

Omolon R.

Indigirka R.

Sea of
Okhotsk

Kamchatka Peninsula

Magadan

0   250   500 km

Map 10

FIGURE 102
Overleaf: Historically, Chukchi armour was made by cutting walrus and bearded seal skins into strips, then linking these with narrow strips of ringed seal skin and allowing the skins to dry in a hoop shape. When warriors had to run, they pulled the collapsible skin hoops up under their arms.

MAP 10
Chukchi homelands

FIGURE 103
Chukchi live in skin or fabric yurangas on the tundra in the Far East. Women set up the complicated pole structure at each camp. Sleeping quarters are formed by tying small tentlike reindeer skin structures to the inside poles.

HE CHUKCHI, WHO number about 15,000, live mainly on the Chukotka Peninsula in the Far East, where they work either as inland reindeer herders or as maritime hunters pursuing marine mammals. Prior to the Soviet era, inland Chukchi herders were nomadic, moving in winter from the tundra, where they spent summers, to the shelter of the forest-tundra (Antropova and Kuznetsova 1964; Birket-Smith 1953; Dall 1881; Gurvich 1979, 1980; Jochelson 1928; Krupnik 1995d; Krushanov 1987; Oakes and Riewe 1997). Coastal Chukchi used dog teams for transportation, but inland Chukchi preferred reindeer-drawn sledges. Historically, herders did not have herding dogs, so they chased any reindeer that tried to escape with the help of boomerangs. Chukchi reindeer are less domesticated than those of other herder groups (Oakes and Riewe 1997).

In the past, coastal Chukchi travelled in kayaks and umiaks similar to those of Siberian Yupik. Before the introduction of rifles, Chukchi used complex bows and arrows and spears for hunting and warfare (Arutiunov 1988b).

Today, Chukchi herders are semi-nomadic, with some women and children living on communes or permanent settlements. Women working in collective farms prepare skins and sew clothing for the herders. Contemporary herders work out of mobile camps as well as base camps established at specific sites in summer and winter (Oakes and Riewe 1997).

Coastal Chukchi live side by side with Siberian Yupik in sedentary communities along the Bering Strait, fishing and hunting seals, walrus, and whales. Every edible part of these animals is consumed after being prepared in a variety of different ways, including drying, aging, and boiling (Antropova and Kuznetsova 1964, Arutiunov et al. 1979, Bogoras 1901, Chlenov and Krupnik 1984).

Inland Chukchi subsist mostly on fish to avoid depleting their herds. The reindeer they do slaughter are completely utilized, providing the materials for clothing, food, shelter, and tools. Herders eat the meat of the reindeer, as well as the blood, fat, viscera, bone marrow, heads, antlers in velvet, and the insides of hoofs. After the major fall slaughter, much of the stomach content gathered is pressed into blocks and frozen for storage. Later it is prepared for eating by boiling it with blood, fat, and pieces of intestines. Rectal contents are used to tan reindeer leg skins, body skins, and skin sleeping bags. Antlers and bones are carved into tools, needles, toggles, and sled crossbeams, and tendons are used for sewing thread. Reindeer urine is kept in a bowl to lure tame reindeer close to camp. Reindeer are also slaughtered or sacrificed to please the spirits (Aburtina 1990; Agche 1990; Bogoras 1901, 1902; Oakes and Riewe 1997).

In addition to fishing, inland Chukchi collect berries, forbs, and seaweed, and hunt ducks, geese, and ptarmigan to supplement their diets. As do Siberian Yupik, coastal Chukchi eat raw, boiled, or fermented seal meat, whale muktuk, and walrus meat (Arutiunov 1988b). During times of starvation, they were known to have hunted ground squirrels and lemmings (Burch 1988).

Inland Chukchi herders trade their reindeer products for blubber, meat, seal and walrus skins, and ropes with coastal Chukchi. In the past, inland and coastal Chukchi families occa-

sionally exchanged places, often as a result of marriage or the loss of a herd. This close relationship continues to be critical to the survival of both groups (Aburtina 1990, Bogoras 1901). Trade with neighbouring Indigenous peoples, as well as with Russians and Alaskans, was historically of great importance to Chukchi, particularly coastal Chukchi, who bartered extensively (Bogoras 1902).

Chukchi have established a social system that includes leaders or bosses. For coastal Chukchi, the umiak helmsman, who is usually the boat's owner, is the boss. Among herders, a similar system is maintained (Bogoras 1901).

Warfare
Historically, Chukchi were fierce fighters with highly effective military strategies, and they often warred with their neighbours. They fought primarily to protect their territory or to

103

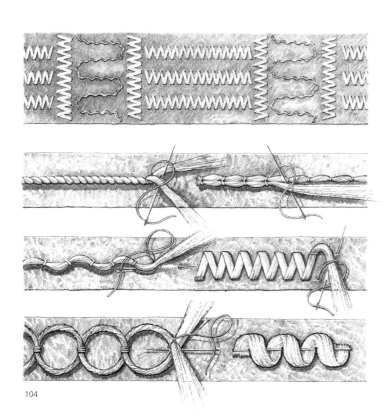

104

capture women and children from other groups to use as slaves. Other types of "bounty" were generally of no interest (Bogoras 1901, 1902; Burch 1988; Czaplicka 1914). In the seventeenth century, inland Chukchi warriors prevented the Russians from invading their region and resisted Russian demands for furs. As pressure from Russians increased in the mid-1700s, Chukchi negotiated a truce with their ancient enemies the Koryak and with two other Indigenous groups in order to once again defeat the intruders. Chukchi warriors maintained control over their lands up until they were subjugated by the Soviet regime, longer than any other Indigenous peoples in Siberia and the Far East (Bogoras 1901, 1902; Burch 1988; Dmytryshin et al. 1985; Forsyth 1992; Krupnik 1995d; Oakes and Riewe 1997).

Until the middle of the nineteenth century, coastal Chukchi living on the Chukotka Peninsula wore armour over reindeer skin parkas. The armour's chest plate, right sleeve, skirt, helmet, and shield were made of bone, ivory, and hardened walrus or seal skin. Hardened skins were impenetrable by the arrowheads and spears used prior to the introduction of firearms. Shields were also made by slipping wooden boards into narrow sheaths of seal skin, then connecting these panels to one another with seal skin thong hinges. Shifting armour plates allowed warriors ease of movement, and collapsible armour hoops surrounding the body could be hoisted up for running. Plate armour was also worn during peaceful trade missions; Chukchi in full armour travelled across the Bering Sea to St. Lawrence Island in order to buy walrus tusks from Siberian Yupik residing there (Varjola 1990b). Chukchi were extremely adept with arrows and spears because of regular training sessions and use of their weapons while hunting (Bogoras 1901, 1902; Burch 1988; Vanstone 1983).

Traditional Beliefs

In the past, inland Chukchi lived in dome-shaped reindeer skin yurangas; coastal Chukchi lived in semi-subterranean houses (Clark and Finlay 1977, Faegre 1979, Jochelson 1907). In the mid–nineteenth century, maritime hunters adopted sedentary yurangas, and they continue to use them today (Arutiunov 1988b). Fire pits are located in the centre of these tents, and the hearth, wooden fire-making tools, and many other household tools are considered sacred. A board used with a bow

FIGURE 104
Chukchi use several different stitches for their hair embroidery. Long white hairs collected from reindeer "beards" are couched into position with a needle and thread.

FIGURE 105
Chukchi seal and bear hunters travel over poorly formed ice wearing snowshoes, which distribute their weight over a larger area. Herders control the direction of their herds by throwing a boomerang over the heads of the lead reindeer. A stone hammer is used for a variety of purposes, including crushing dried meat. *Top to bottom:* BSM P90.0297.ab, REM 2083.45, REM 8261.6

drill to create a spark is carved with a headlike shape at one end, symbolizing the power of women and indicating woman's role as matron of the hearth. In the past, it was critical that household fires be lit with a bow drill and a woman's wooden board rather than with matches or flint and steel, or with a drill board taken from another fire (Bogoras 1901, 1909 [1975]).

Chukchi shamans journey into many worlds, including the upper, the lower, and up to six other layers of worlds inhabited by spirits of the dead and mystical creatures. Ordinary humans and animals live in the middle world. Shamans make their journeys while in a trance, with the help of effigies, chants, and spirit helpers. Under the Soviet regime, shamans were persecuted and their ceremonies banned (Krupnik 1995d, Van Deusen 1994).

Shamans communicated with the spirits in a dark, inner room of the home where it was so warm they usually took off their coats. Original coat designs, such as those obtained from recycled Alaskan coats from the shores of the Bering Strait, were preferred. On some coats, fringes and strips of leather woven through slits in the sleeves were used to represent the Milky Way (Czaplicka 1914).

Traditionally, clothing was removed from the recently deceased, and the corpse was wrapped in reindeer skin and watched by the next of kin for several days. A ceremonial meal was eaten with the deceased by passing food and tea through a hole in a serving board placed over the corpse's mouth. Then the body was dressed in a special hooded parka, which acted as a shroud. The parka was sewn with extra-large stitches made from right to left (rather than the standard left to right) to allow the person's spirit to escape through the seams. Some Chukchi took the dressed corpse out on a funeral sledge and set it on a pyre for cremation. Others buried the corpse with sacrificial reindeer meat placed on the body (Bogoras 1901, 1910 [1975]).

Traditional Clothing
Men's Clothing
There is no difference between clothing worn by coastal and inland Chukchi men, except that inland herders have access to finer reindeer skins and maritime hunters have better access to seal skins. Reindeer skins are preferred for winter clothing;

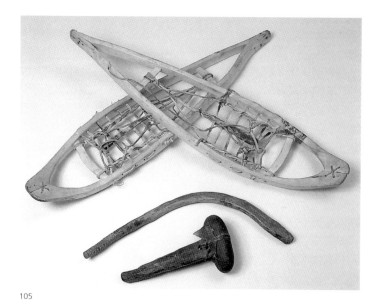

105

seal skins provide protection in damp weather and wear better in spring and summer. In the past, coastal Chukchi often traded for the castoff clothing of inland herders, who had new parkas made every year (Bogoras 1901, Prytkova 1976).

Chukchi men wear hoodless pull-over reindeer skin inner parkas with the fur to the inside and outer parkas with the fur out. The collar of the inner parka is trimmed with a broad strip of dog, wolf, or wolverine fur. Parkas are worn with double-layered fur bonnets. Men also wear square bibs made of reindeer leg skin around their necks to prevent frost formed by their breath from collecting on their parkas. Even living in the Far East, who normally wear narrow, open coats and aprons (Kalashnikova 1990), often don Chukchi-style parkas when driving reindeer sledges, since their own clothing does not provide as much protection from the wind (Bogoras 1901).

During extremely cold weather, a third parka is worn. These overcoats, which have loose hoods and full sleeves gathered at the wrists, extend down to the knees. Strips of fur and leather trim the hemline (Bogoras 1901, 1909 [1975]).

Chukchi men often wear a cloth cover over their reindeer skin clothing to protect it from getting damp or worn out (Bogoras 1901). Key features of these outer shells are their lack of a gathered hemline and the addition of a strip of reindeer skin along their lower edge.

106

Intestine parkas were worn as a cover before fabric was available; they were also used for warm, wet conditions and for ceremonial purposes. At other times of the year, these parkas were kept in storage. Historically, intestine parkas were made from walrus and bearded seal intestines (Smolyak 1988). The intestines were cleaned, inflated until dry, then cut lengthwise; the strip was then sewn together in one continuous spiral, omitting side seams. The hemline of the parka was finished with a strip of fabric or dehaired reindeer skin (Antropova and Kuznetsova 1956 [1964], Bogoras 1901, Varjola 1990a).

Today, depending on the season and the availability of skins, men wear trousers made of seal skin, reindeer leg skins, fawn skins, or fabric. Pants are held in place with a drawstring that passes through a casing around the waist. The pants have tight-fitting legs that extend down to the ankles, where there are gathering strings which can be drawn tight. Short boots are often worn inside the pants. One style of outer trousers, known as "wrestler trousers," are decorated with numerous tassels of red-dyed seal skin. During festivals and holidays Chukchi men regularly compete in tests of strength and

wrestling matches, and those wearing these special trousers are recognized as accomplished wrestlers.

Short snowshoes, about 70 cm long and webbed with bearded seal thongs, are worn through the long cold winters by inland herders. In the spring, since wet snow destroys seal thong webbing, herders switch to broad wooden skis (Pelyrmagen 1990, BSM P90.0297.ab).

Women's Clothing

Traditional Chukchi women wear reindeer skin combination suits, similar to a snowsuit, with long baggy sleeves and pants, and a wide neckline cut low in the back and front and trimmed with wolf skin. This garment, entered through the neck opening, is large at the shoulders and closer-fitting at the waist. The pants, which are gathered just below the knees, are tucked into boot tops. This garment is made with two layers, like a man's inner and outer parka (Bogoras 1901). It is also worn by some older Koryak, Yupik, and Itelmen women on the Kamchatka Peninsula.

Women's combination suits do not appear to be as well adapted as men's clothing to the harsh tundra climate.

Bogoras (1901) heard young women complain about the inconvenience of their garments. Because of the excessively long sleeves, a woman must thrust her arm, shoulder, and breast out of the neck and leave the sleeve hanging down her back while she works. In order to relieve herself, a woman must entirely remove her garment—an unenviable position in the wind. In the winter, she must throw an overcoat around her shoulders to protect her naked body. The combination suit also influences women's gait; the Even describe Chukchi women as walking with their legs spread apart. (Chukchi retaliate by saying that Even girls are chained like dogs because they wear metal decoration on their clothing.) Some women have adopted men's style of dress instead.

Despite the inconvenience of the combination suit, it has its admirers. Sverdrup (1978) reports that

> one of the prettiest Chukchi interjections was used by a man . . . when his wife was wearing for the first time a new suit of black-and-white spotted fur. Then he would stand in front of her, look her over carefully from head to toe and say, hra-a, with an "r" way down in his throat. This means, "My dear, how perfectly charming."

Inland Chukchi women also wear a hooded overcoat similar to that worn by men. Sometimes this overcoat is layered over a combination suit when going for a walk or performing ceremonial dances (Mitlyanskaya 1976). Overcoats are constructed from thin summer skins, with the hair worn to the inside. They are dyed red with alder bark and decorated with fringe, embroidery, and patches of fur on the back and front using designs distinct to Chukchi (Kocheschov 1989).

Children's Clothing
Babies and toddlers wear a one-piece combination suit made of reindeer fawn skin with the hair to the inside that features a large fur-trimmed hood. The open crotch is covered with an attached reindeer skin diaper lined with moss. Once a child begins to walk, the suit's sleeves are slit near the palm of the hand so that the child's hand can extend outside the garment or quickly be withdrawn inside the sleeve, which ends in a mitt. The bottoms of the pants are also slit. Children are dressed in short fawn skin boots (Bogoras 1901, Oakes and Riewe 1990).

Footwear
Chukchi, Koryak, and Yupik wear similar boot styles made from primarily seal and reindeer skins (Vasilevich 1963a). Chukchi and Koryak living inland trade reindeer skins for seal skins with coastal Chukchi, Koryak, and Yupik. Soles of summer and winter footwear are either boat-shaped, with vertical pleats evenly spaced around the toe and heel, or flat and

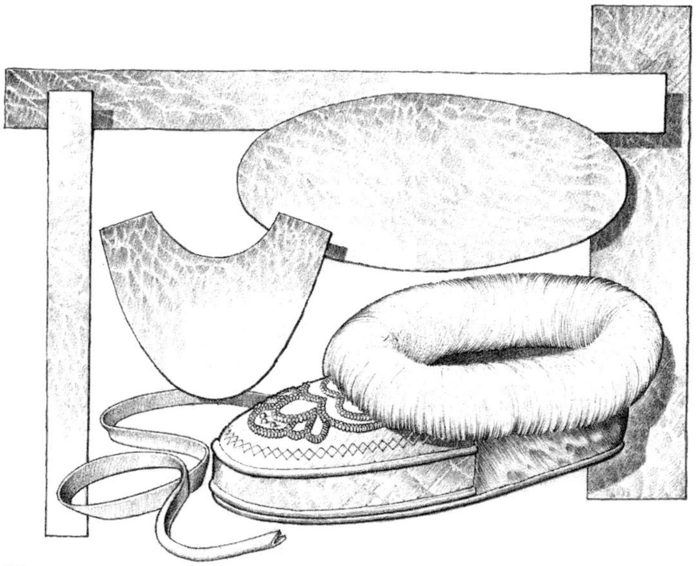

FIGURE 106
Chukchi wear colourful fabric shells over their inner parkas to prevent snow from sticking to the skin and for decoration. On women's fabric shells, the sleeves are extra long and gathered. REM 3949.22

FIGURE 107
The slipper shown here is often made from vinyl lined with imitation fur. It has an unpleated sole, a vertical side strip, a vamp decorated with embroidery or skin mosaics (often machine-stitched), and folded vamps in the toe seams. This modern version of a traditional style is made and sold by contemporary women in many brigades throughout Russia.

unpleated. The stiffly pleated boat-shaped sole was also used by ancient arctic Aboriginal hunters. It is made from dehaired bearded seal, and occasionally from split walrus hide. Flat soles are made from bearded seal, split walrus, bull reindeer, or reindeer toe skins.

Boots are made with or without a vamp. Vamps either encircle the foot or are cut in a distinct shape with a rounded point that extends up to mid-shin. Extra room is sometimes added across the toes. Leg sections, constructed from haired or dehaired reindeer and seal skins, are cut straight across at the shin or knee. Before bear skins became valuable in the fur trade, coastal Chukchi wore polar bear leg skin boots, which are extremely tough as well as warm (Bogoras 1901).

Chukchi continue to make traditional winter skin boots but wear mostly manufactured rubber boots in summer. Today, knee-high boots into which trousers are tucked are often worn by men, even though this was originally considered a women's boot style (Oakes and Riewe 1990). In the past, men wore these boots only when shamans or spirits ordered them to do so, as a means of concealing their identity or as the first step in their symbolic transformation from men to women, which was practised when men needed to gain more spiritual power (Bogoras 1901).

Leg Skin Boots
Coastal Chukchi leg skin boots have stiffly pleated boatlike soles or unpleated soles, while those of inland Chukchi have flat, oval-shaped, unpleated soles. Coastal Chukchi boots are

flatter-looking, with a strip of unfolded skin sewn into the sole seam. Neighbours of the Chukchi generally wear footwear with slightly pointed soles; in a Russian legend about the Chukchi wars, a party of warriors was detected by the Russians because their distinctly shaped grass insoles floated downstream past the Russian camp (Bogoras 1901, 1909 [1975]).

In one style of leg skin boot, a side strip with a centre front and centre back seam encircles the foot. Another common side-strip design begins with a centre front seam and extends only to the edge of the back panel. These variations produce a toe silhouette that has a clifflike appearance rather than the slanted-toe silhouettes of boots made by Evenki, Nenets, and other groups in the west. Some boots are made with a gusset that tapers to a point on each side of centre front and extends back to the back panel.

Leg sections are made from light- or dark-haired skins, using four panels per leg for inland Chukchi knee-high boots (BSM P90.0298.2, P90.0300.2, P90.0301.2, P90.0302.2, S90.0030.4, P90.0296.3; EMO 28.157, 27.559, 28.156, 28.155; NME 1070.35) and two panels for shin-high coastal Chukchi boots (EMO 28.154). Similar-coloured panels are usually selected, although panels of different colours are alternated occasionally. The upper edge of the boot is cut straight across. It is finished with either a casing and drawstring or a strip of skin sewn with the hair to the inside. If the latter technique is used, ties are sewn to the upper edge. Ankle straps are sewn directly to the sole or threaded through loops sewn into the sole seam. Chukchi often decorate leg sections with one or two short strips of light- and dark-haired skins placed parallel, staggered, or arranged in a V shape. Like Koryak and Yupik, Chukchi sometimes use geometric fur mosaics, and hair and skin embroidery is sewn around each boot's upper leg, centre front, vamp, and ankle straps (Turner 1976).

Summer Skin Boots
Historically, coastal Chukchi used shaved bearded seal or split walrus hides blackened with soot (MVB IVA 498, 497). When seal skins were unavailable through trade, inland Chukchi and Koryak made their summer boots from heavily smoked reindeer skins, which are almost as water-repellent as seal skins and will not shrink after getting wet (Vasilevich 1963a). Today, traditional herders continue to wear smoked reindeer or seal

109

FIGURE 108
Chukchi boot patterns are passed down from grandmother to grand-daughter. Slight alterations may be made; for example, the leg section is cut with fewer panels on short boots when larger-sized reindeer leg skins are available. The large sole is trimmed to fit the foot of the wearer.

FIGURE 109
The soles of Chukchi winter leg skin boots are made from reindeer toe skins, which have stiff, dirty-white bristlelike hairs swirling in all directions. These skins provide warmth as well as traction.
BSM P90.0301.ab

FIGURE 110
Reindeer hair embroidered designs decorate Chukchi leg skin boots for special occasions. Stiffly pleated soles are seen on the footwear of coastal Chukchi and Yupik in the Far East and Alaska and of Inuit in northwestern Canada.
REM 7396.3/1,2

FIGURE 111
Inland Chukchi wear knee-high leg skin boots with flat soles and a stove-pipe–shaped leg section.
BSM P90.0266AB

FIGURE 112
Traditionally, Yupik made slippers with stiffly pleated bearded seal skin soles. They were finished as unpleated slippers are, or had a vamp similar to that of a European bedroom slipper, decorated with skin or fur mosaics and embroidery. REM 2106.13/1,2

FIGURE 113
Bleached seal skin welts, ankle straps, and an upper leg band are common features on Chukchi seal skin footwear. Shin-high boots are used during mild weather when deep water is not expected. The upper edge of these boots is decorated with hair embroidery and skin pieces. MVB IVA 599

FIGURE 114
One style of Chukchi women's summer boots is made with bleached ringed seal upper leg sections and dehaired (black) lower leg sections, and decorated with skin mosaics and hair embroidery. Circles are created using a handmade chisel with two points on the tip, which is used like a compass. REM 8762.15258/1,2

112

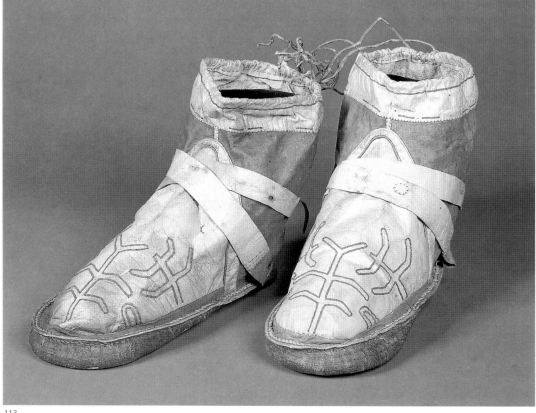

113

skin boots with pleated soles, vamps with a slightly rounded point extending up to mid-shin, and knee-high or shin-high leg sections. Cowhide is sometimes used as a substitute for seal and reindeer, as skins quickly wear out on abrasive rock surfaces. Occasionally, small skin guards are placed around the boot front to protect toes from stones and exposed roots (Bogoras 1901).

Vamps either encircle the foot, have a second small vamp placed at the top centre front, or are cut with a steep triangular point that is rounded off. Seams are either top-stitched or sewn with folded welts in the seam. Leg sections, cut straight across, are finished by folding the skin to the inside and top-stitching it, or by sewing on a casing, which usually has a drawstring threaded through it. Knee-high or mid-shin leg sections are close-fitting, with very little flare at the top. This snug fit ensures that the little water that enters is forced out through two rows of small holes pierced in the sole. After a long walk through a wet bog, this style of footwear dries out within half an hour (Bogoras 1901). It is worn with grass insoles and no socks.

An adaptation of this style is made for special occasions in modern homes. These boots are elaborately decorated with semicircular designs made from hair and skin embroidery, and geometric designs created by combining white bleached skins and dark shaved skins (Antropova and Kuznetsova 1956 [1964]). This style is also worn by Koryak and Itelmen.

In a manner similar to Koryak and Yupik, each of these boot styles is sometimes decorated with fur mosaics using bleached (white), stained (reddish), shaved (black), haired seal (silver and black) and haired reindeer (white, light brown, and dark brown) skins. One or more bleached skin welts may be added to the centre front seam of black dehaired skin boots (MVB IVA 532, IVA 598). Sometimes several rows of welts are used, with pieces of white and black skins placed adjacent to one another. A band of bleached skin is often sewn around the top of the leg section. Black thread and reindeer hair are used to embroider lines along this band. Circles, crisscrosses, and zigzag patterns cut from bleached and shaved skins are sewn to the upper band for extra decoration.

Boot Straps
Chukchi have wide ankle straps cut from dehaired skins on almost all of their footwear. Some straps are sewn into the sole seam on each side towards the back; others are threaded through one or two loops sewn on each side of the foot towards the back. These straps are crossed over the toe, wrapped around the ankle, then tied securely. Casings with drawstrings are sewn around the top of most boots, regardless of height.

Stockings and Grass Insoles
Winter boots are worn with short, thin reindeer socks (MVB IVA 502). Chukchi herders wear thinner fur socks than do Yakut, who travel by horseback, because Chukchis' feet are kept warmer by walking and tending herds. Except for the pleated boatlike sole style, patterns used for boots are also used for stockings.

Grass insoles, which take on the shape of the boot sole, are worn at all times of the year, even in summer when boots are worn without socks. Women harvest enough long grasses in the autumn for their family's use all year round.

Summary
Chukchi footwear styles are similar to those of Koryak and Yupik but are easily distinguished from those of other groups in western and central Siberia. Soles are either unpleated or crimped into stiff, vertical pleats. Leg sections are usually made with four or six panels, with the top cut straight across. Loops for ankle straps are sewn into the ankle seam, or ankle straps are sewn directly into the sole seam. The upper edge of boots of all heights is finished with a casing and drawstring; ties are used on some thigh-high boots. Boots are made with single and double vamps. Dehaired, stained, bleached, haired, and cropped seal and reindeer skins are used to make footwear and for decorative skin mosaics. Hair embroidery and ochre are also commonly used for decoration.

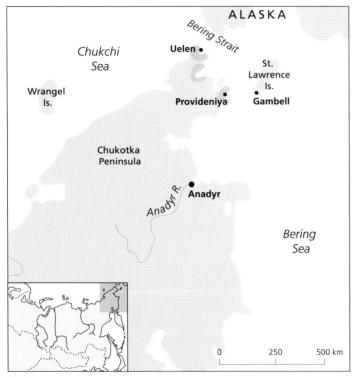

CHAPTER 10

ALASKA

Bering Strait

Chukchi Sea

Uelen

Wrangel Is.

St. Lawrence Is.

Provideniya

Gambell

Chukotka Peninsula

Anadyr R.

Anadyr

Bering Sea

0   250   500 km

Map 11

FIGURE 115
Overleaf: Yupik hunters search for walrus and whales in the fog-shrouded waters of the Bering Strait.

MAP 11
Siberian Yupik homelands

FIGURE 116
The Yupik were gradually pressed out of their expansive Bering Strait territory and forced into mountainous areas along the southeastern and northeastern edges of the Chukotka Peninsula.

URING THE SEVENTEENTH and eighteenth centuries Siberian Yupik, who now number only about 1,700, occupied a broad area along the Bering Strait coastline. Well into the twentieth century, they lived a traditional way of life in temporary settlements, harvesting marine mammals, sea birds, fish, and invertebrates (Bogoras 1913 [1975], Hughes 1984, Jochelson 1928, Krupnik 1995c, Rudenko 1961). Today, Yupik occupy a much smaller area and are closely related in lifestyle, traditions, language, and appearance to Koryak and Chukchi. They are commercial fur farmers, hunters, bakers, butchers, and labourers as dictated by the Communist Party. Traditional hunting and ceremonies have almost disappeared as a result of these changes.

Contemporary Yupik live on both sides of the Bering Strait in villages; families on the eastern coast of Siberia often have American relatives only a few kilometres away on St. Lawrence Island in Alaska (Kairaiuak and Orr 1995, Oakes and Riewe 1997). The two groups share the same language dialects, material culture, and cultural characteristics (Alekseyev 1979a, 1979b; Apassingok et al. 1985, 1987; Arutiunov et al. 1979; Bogoras 1913 [1975]; Chlenov and Krupnik 1984; Issenman 1997; Jochelson 1926a, 1928; Krupnik 1995c; Menovshchikov 1964; Michael 1961-1974; Michael and Vanstone 1983; Moore 1923; Okladnikov 1965; Rudenko 1961; Swadesh 1962).

Due to the shortage of wood in traditional Yupik territories, animal parts provided materials for many tools, as well as for clothing, household supplies, and other possessions. Baleen and ivory were made into storage containers. Ladles and spoons were carved from antler, ivory, whalebone (jaw or scapula), and walrus scapula. Walrus and bearded seal intestines were used for waterproof parkas, and walrus stomachs were used for sewing kits, assorted bags, and drums. Seal skins were made into parkas, boots, pants, mittens, and packs, and these traditions continue today (Mitryukova 1988, Oakes and Riewe 1989).

Historically, split walrus skins served as covers for umiaks and for the roofs of houses. People today still employ umiaks and seal skin harpoon floats when hunting whales and walrus. If a walrus punctures the hull of a skin boat, a quick patch can be made easily by stuffing the hole with a piece of skin.

In the past, the Yupiks' primarily meat diet was supplemented by local berries and roots. Today, rice, pasta, and dried vegetables are often added to boiled meat. The traditional marine diet of the Yupik and their maritime neighbours ensured low rates of hypertension and cardiovascular disease (Nobmann et al. 1994, Oakes and Riewe 1989).

In addition to being hunters, Siberian Yupik, like Chukchi, were formidable warriors, with weapons inspired by those of China and Japan. By A.D. 800 or 900, armour plates made from bone or ivory were used by Siberian Yupik as well as by Chukchi and Koryak. The oblong plates were lashed to one another with seal skin thongs. Shoulder, wrist, chest, groin, and head guards were worn (Ackerman 1984, Rudenko 1961, Vanstone 1983).

Traditional Beliefs

Hunting on moving sea ice is extremely dangerous (Nelson 1899; Nelson 1969; Riewe 1992, 1991), and Yupik acquire protection by showing respect to the spirits (Fitzhugh 1988). Protective bundles, whose contents include ivory or wooden carvings of whales, seals, bears, foxes, and dogs, are carried in

walrus skin boats (Bogoras 1909, Milovsky 1991, Murdoch 1892, Nelson 1899, Rudenko 1961).

The Yupik whale ceremony is an extremely important event. When a whale is killed, the whole community celebrates with a blanket toss, a feast, dances, and games. A dance called "Hunting the Whale," performed while sitting on benches, uses hand movements to depict the story of the hunt. Other dances performed by the Yupik as well as the Chukchi and Koryak include "Sewing," "Dance of the Cranes," "Scraping Skins," "Raven," and "Mating Reindeer." These dances are used to communicate with the spirits that manifest themselves in animals or in human activities (Arutiunov et al. 1979, Istomen 1990, Rultineut 1989, Sapronov 1985, Yemelyanova 1988, Zhornitskaya 1988). Yupik also hold ceremonial dances to celebrate a young person's first kill or first berry-picking expedition (Wallen 1990).

According to Yupik, it is the spirit of the animal, rather than the skill of the hunter, that determines whether or not a hunt is successful. An animal that has been shown respect

116

117

will give its spirit up to the hunter. In order for men to have a successful hunt, women communicate with the spirits of the animals through sleeping and waking dreams and through their elaborately decorated clothing (Apassingok et al. 1985, 1987).

Hair-embroidered symbols, ochre-painted designs, and skin piecework represent helping spirits and bring life to the objects depicted. Ochre is used as a substitute for blood, which is seen as a critical element for life, youth, and strength. Yupik and Chukchi draw animal symbols with ochre so they can become real, thus increasing the number of animals available to hunters. A minute strip of skin representing a whale's tail is embedded into the centre front seam of footwear to please the spirit of the whale (Chernetsov 1963; BSM P90.0040.ab). Men also speak to helping spirits by carving artistic images of them on their tools and weapons. However, if men return empty-handed from the hunt, women are held responsible for not focussing their attention on the animals (Kuz'mina 1988a, 1988b).

Traditionally, female shamans were considered to be stronger than males. The relative strength of a male or female shaman was expressed in the preservation of his or her teeth; the incantations of a toothless shaman were considered to be very weak. Strong, sharp teeth supposedly lent the shaman strength during seances. Since cracks in damaged teeth accumulate food particles, giving rise to unpleasant odours, spirit helpers would refuse to visit such a person. Shamans generally lost their powers in old age, and this was reflected in their clothing; the white parkas, pants, mittens, and boots of the elderly symbolized weakness (Morrow 1984, Tein 1994). On St. Lawrence Island, Yupik wore different clothing when they were ill to trick the evil spirits and direct their negative energies elsewhere (Fitzhugh and Kaplan 1982).

Traditional Clothing
Skin clothing is a necessity for successful arctic coastal hunting; however, since this clothing is biodegradable, ancient examples of it are rarely found. Nonetheless, archaeological

118

remains of stone, ivory, and antler scrapers, awls, needles, needle cases, and knives indicate that tailored clothing was worn by ancient societies in the northern Far East (Ackerman 1984, Levin and Sergeev 1964). Similar Yupik clothing styles still appear on both sides of the Bering Strait.

Some traditional women still wear the combination suits also worn by Koryak and Chukchi. The suits are often decorated by placing two vertical strips of white-haired reindeer skin down each side of the front and one strip down the back. Several short strings of beads are sewn to the neck opening for decoration. A bib cut from white- or dark-haired reindeer calf skin is worn across the chest (Apassingok et al. 1985, Chubarova 1988, Oakes and Riewe 1989). Contemporary women wear cotton pull-over shells every day and for special occasions. This fabric garment was originally designed to prevent snow from sticking to skin clothing; however, today it is often worn alone.

Intestine and seal skin clothing is worn in mild, damp weather. Intestines are semipermeable membranes that allow

FIGURE 117
These Yupik hunters work as professional walrus butchers for their brigade.

FIGURE 118
Fish is smoked in order to preserve it for longer periods of time and to add variety to the Yupik diet.

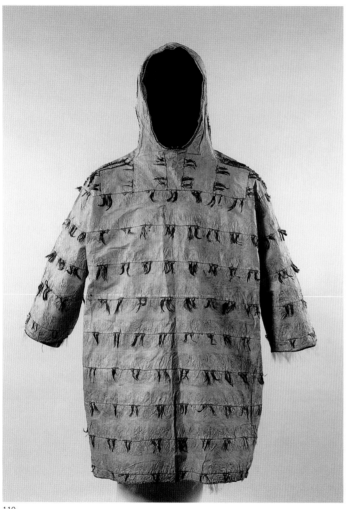

119

body vapours to escape yet prevent large water molecules
from entering, making this traditional material far more effective than modern manufactured "breathable" clothing. Durable raincoats and fancy parkas are constructed from the large
intestines of walrus and bearded seals. Raincoats are made
from unbleached intestines, whereas fancy parkas are assembled from bleached intestines. Seams are decorated with scalps
of crested auklets, red yarn, or strips of unborn seal fur dyed
red. Grass is placed on each side of the seam to act as rein-
forcement, allowing stitches to be pulled tight without tearing
the skin; the grass swells when wet, making the stitches even
tighter. Parkas are sewn with the intestines running either
horizontally (for unbleached intestines) or vertically (for
bleached or unbleached intestines) over the torso. A woman's
fancy parka has more gathers at the back of the hood than a
man's. Some elders say that men's parkas have horizontal
strips of intestines and women's parkas have vertical strips,
and that men's intestine parkas are sewn on the outside while
women's are sewn on the inside. These differences are less
pronounced in clothing made by younger seamstresses today.
Some Siberian Yupik in Alaska also still make these garments
(Apassingok et al. 1985, Fitzhugh and Crowell 1988, Fitzhugh
and Kaplan 1982, Issenman 1997, Oakes and Riewe 1989).

Yupik men wear hoodless pull-over reindeer parkas with
inner and outer trousers like those of coastal Chukchi. Outer
pants made from haired ringed seal or spotted seal skins
extend over the man's skin boots and are tied at the ankle.
Inner pants are made from dyed reindeer skin. On St.
Lawrence Island, skins are dyed with a fine powder mixed
with oil. The powder is made from clay collected from the
cliffs near Gambell. The clay is shaped into thin bars and dried
in the sun; once dry, the bars are baked to turn them colours
ranging from orange to red.

In the past, pull-over parkas were also made from bird
skins if reindeer skins were impossible to obtain. Murre,
cormorant, crested auklet, old squaw, and Steller's eider skins
were commonly used (Apassingok et al. 1985, Oakes and
Riewe 1989).

Babies wear combination snowsuits with a built-in pad for
moss "diapers"; older children dress in miniature versions of
adult clothing. Mittens and hats are worn for protection while
travelling. On mittens, hoods, or hats made from reindeer

head skins, the reindeer's eyes are sewn shut; this helps protect the wearer from being seen by the harmful spirits of the dead (Aburtina 1990, Oakes and Riewe 1989).

Men used to wear ivory labrets and have short, blunt haircuts. Women tattooed their faces, arms, and hands with distinct designs. Soot was collected from seal oil lamps or from the bottom of cooking containers. Sinew was soaked in a mixture of soot and urine, preferably from an elderly woman, and the stained sinew was drawn under the skin with a needle. Another technique was to dip the needle in the solution and then prick the skin (Apassingok et al. 1985, 1987). Today, only a few elderly women are seen with tattoos (Oakes and Riewe 1989). Contemporary Yupik women of all ages wear beads strung on pieces of sinew braided into their long hair (Afanasev and Pitkzu 1987); these are also used as body jewellery.

Footwear

Footwear plays a major role in the lives of Yupik; boots provide protection from the physical elements and are important in ancient rituals. Elders say that when a woman is pregnant her husband must leave his boots' ankle straps untied; if he ties them, the foetus will choke to death (Apassingok et al. 1985). Another tradition is that of using footwear to find lost hunters. Hunters on the Bering Sea are exposed to treacherous currents, rapidly changing weather systems, and erratic ice conditions. When a hunter does not return, his wife hangs a pair of his boots over a pole inside the house. The boots are carefully watched to determine whether or not the hunter is still alive. Women are able to observe slight movement over weeks, but as soon as the boots stop moving, the hunter's wife knows that her husband has perished (Fortier 1978, Oakes and Riewe 1989).

Yupik make two main types of footwear: reindeer leg skin and seal skin styles. Many variations in height, decoration, and combination of materials create a wide range of boots for different seasons and activities.

Leg Skin Boots

Leg skin boots are made with either flat, unpleated, reindeer skin soles (BSM P90.0298.ab, NME 1070.34, REM 8023.16/1,2) or stiffly pleated boat-shaped soles of bearded seal skin (BSM

P80.0839.ab; EMO 27.972). The seal skin sole is attached to a vamp and leg section with welts in the seams. A side strip is often inserted between the sole and the vamp (Gorbacheva 1997, Oakes and Riewe 1996). Felt soles are used occasionally for dry conditions (BSM P90.0288.a-d). A strip of skin or vinyl (not folded) is used as a welt in the flat sole seam, and folded welts are used in the pleated sole seam version of this boot. Some flat-soled boots are made without a side strip; others have a partial side strip that begins with a centre front seam and extends back to the back panel. Sometimes the side strip encircles the foot and has a centre back seam. This latter design is often used for women's boots. Leg skin boots are also made with vamps that encircle the foot.

Reindeer leg skin boots are made either knee-high, with front, back, and side panels, or mid-shin–high, with front and back panels (BSM P85.0016). Winter leg skins are used for mid-shin winter land-hunting boots. In more elaborately decorated leg skin boots, a narrow strip of leg skin is inserted in the seam on each side of the front panel (BSM P84.0143, P88.0083; EMO 27.972). Some leg sections are made with the lower portion cut from reindeer leg skins and the upper from seal skin (REM 4979.6/1,2). The boot top is cut straight across and finished with a casing and drawstring.

Seamstresses decorate everyday and special occasion boots with braided or woven multicoloured strips, fur mosaics, skin appliqué, and hair or thread embroidery. "Tongues," ovals, semicircles, lines, and zigzags are common Yupik design elements (Ivanov 1963). Hair embroidery is especially common on traditional Yupik footwear. Contemporary boots are trimmed along the upper edge with polar bear, muskrat, or other skins available to the seamstress.

An undecorated version of this boot style is regularly made and sold by women who work on collective farms. Undecorated leg skin boots are also used for work boots.

Dehaired Seal Skin Boots

Waterproof seal skin boots are worn by Yupik men for late spring hunting and by the elderly throughout the summer. Most people have substituted manufactured rubber boots for traditional waterproof boots today.

Waterproof skin boots are made with scraped, pleated, or unpleated bearded seal skin soles. Each sole is sewn to the vamp and leg with a depilated seal skin welt in the seam. A narrow side strip is sewn to the sole seam of some pleated soles.

The vamp either encircles the foot, encircles the foot with a second smaller vamp sewn to the top centre front (BSM P92.0089.ab), has a long pointed front seam, or has a long pointed front seam with the point rounded off (REM 6779.83/1,2). The vamp, leg, and ankle straps are made from dehaired, bleached, smoked, blackened, ochred, or alder-barked ringed seal skins. The vamp-leg seam is sewn with a double row of running stitches. Seams are sewn with thick sinew threads; if they start to leak, they are lubricated with seal oil. The leg section has a centre front seam that is reinforced with strips of depilated seal skin. In one variation, the central welt of depilated skin extends past the centre front seam about .5 cm and is cut in the shape of a whale's tail (REM 8762.15256/1,2, 8762.15249/1,2).

Waterproof boot legs are finished with a bleached seal skin band. A casing is made by stitching through the upper band; black thread is often used as it adds a decorative touch. Drawstrings are threaded through the casings, and ankle straps are sewn to each side of the foot near the front. A short piece of scraped skin is attached to the base of the ankle strap before the strap is sewn on. Straps are crossed over the toes and threaded through loops sewn near the heel.

A hip-high waterproof boot (BSM P85.0307) is used by men during late spring hunts. It is identical to the knee-high boot, except that the leg section is extended with a piece of dehaired seal skin. Sometimes a bleached skin casing is sewn to the upper edge and around the knee.

Waterproof boots are often decorated with welts, skin mosaics, and hair embroidery (Gorbacheva 1997; BSM L84.0003; EMO 27.975, 27.973; MVB IVA 599; NME 1070.54). An exceptional example of Yupik decorative techniques was collected by Captain James Cook in the early 1700s (BM Q78.AM.38). Squares, circles, semicircles, zigzags, triangles, and lines are common design elements. Women also alternate the colour of skins used for the upper and lower leg, then use contrasting coloured welts in the seams to create additional decoration (REM 8762.15258/1,2). Bleached (white), dyed (red), and dehaired (black) skins are commonly used for welts and for skin mosaics. Clusters of five or six red, blue, and white beads are also spaced evenly around the leg on more elaborately decorated boots.

Haired Seal Skin Winter Boots

A classic silhouette seen in Siberian Yupik footwear is a boot with a puffed-up toe (Vasilevich 1963a). Extra room across the toe enables a hunter to wear an extra pair of boots or extra-

FIGURE 120
Yupik use a boot construction process identical to that of Inuvialuit in the western Canadian Arctic and Yupik in Alaska. Hard soles are sewn with a running stitch that goes through a welt in the seam and over an extra thread placed along the seam allowance (a). Loops for ankle straps (b, c, and d) are included in the seam while it is being sewn.

120

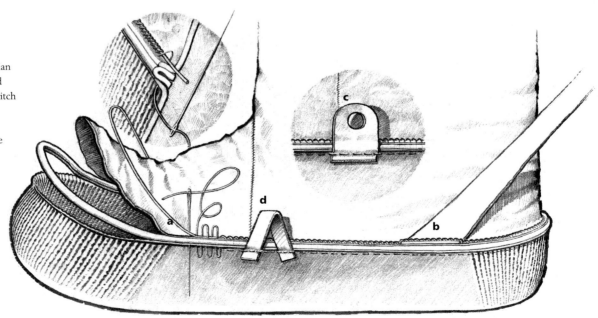

thick grass insoles and thick inner stockings when travelling in extremely cold weather. An example of the complete footwear system is shown by a boot made in the early 1900s, which still has the inner boots inside (Oakes and Riewe 1989; BSM s82.0052, s82.0030).

Boots for inland hunting trips during dry, cold winter weather are made from haired spotted seal skins (BSM P82.0030). An identical style used for coastal winter hunting is constructed from ringed seal skins (BSM P82.0040, P82.0052, s80.1023). Haired seal skin boots are either knee-high or ankle-high. They have a sole of shaved, pleated bearded seal skin sewn to the vamp and leg with a depilated welt. The haired seal skin vamp extends up the shin and is either pointed or has the point rounded off. It has extra room across the toes, creating the puffy silhouette.

The leg and vamp are sewn with the hair to the outside. A close-fitting stovepipe cut is used for the leg section, and the upper edge is cut straight across. A bleached seal skin or canvas casing is sewn to the upper edge and a drawstring threaded through. Ankle straps are sewn to each side near the front and an extra piece of shaved skin is sewn between the ankle strap and sole seam. Ankle straps are crossed over the toes and threaded through a loop sewn on each side towards the back.

Before polar bear skins became valuable in the fur trade, Yupik wore polar bear skin boots while hunting during the coldest part of winter. Polar bear boots were introduced to Yupik living on the western shores of the Bering Sea by Inupiat from northern Alaska. The boots were made using the same pattern as that described for haired seal skin boots. The pads of polar bear feet provide excellent traction on snow and ice (Manning et al. 1985) and are ideal for boot soles.

Red Seal Skin Boots

Another variation of the haired seal skin boot style has a vamp and leg sections made from recycled seal skin pants, which are washed, then stained with ochre or dyed red with alder bark. This style is also worn by Yupik living in Alaska and is made with or without a side strip (Apassingok et al. 1985).

A dehaired variation of this style is also stained red; it is used as a "runner" boot. Historically, Yupik regularly practised running and wrestling to hone their skills for hunting, athletic

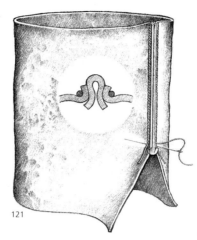

121

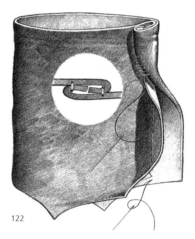

122

FIGURE 121 & 122
Coastal Chukchi, Koryak, and Yupik sew welts into their centre-front boot seams; welts are anchored with strips of contrasting skins placed on each side of the seam allowance. The complicated welt used by seamstresses to depict a whale's tail helps women to communicate with the whale's spirit even when they are absent from the hunt. These maritime peoples also occasionally execute a complex waterproof seam using two rows of running stitches. The needle never pierces both skin layers, thus preventing water from leaking into the boot.

competitions, and warfare. The polar bear, a predator that hunts by ambushing and stalking, cannot run as long as can a highly trained hunter wearing handmade skin boot runners. An exhausted bear will turn to face a hunter, allowing him to approach with his killing lance (Apassingok et al. 1985).

These running boots have soles made of shaved, pleated bearded seal skin. The soles are sewn to the vamp and leg with a depilated seal skin welt in the seam, and the vamp and leg section are cut from depilated skins dyed red. The vamp covers the entire toe area and has a decorative piece of skin inset along the vamp-leg seam. The leg has a centre front seam, and the back of the leg extends down to the sole. The upper edge of the boot is finished with a band of bleached seal skin folded over and topstitched into a casing. Drawstrings are omitted. Ankle straps are sewn into the

FIGURE 123
A combination of sea and land
mammal skins are used in this
Yupik boot, reflecting the diversity
of wildlife in the region and the
extensive trading between Yupik
marine hunters and Chukchi reindeer herders. These boots have
reindeer leg skins on the lower
leg section, with ringed seal skin
used for the upper portion. REM
4979.6/1,2

FIGURE 124
Boots with double vamps are worn
throughout the northern Far East.
They are decorated with reindeer
hair embroidery using traditional
Yupik designs. In the early 1950s,
expert Siberian Yupik hair embroi-
derers reintroduced their skills to
Yupik living on the Alaskan side of
the Bering Sea, but few people
continue this type of embroidery
today. BSM P92.0089.AB

123

124

126

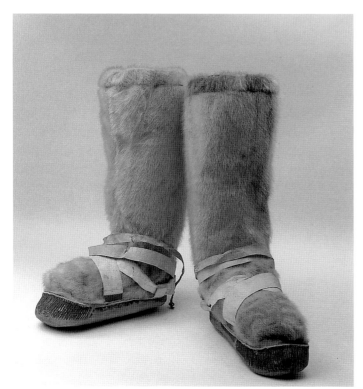

125

FIGURE 125
Yupik winter work boots are made from seal skin and have broad ties around the ankle. The large roomy area over the toes is necessary since these boots are sometimes worn over an inner pair of boots and stockings. BSM P90.0078.ab

FIGURE 126
Waterproof boots are worn by Yupik marine mammal hunters. Even the plainest hunting boot has some decoration, such as a complicated welt, for spiritual reasons. The extra room across the toe allows for additional insulation. REM 8762.15249/1,2

FIGURE 127
In 1744, Captain James Cook collected the boots depicted here from people living along the Bering Strait. The wide ankle straps, narrow boot leg, small vamp insert, oesophagus and hair embroidery, and design motifs are typically used by Siberian Yupik, Koryak, and Chukchi. BM Q78.AM38

127

sole-vamp seam, crossed over the toes, and threaded through loops sewn towards the heel. This style is rarely made today.

Crampons

In the past, one or two crampons made from whale rib bone or walrus ivory were lashed to each skin boot to provide traction on ice. Some ice creepers had spikes carved into the bone or ivory; others had spikes attached (Rudenko 1961). In the latter design, about six holes were drilled into the bone or ivory using a mouth bow drill. Then bone pegs were sharpened and inserted into the holes on the inner, concave side.

Snowshoes

On the Bering Sea, Siberian Yupik hunters often travel by snowshoe over treacherous ice and slush that is always moving and breaking up in the fast currents. Snowshoes are only about 60 cm long and are webbed, with heavy latticework of bearded seal thong beneath. Unlike snowshoes designed for dry arctic snow, these ice snowshoes are not webbed in the toe or heel sections.

Slippers

Seal and reindeer inner and outer slippers are used by Yupik. Inner slippers are short versions of stockings. Outer slippers have pleated or unpleated bearded seal skin soles with ringed seal skin vamps. The vamp is embroidered or decorated with skin mosaics, then a folded welt and side strip are sewn to the seam allowance of the vamp with a running stitch. Following this, the back portion of the slipper is overcast to the side vamp seam. Once the upper portion of the slipper is assembled, the sole is attached with a folded welt placed in the seam. This welt extends around the toe area or encircles the foot. Some slippers are made using patterns influenced by non-Indigenous peoples; however, skin selection and decorative details are distinctly Yupik (BSM P89.0031.ab, P79.0032.2; REM 2106.13/1,2).

Stockings

Female knee-high seal or reindeer skin stockings are made with soles softly pleated to a vamp and back piece. The leg section has a centre back seam. The skin is stained with alder bark, and pieces are all sewn with the hair to the inside.

Stockings extend well above women's boots and are tucked under their combination suits. Drawstrings on the boots hold the stockings in place. Men's stockings extend up to the shin and are made without the leg section used by women. Men also wear a stocking with a side strip that extends around the front panel (Apassingok et al. 1985).

Summary

Yupik, Chukchi, and Koryak footwear reflects these peoples' close interactions with one another and also reflect the arctic marine climate, the range of available resources, and the diversity in lifestyles. Seal and reindeer skin boots are extremely common, reflecting the importance of these animals and the ways of life that have evolved around them for coastal and inland Indigenous peoples of the northern Far East.

Yupik boots are often made with a sole, vamp, and leg section with a centre back seam. They are made with either an unpleated sole or a stiffly pleated boatlike sole cut from dehaired bearded seal or reindeer skin. The vamp has extra ease over the toes, creating a large puffy area. It extends up to the lower shin and is either sharply pointed or has the point rounded off. One-piece vamps with an insert and vamps that encircle the foot are also used. Leg sections are shin-, knee-, or thigh-high. Boots made from leg skins are cut from four or six panels. Thigh-high leg skin boots are sometimes cut on an angle, but all other boot legs are cut straight across. Depilated seal skin welts are sewn into the sole seam and leg seams, and some welts terminate in the shape of a whale's fluke or tail. Skins are decorated with red ochre, hair embroidery, and skin mosaics. Wide skin ties are sewn either into the sole-leg seam towards the back or into the back panel seam. Bleached skin casings are sewn to the upper edge, and drawstrings are used on some boots.

Evidence of linkages to ancient arctic Aboriginal cultures is even stronger in Yupik footwear than in Chukchi and Koryak footwear. Ancient design elements include the bulge over the toe of the vamp, stiffly pleated soles, and welts inserted in the seams. Winter footwear shows evidence of ancient connections with taiga hunters and peoples of the Altai Plateau through the sewing of the sole and leg section together without any side strip, vamp, or gussets (Pitul'ko and Kasparov 1996, Vasilevich 1963a).

CHAPTER 11

Map 12

*A*T LEAST SEVEN distinct groups of Indigenous peoples occupy the Amur region of the Far East, which served as an ancient travel and communication route between the Pacific and polar shores and the interior of Asia (Black 1973, 1988; Levin 1963; Levin and Potapov 1956 [1964]; Vanstone 1985). In 1989, there were 12,023 Nanai living on the Russian side of the Amur region (the remainder reside in China); 622 Negidal in the mountains north of the Amur River; 4,673 Nivkhi on the northern tip of Sakhalin Island and at the mouth of the Amur River; 915 Orochi inhabiting coastal areas; 190 Oroks (along with 1,300 Ainu, Indigenous people of Japan) on Sakhalin Island; 2,011 Udege inhabiting the taiga of the Ussuri River basin and the Sikhote Alin mountains; and 3,233 Ulchi along the Amur River (Dahl 1990). All of these groups interact with one another as well as with their numerically dominant neighbours and overlords the Chinese, Manchu, Japanese, Koreans, and Russians. Indigenous peoples in this region have exchanged ideas and materials over the centuries. They now share similar economies, material culture, rituals, and beliefs. Nonetheless, these groups have developed independent ethnic identities (Black 1988, Nagishkin 1980).

Negidal, who descended from Evenki reindeer herders, continue to breed reindeer and hunt in the taiga but have in the main adopted the sedentary village life. Orochi have retained their reindeer-herding way of life. Nivkhi and Nanai are sedentary fishers living in permanent summer and winter villages; a few raise horses and other livestock. Nivkhi and Nanai people are master metalworkers well known for their elaborately designed weapons, including armour, helmets, spearheads, and daggers (Black 1988).

Fishing

The Amur River is inhabited by more than one hundred species of fish, the most prolific being the migratory Pacific salmon. Many Amur peoples rely primarily upon fish for their sustenance and have developed numerous fishing techniques, including nets, weirs, seines, spears, and hooks (Margolina 1997a, Vanstone 1988).

Fish is prepared in a variety of ways. Sometimes it is dried or smoked with the skin intact. Sometimes the skin is removed in one piece with a long narrow knife on a

FIGURE 128
Overleaf: In the Amur River region, women visit at a local cultural centre while they cut out designs.

MAP 12
Homelands of the Amur region peoples

skinning table, and the meat and skin are dried separately. Skins are then kneaded with a skin softener and moistened with fish soup until they become soft and elastic. Afterwards skins can be smoked, sewn into large panels using fish skin thread, and finally made into clothing. Fish glue, made from simmered skins and heads, is used in clothing, footwear, household items, boats, and birch bark tarps (Black 1988).

The lightweight, water-repellent, and durable features of fish skins make them ideal for clothing and shelters. In the past, carp, catfish, and especially salmon skins, which are quite large and readily available, were preferred for robes and pants. Salmon and pike skins were used for footwear, mittens, and leggings. Skins from other marine animals, reindeer, and dogs are also used for clothing. Today, few women make fish skin clothing (Black 1988).

Hunting and Gathering

Their diverse coastal environment supplies Amur peoples with a variety of marine mammals, such as bearded, ringed, ribbon, and harbour seals, sea lions, dolphins, and whales. Traditionally, marine mammals were harvested for their meat, oil, skins, and teeth, which were used locally and traded with neighbours. The taiga and mixed forests support a wealth of wildlife, which provides sustenance as well as spiritual well-being for hunters. Some Amur peoples relied heavily upon hunting, whereas many of the riverine peoples hunted only to supplement their fish diets (Black 1988).

Hunting is a communal activity. Land animals are hunted on foot or with dogs; marine animals are harvested from the ice surface, on the open water, or from shore. Various types of harpoons, lances, clubs, and traps are employed. To prevent evil spirits from interfering with the hunt, strict taboos are obeyed by hunters as well as by their wives, who remain in the village (Buijs 1984, Smolyak 1988). When hunters return with sleds filled with game, they show their respect to the animal spirits by parading through the village wearing their most elaborately decorated clothing. As for other groups in Siberia and the Far East, in the Amur region clothing decoration carries the powers needed to appease the animal spirits. Without these powers, animals would not give themselves up to the hunters (Kuz′mina 1988b).

The Amur region also provides a wide variety of terrestrial plant resources. The mixed forests contain fruit-bearing trees and bushes, other edible plants, grasses, and medicinal plants such as ginseng. A wide variety of wood, including birch, elm, oak, larch, and pine, is used to construct homes, boats, and elaborately decorated implements. Ainu from Sakhalin Island also made their summer clothing from elm bark. Grasses, nettle fibres, and other vegetable fibres are used for the production of cordage, mats, nets, and baskets. In the past, nettle fibres were used to make armour shirts and helmets. Traditionally, men carried fresh grasses while hunting marine mammals; they fed the grass to an animal after it had been killed, to signify a gift to the sea world from the land (Black 1973, 1988; Levin and Potapov 1956 [1964]; Okladnikov 1981).

Woodworking skills are highly developed by the peoples of this region; the exquisite workmanship and aesthetic designs they apply to boats, houses, domestic utensils, sleds, and boxes warrants their recognition as outstanding artists (Black 1988, Buijs 1984, Levin and Potapov 1956 [1964]).

Transportation

Boat building is well advanced among the coastal and riverine peoples. Boat styles vary from group to group, from skin or birch bark canoes to large plank vessels. The flat-bottomed plank boats, which range in size from those with three or four pairs of oars to those with as many as twenty, were widely used by Amur peoples in the past. Beautiful dugouts made of poplar, with shovel-like extensions on both ends, were ideal for navigating the Sea of Okhotsk coastline. For transporting heavy loads, two or three dugouts were lashed together with cross poles. Nivkhi regarded their boats as living entities and depicted eyes on their prows. The launching of a boat was an important event surrounded by rituals (Margolina 1997a).

During the winter, Amur peoples use skis and dogs for hunting and pulling sleds. Skis are hand-carved from larch or birch. They are quite wide and long, with pointed tips that curve up slightly at the front. Hand-carved ski poles have broad, T-shaped handles resembling the butt of a paddle (Shrenk 1883-1903, Taksami 1967). Distinctive styles of skis are worn for different snow conditions and activities. For hunting, several layers of moose, reindeer, or seal skin are attached to the ski bottoms with fish glue, improving traction, increasing

129

130

FIGURE 129
Nanai wooden cutting boards are decorated with intricate relief carvings to appease the spirits. REM 1524.27

FIGURE 130
Bears are kept in captivity for several years and then killed and eaten. They are fed from a ceremonial wooden bowl decorated with figures depicting their capture and imminent demise. REM 8761.9468

FIGURE 131
A bear feast creates, strengthens, or restores linkages between families. During part of the ceremony, the bear's head is placed on a mantel. REM 2449.5

speed, and silencing the skis. Whalebone edges are occasionally added to these hunting skis. Skis without skins are used for travelling across deep snow to go winter fishing, woodcutting, or visiting neighbouring villages. These skis make more noise on the snow surface but require less energy to use. Dogs often pull hunters on skis in winter; in summer, people use dogs to tow their boats upstream (Black 1973, 1988; Levin and Potapov 1956 [1964]; Vanstone 1988).

Traditional Beliefs

Bear hunting, conducted by all Amur Indigenous groups, is considered a very prestigious activity. The hunt and the feast that follow are surrounded by complex rituals, especially for Nivkhi and Ainu (Black 1988, Buijs 1984).

The bear feast possibly arose as a rite of "feeding" the Lord of the Earth, Forest, and Mountains, the master of all animals, in order to secure good hunting, gathering, and health. The equality and unity of people and nature is the foundation of the feast—and of the entire spiritual culture of the Amur peoples. Bears and tigers are associated with men, and it is believed that these supernatural animals can transform into humans and enter into sexual relations with other humans (Buijs 1984).

A bear feast is used to commemorate deceased ancestors, join two distinct families, or adopt someone into a group. Marriage is crucial both for the continuation of a family group and the creation of a link between two groups. When someone dies, this link is broken (Buijs 1984).

Amur peoples also capture bear cubs and raise them in captivity for two or three years. While in captivity, a cub is fed with a long-handled wooden spoon. Before a bear is due to be killed, it is led through the village while men dressed in fur coats worn backwards demonstrate their manliness by trying to get close to it. The bear is killed, cooked, and then eaten with special carved utensils depicting the bear's capture, feeding, and sacrifice (Black 1988, Buijs 1984).

In preparation for weddings, dog harnesses are decorated and dogs wear special headgear. The bride's father carves spoons that will be used by the bride and groom to ritually feed each other. Fathers provide a dowry of prestigious goods, such as ornately inlaid knives; these items are stored as symbols of wealth and of the bride's importance. At the end

131

of the marriage feast, a kettle (a female utensil) and an axe (a male utensil) are exchanged between the two families (Black 1973, 1988). Symbols of elements of nature and the universe are placed on footwear, spears, knives, household implements, and clothing used by the bride and groom to ensure health, happiness, and prosperity. Fish scale symbols and Chinese shell motifs are common in the Amur region (Hsio-Yen 1963).

Shamans

Traditionally, Nivkhi and other groups living in the Amur region were animists who endowed all living entities with a soul and either a good or an evil spirit. People befriended good spirits and fought evil spirits by observing many taboos, such as not hurting a wounded animal or braiding grass that is still growing. There were so many spirits that shamans, the

keepers of traditional culture and medicine, were required to act as mediators (Siikala 1978, Smolyak 1988).

Shamans inherited their special gifts. Both men and women could be shamans; some were ordinary shamans and others were "big" shamans who could send the souls of the dead to the afterworld and cure the most serious illnesses (Margolina 1997a, Siikala 1978).

The costume of an eighteen-year-old female shaman in the collection of the Russian Museum of Ethnography consists of a short jacket, skirt, apron, and headpiece made of cloth and decorated with images of spirit helpers in the form of birds, fish, snakes, and lizards. Little ribbons are sewn along the edges of the jacket and skirt. The shaman wore wood and metal representations of spirit helpers, and a metal lattice representing the universe hung around her neck.

FIGURE 132

The back of this Nanai wedding robe is made from four panels. The first panel is decorated with bird symbols, the second with fish symbols, and the third with dragon symbols; a tree of life design, which includes birds, reindeer, and other important elements of nature, is embroidered on the fourth. The combination of the symbols depicted creates powerful spiritual support for good health, happiness, and prosperity for the bride and groom. REM 7247.2

A male shaman's costume, also in the Russian museum's collection, consists of a coat with a jacket over top, along with a skirt and a suede apron bearing images of spirit helpers. Long strips and numerous figurines of spirit helpers were hung on the back of a belt. Similar but smaller pendants were located on the headpiece (Margolina 1997a; REM 4871, 212-217).

To celebrate their reverence for nature, people of the Amur region traditionally held feasts to mark the changing seasons. "Feeding of the Waters" celebrated freeze-up; "Feast of the Opening of the Amur" occurred when the river ice broke up in spring; and "Feast of the Sea" was held upon the breaking up of the sea ice. For each feast, dishes and implements were made with zoomorphic representations of fish, birds, or sea mammals. Festivals were conducted before hunting began (Buijs 1984, Smolyak 1988).

Today, under the process of democratization in Russia, people are returning to some of their traditional settlements and revitalizing Amur folklore, sagas, lyrical songs, applied and decorative arts, and cultural activities, including feasts (Margolina 1997a).

Funeral Rites

To prevent contaminating a funeral pyre, traditional Nivkhi prohibit the dressing of a corpse in skin clothing. Neither is clothing with elaborate decoration allowed, as the deceased could lose his or her way to the underworld. Nivkhi funerary garments are made from white fabric and stitched with very large loose stitches. A corpse is dressed in leggings and short cloth slippers on naked feet. Once the corpse is properly dressed, the funeral ceremony begins.

Later, when it is time for the cremation, expensive furs are heaped upon the deceased, in multiples of three for a deceased man and two for a deceased woman. In the past, individuals prepared for their deaths by collecting expensive fur mantles. After the body is cremated, a piece of cranial bone is retrieved, wrapped in white cloth, and placed between two small planks that are fastened together with the umbilical cord of the deceased, which has been stored in an inner bag inside a sewing bag. A miniature wooden image of the deceased is carved and set nearby with several sticks, one of which has a piece of human hair tied to it. This hair symbol-izes the inner soul of the footwear needed to "cross into the other world." The other sticks have items attached that all provide assistance on the journey (Black 1973).

Traditional Clothing

Amur fish skin clothing, particularly shamans' robes and special occasion clothing for weddings and burials, is exquisitely decorated. The aesthetic influence of Chinese and Manchu decorative arts is evident in the complex designs (Black 1988; Ivanov 1937, 1954, 1963, 1970; Laufer 1902 [1975]; Mitlyanskaya 1983; Shrenk 1883-1903; Shternberg 1904).

Women's and men's outer wear is similar, except that women's clothing is longer and more elaborately decorated. It was traditionally created with a greater variety of skins than men's clothing and is now made mainly from fabric (Margolina 1997a, 1997b, 1997c; Vanstone 1985).

In the past, women preferred inner clothing made from young dog skins trimmed with fox, muskrat, squirrel, or sable. Wealthy women usually wore fox. Men often wore lynx coats on special occasions. Hemlines were trimmed with Chinese coins, medals, and shells. Robes were worn indoors in the winter, and an insulated robe was added over other clothing outdoors. Shorter fish skin robes were worn in summer (Black 1973, Shrenk 1883-1903, Taksami 1967).

Nivkhi clothing was traditionally made from fish, seal, and dog skins. It consisted of a robe that wrapped to the right, pants, footwear, leggings, and headgear. Black or dark brown dog and seal skins were used for men's outer winter clothing. Black dog skin coats were the most prestigious, as matching skins were the most difficult to find. Men's inner garments were made from the skins of seal pups, puppies, or other young animals. Outer garments, including the outer skirt, were made from large spotted seal skins with a fish or seal skin casing at the waist (Black 1973, 1988; Margolina 1997a, 1997b, 1997c; Shrenk 1883-1903; Shternberg 1904, 1933; Vanstone 1985).

Lynx hats, especially prized by women, were worn to bear festivals. In the winter, men wore hats with or without earmuffs, and in summer birch bark and cloth hats were worn. Mittens were made from seal, dog, reindeer, fox, or sable (Black 1973).

Both men and women traditionally wore belts. A hunter's

133

as well as Oroks and Negidal, make their clothing mainly from reindeer skins. These groups, however, spend part of the year at the coast, so fish and seal skins are also used. Cotton fabric and metal ornaments are obtained in trade with Nivkhi. Except for the frequent use of reindeer skin, the styles and decorations of Orochi, Oroks, and Negidal clothing are heavily influenced by Nivkhi and Even (Hatt 1916, Vanstone 1985).

Clothing is decorated with complex scrolls depicting animals or mythical beasts (Anisimov 1963b, Buijs 1984, Klimova n.d.). Ancient designs are passed from mother to daughter and have culturally distinct characteristics. For example, Nivkhi use stronger, more defined spirals than those of Nanai; Nivkhi floral and anthropomorphic motifs are bolder and more stylized than those of Negidal. Nivkhi are also known for their extensive use of turtle, toad, lizard, snake, and fish symbols (Black 1973).

Nanai symbols depict ancient beliefs and values, as explained by Krupnik (1995b):

> According to Nanai legend, the earth was originally smooth and covered with water, until a giant serpent ploughed deep valleys with his body. The water flowed down the valleys, leaving dry land for humans and other creatures. Serpent images appear in the form of spirals and zigzags.

Brightly coloured scrollwork is painted, dyed, appliquéd, or embossed onto skin garments, birch bark, and tools. On skins the designs may be painted with red or orange ochre; blackened with a mixture of caviar and soot; embroidered with hair or silk embroidery; appliquéd with complex curvilinear designs; embossed using a method similar to trapunto; or dyed with plant dyes.

Clothing and tools are displayed before and after each hunt (Black 1988). The power of a woman rather than the prowess of a man determines the success of a hunt (Bodenhorn 1990). According to Smolyak (1988), a Russian scholar,

> Each woman strived to make one-of-a-kind garments for her husband or son for festive occasions or for hunting. Usually no two identical designs could be found in the entire village. The men cherished the craftsmanship of the women. Among the Nanai and the Udege, the departure for hunting was a sort of

belt was considered his most important item of clothing, and it was also an essential part of funeral apparel. Men's belts, which were made from seal skin, carried a variety of tools and implements, including a flint, tinder pouch, dagger, fish knife, carving knives, tobacco pouch, drill, pipe cleaner, needle case, and amulets (Black 1973).

Nivkhi associate the colour white with the sea and with power, violence, and death, and generally do not use white for clothing. Black, which symbolizes good luck, is for festive clothing, and grey or blue for undergarments. Silk and cotton fabrics imported from China and Japan are used for summer and funeral clothing (Black 1973).

Orochi hunters living between inland rivers and the coast,

134

FIGURE 133
Udege women commonly wear rings in their ears and noses, as well as necklaces and bracelets. REM 4907.25

FIGURE 134
Stylized fish scales on the back of Nanai coats provide extra spiritual protection, as evil spirits generally attack from the rear. Scales, dragon symbols, and Chinese coins help the wearer to achieve happiness and good fortune. REM 7006.1

exhibition of the women's applied art. Hunters often left the village in groups of five to seven men. On a designated day and hour they would leave their homes, accompanied by relatives, and proceed ceremoniously through the village wearing jackets embroidered with different coloured threads, ornamented hats with plumes on top, balaclava helmets, aprons, gauntlets and footwear. It was a parade of splendour. Deeply appreciating the women's efforts, the men would take off the beautiful garments before actually going on the hunt. After the hunt, each man would remove his work clothes and don his elegant attire before actually returning to the village pulling his sled of game or other items. The hunters were welcomed by the villagers as "victors" and there was a celebration of the successful hunt and the splendour of the hunters' attire.

Footwear

Today, most people in the Amur region wear mass-produced boots purchased from local stores. Footwear worn by traditional Nanai, Negidal, Nivkhi, and Ainu of Sakhalin Island is made from seal or fish skin. Salmon and pike skins are preferred by fishers of the lower Amur River because they are light, strong, and waterproof, and provide good traction on ice (Smolyak 1988). The few people who are reindeer herders use reindeer skin footwear.

Leg Skin Boots

Reindeer leg skin boots are commonly made with seal skin soles and a gusset that tapers to a point on each side of the

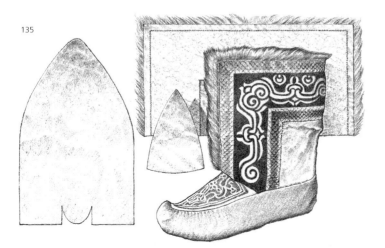

135

centre front panel and extends back to the side panel. Leg sections are made from four panels: front, back, left side, and right side. They are cut straight across the top and finished by sewing a band of fabric and possibly a strip of beaver fur around the upper edge. Seal skin ties are sewn to the lower back and tied around the ankle. Leg skin footwear is worn with skin stockings and grass insoles (Vanstone 1985).

Another variation of reindeer leg skin boots has either a seal skin or a reindeer skin sole. Side strips are usually omitted. The front panel is relatively narrow and the back panel is much wider, similar to the Yukagir leg style. The upper edge is cut straight across and trimmed with embroidery, appliqué, fur, and strips of fabric (BSM P95.0134.4).

Ulchi Seal Skin Boots

The pattern used to make reindeer leg skin boots is also used for Ulchi thigh-high seal skin boots. The flat, unpleated soles are cut from bearded seal skin. A haired seal skin gusset tapers to a point on each side of the front panel and extends back to the side panel. The leg section consists of front, left side, and right side panels cut from light- and dark-haired seal skins. The upper edge is cut straight across and finished with a band of embroidered or appliquéd fabric. Pieces of light- and dark-haired skins are cut into curvilinear designs and inlaid into the front panel (REM 8762.18501/1,2).

Pleated Pointed Sole Boots

Seal, fish, or moose skin soles are made with a pointed, slightly curved pleated toe and a Y- or T-shaped heel seam. The size and curvature of the point varies along the Amur River and was more prominent in the past (REM 2914.81/1,2). To make a larger point, seal or moose skin soles were pleated while wet, moulded into position, then allowed to dry hard. Smaller points are created with the help of pleats.

The vamp has either a triangular or a tongue-shaped lower seam and a slightly arched top seam. Tongue-shaped vamps create a broader, less pointed upturn at the toes (REM 2914.80/1,2). Vamp width varies; for example, Nivkhi and Ainu use narrower vamps than do Nanai. Some vamps have a centre seam. A skin flap is sewn around the ankle of some footwear (EMO 9229). Curvilinear designs are appliquéd (BM 72.3.18.3; MVB IVA 391, IVA 1328), painted (EMO 9219, 9229;

136

FIGURE 135
One typical sole style for the Amur region has a turned-up toe; the amount the toe turns up increases as one progresses down the Amur River. Decorative details, and the width and degree of curvature in the vamp, also change slightly from one group to the next.

FIGURE 136
Nanai paint their boots and leggings with ancient designs using natural paints. Symbols are outlined with fine black lines. Neighbouring groups use wider black lines and thicker designs. REM 1524.17/1,2

138

139

FIGURE 137
This pair of Amur region boots has a mixture of soot and eggs painted around the foot to increase water-repellency. REM 1998.394/1,2

FIGURE 138
Stockings and boots like these are often warn with colourful fabric leggings. Traditionally skin was used, but today fabric leggings are more common. BSM P95.135.a-i

FIGURE 139
Elaborately decorated fabric stockings are often worn with fish-skin winter boots that are wrapped around the ankles and held in position with a tie.

140

FIGURE 140
Ulchi and Nivkhi decorate the sides of their boot soles and vamps with hair-embroidered curvilinear or embossed designs. Skin is embossed by dampening the skin, pinching it into position, stitching the ridge in place, and then allowing the skin to dry. REM 7005.83/1,2

FIGURE 141
Reindeer hair and silk embroidery thread decorate the vamp of this boot. The dragon symbol woven into the silk fabric used for the leg section reflects Amur peoples' strong trade links with China. REM 2914.81

141

142

FIGURE 142

One distinct sole style used by Ulchi, Nivkhi, and other groups in the Amur region has a pleated horizontal seam and a vertical seam that extends up the centre of the toes. A triangular vamp is added on these boots. The leg sections are made from fish and seal skin.
REM 6948.6/1,2

FIGURE 143

In this Amur region boot style, harbour seal skin is cut into light- and dark-haired strips and used in panels similar to leg skin panels. Curvilinear designs are created with fur mosaics and embroidery. This boot is worn for special occasions and in cold winter conditions, since snow will not stick to the hair.
REM 8762.18501/1,2

144

REM 1871.31/1,2), embroidered, or embossed (MVB IVA 1333, IVA 1805; REM 7005.83/1,2) on the vamp and the ankle flap before these pieces are sewn to the sole. Nanai outline their designs with a fine black line. Undecorated boots are used for work wear (EMO 9221; MVB IVA 1521; NME 1202.61, 1202.62). An extra row of stitching is placed on the sole about 2 cm below the vamp-sole seam on some Ainu boots from Sakhalin Island (Hatt 1916).

Shin-high and knee-high leg sections are cut from haired seal skin (MVB IVA 4702), fish skin (BSM P95.0135.a-d; MVB IVA 1335), dehaired moose hide (BSM P95.0183, EMO 9466, NME 1202.61), or several pieces of fabric sewn together (BSM P96.0182.ab, P95.0136.a-d, P95.0185.ab, P95.0139.a-d, P95.0140.a-d, P95.0137.a-d; REM 1871.32/1,2). These sections are appliquéd

with stained skins, trimmed with fur or fabric, and sewn to the boot with a centre front opening. One side of the opening is wrapped over the other. A boot tie is threaded through holes cut around the ankle and wrapped around the leg section to hold the front opening closed (Hatt 1916).

Nivkhi Winter Boots
Another boot style also has a pleated sole and a separate vamp made from seal or fish skin. The sole has two toe seams (MVB IVA 961, IVA 1843; NME 1202.286, 1202.285, 1202.267; REM 6948.6/1,2). Pleats are held in position with a separate row of stitches placed close to the seam. The broad, triangular vamp, made from dark or light seal skin, is often pinched down the centre front fold line, leaving a permanent crease

(Hatt 1916). The leg sections are mid-shin height or knee-high and are made from fish skin, seal skin, or fabric. Some leg sections are made with a centre front opening that is held closed with a boot tie. Others have a centre back seam and a strip of skin sewn around the upper edge. This boot style, which may be left undecorated or decorated with a few small skin and fabric appliqués, is often used by Nivkhi. Nanai make this boot style with a fabric leg section appliquéd with curvilinear stylized animal designs (Levin and Potapov 1956 [1964]).

Nivkhi Women's Wraparound Boots

A slight variation of this style, worn by Nivkhi women of Sakhalin Island, is made with the vamp and sole cut in one piece. Fish and seal skin are usually used for the sole. The heel has a Y-shaped seam, and the toe has an elongated T-shaped seam that arches from the toe up towards the ankle. Pleats are formed around the toe area. The shin-high leg section is usually cut from linen, although fish and seal skins are also used occasionally. It has a very short centre front seam (about 1 to 2 cm long) that ends in a centre front opening. The leg section is folded around the ankle and held in position with ties or leggings (Hatt 1916, Vanstone 1985). This sole style is also used with knee-high leg sections and leggings.

Orochi Winter Boots

In the winter, Orochi wear a knee-high boot style with the sole cut from heavy skins, sometimes cowhide. The sole has a T-shaped heel seam and a few pleats at the heel and toe. A narrow side strip either encircles the foot or extends to the edge of the vamp, which is cut with a vertical instep seam and a horizontal shin seam. The centre front fold on the vamp is pinched into position when wet and remains as a pinched seam for the life of the boot. The leg section varies in height and has a centre back seam or side seams, depending on the materials used. It is made from moose skin (hair inside), reindeer leg skin, or other available materials (Hatt 1916).

Nanai Winter Boots

Nanai wear a style of boot in winter with bleached seal skin soles and reindeer body skins for the vamp and leg sections (MVB IVA 1340). The sole is pleated around the toes and has a

Y-shaped heel seam. The vamp has an oval-shaped lower seam and a concave upper seam. The leg section extends down over the top of the foot to the vamp. It has a centre front and centre back seam. The leg section is knee-high, cut on an angle, and trimmed with a strip of dark green velveteen commonly used by Yakut. Dark green and black welts are placed in all the seams.

Wet Weather Boots

Nivkhi of Sakhalin Island use the following style of boot for working in wet conditions. The sole is made from dehaired seal skin and fish skin with either a straight, a Y-shaped, or a T-shaped heel seam and a straight, centre front toe seam (MVB IVA 1804, IVA 1801; MVD 27082; NME 1202.264; REM 1997.110/1,2). The toe seam extends under the toes a short distance and is

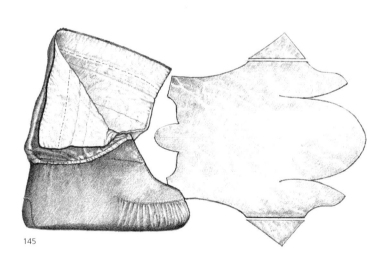

145

FIGURE 144
Ulchi footwear is embroidered with floral and stylized animal faces on moose (*right*) or seal (*left*) skins. This boot style is ideal for travelling in the winter on snowshoes. *Left:* BSM P90.0285 *Right:* REM 7436.9/1,2

FIGURE 145
A typical Nivkhi boot style has the side and bottom cut in one piece. The sole has a vertical and a horizontal seam. The vamp may be cut together with the rest of the sole or sewn separately, often from bleached seal skins. When the skin is still damp, the vamp is folded down the centre front and pinched into a ridge, which is then sewn into position.

made without any pleating. A dehaired, often bleached, seal skin is used for the short, triangular-shaped vamp. As in Orochi boots, a centre front fold is usually pinched into the vamp while the skin is prepared, creating a distinct fold that remains for the life of the boot. The leg section is either shin-high with a centre front opening or knee-high. Knee-high leg sections are made with either a centre front or a centre back seam; boots with a centre back seam on the leg section are usually worn without leggings and ties are omitted. A strip of skin is sewn around the upper part of the leg. Haired seal, dehaired seal, or fish skin is usually used for the leg section, although sometimes it is cut from linen instead (Hatt 1916, Taksami 1970, Vanstone 1985).

A variation of this style used by Nanai has the sole and vamp cut in one piece with a centre front and centre back seam. Sometimes the vamp is cut separately. The centre front seam comes to a point rather than curving around under the sole (MVB IVA 1338, IA 1523).

Ulchi Boots with Triangular Vamp
Ulchi make a boot style with an unpleated sole, a vamp with a triangular upper seam, and a mid-shin–high leg section cut straight across the top. This style is made from dehaired moose or reindeer. It is left undecorated or mystical faces are embroidered on the vamp and leg section (REM 7436.9/1,2). A band of embroidered or appliquéd fabric and fur is sewn around the upper edge. Ankle straps are sewn to the back.

Orochi Boots with Yakut Sole
Orochi use a combination of leggings and low-cut footwear in the summer. One women's boot style has a seal skin sole that narrows to a point at the centre front and extends up over the toes, like Yakut soles (Vanstone 1985). Nanai also wear footwear styles similar to Evenki and Yakut which are decorated using traditional Nanai designs (Vasilevich 1963a).

Slippers
Modern seamstresses produce slippers for sale in the urban centres that are made of commercially tanned skins, fabric, and seal skin. The decorative beading, skin appliqué, and strips of fur echo the traditional designs used by people of the Amur River region (NME 5517.4, 5517.6, 5708.1).

Leggings and Stockings
In the past, men wore skin leggings made with two layers of reindeer leg skins, moose leg skins, ringed seal skins, fabric, or fish skin (NME 1202.455, 1202.275, 1202.454, 1202.276, 1202.274, 1202.73, 1202.53, 1202.52). Cloth leggings used in winter were insulated by stuffing hay between the two layers of fabric. Leggings were worn with either seal or fish skin boots (Black 1973, Vanstone 1985). Oroks wore reindeer skin or fabric leggings with short pants (Vanstone 1985).

Stockings are usually made from several layers of fabric quilted together and appliquéd or embroidered around the upper leg. The sole is sometimes quilted for added insulation and durability (BM Q72.AS.46). Grass is used as insulation between the layers of quilted fabric. Skin stockings are also made with an oval sole, a vamp that encircles the foot with centre back, centre front, or side seams, and a broad panel sewn to the upper edge (DL 11163, REM 1998.394/1,2). Nanai make reindeer skin stockings with the hair worn to the inside. The soles are unpleated, with rounded toes and pointed heels. The leg section has a centre back seam and extends to mid-shin or the knee, with the top cut on a slant. The upper edge is trimmed with a strip of fabric or stained skin (MVB IVA 1336).

Summary
Amur region footwear styles show evidence of connections with ancient hunters. Footwear is made from locally available materials, and the pointed sole is adapted for more efficient use on skis. Tungus-speaking people in the Amur region use winter footwear typical for taiga hunters. Ulchi, Udege, and Orochi footwear shares some features with that of Nivkhi and Negidal. Orochi footwear has pleated soles, vamps, and leg sections, reflecting the historic connections between Orochi and Evenki from the Yenisey River and the Sea of Okhotsk, who are also connected to Yukagir and use leg sections with a narrow front and wide back. Orochi also borrow Nivkhi and Yakut styles, indicating their contemporary interrelationships. Nivkhi footwear styles have little in common with those of their Tungus-speaking neighbours or other groups in northern Asia, although their use of a wide leg section suggests that their ancestors were river fishers.

IDENTIFYING SIBERIAN AND FAR EASTERN FOOTWEAR

FOOTWEAR IS LIKE an unwritten history text: it reveals much about interactions among groups, life ways, availability of local resources, spiritual beliefs, and cultural values. During our research we studied thousands of pairs of boots, both those belonging to the people we met and those located in museums and cultural institutions or depicted in photographs, illustrations, films, videos, legends, songs, and folklore. Our survey indicates that the most common form of footwear used across Siberia is reindeer leg skin boots. Temporal, cultural, and lifestyle variations are evident in the cut of soles and vamps, the type of skins used, the number of leg skin panels, the shape of the side strip, the type of gusset, and the decorative techniques employed. Classic sole, vamp, and leg features used by various groups are combined in different ways, creating distinct styles. For example, many groups use vamps that encircle the foot; however, coastal Chukchi, Koryak, and Siberian Yupik are the only groups who use this vamp style with a stiffly pleated sole. By studying the sole, vamp, leg sections, and decoration of boots produced within this region, experienced seamstresses are able to identify who made them.

The following key builds on Vasilevich's (1963a) analysis of regional diversity in Siberian footwear. Important features are highlighted and sample styles shown; however, many variations in sole, vamp, and leg style combinations exist. Indigenous peoples from northern Alaska, Canada, Greenland, and Scandinavia use other types of pleated soles, vamps, leg sections, and decorative techniques, and different combinations of materials. Numerals in bold type refer to the line drawings of Siberian footwear on pages 187–89.

FIGURE 146
Overleaf: In the Amur region, a wooden hammer is used to pound skins into a slot cut in a wooden plank. Pounding continues until the skin is softened. REM 953.4/1

Soles

Soles are either pleated or unpleated. Both styles are found across Siberia; however, flat, unpleated soles are most common.

Unpleated soles may be:

a) oval-shaped (Chukchi, Koryak, Yupik, Nenets) **11, 14**

b) oval-shaped with a slight point at centre front (Nenets, Khanty, Even, Evenki) **6, 7**

c) oval-shaped with a long, narrow extension that folds up over the toes (Yakut, Evenki, Yukagir) **9**

d) made with a vertical or horizontal seam across the toes (Amur region groups) **8**

Pleated soles may have:

e) a round toe and soft pleats (Evenki, Khanty, Mansi, Selkup, Ket, Nenets, Komi) **3**

f) a pointed, upturned pleated toe on a sole cut with a separate vamp (Nanai, Ulchi, and other Amur region groups) **4**

g) a rounded, upturned pleated toe on a sole cut in one piece with the vamp (Amur region groups) **5**

h) a stiffly pleated heel and toe (coastal Chukchi, Koryak, Yupik) **1, 2**

Vamps

Vamps either encircle the foot or cover the front part of the foot.

Vamps that encircle the foot may be:

a) U-shaped (Chukchi, Koryak, Yupik, Khanty, Mansi, Even, Evenki) **11**

b) cut at a slight angle (Khanty, Mansi, Komi, Nenets, Ket, Selkup) **12**

c) combined with an extra vamp added higher on the foot (Chukchi, Koryak, Yupik, Even, Evenki) **1**

Vamps that cover the front part of the foot may have:

d) a triangular-shaped upper edge with a curved front edge (Khanty, Mansi, Ket, Komi, Selkup, Nenets, Evenki, Yakut) **3**

e) a truncated upper edge (Yakut, Even, Evenki, Yukagir, Ket) **9**

f) a truncated shape with gathering over the toe (Yukagir, Yakut) **10**

g) a rounded upper edge (Chukchi, Koryak, Yupik) **2**

h) a small triangular-shaped piece set high up on the foot (Nivkhi and other Amur region groups) **8**

i) a triangular shape with a concave upper edge (Nivkhi) **4**

j) a very inflated toe area (Yupik, coastal Chukchi) **2**

Leg Sections

Leg sections cut from leg skins may have:

a) a front panel and a back panel (Chukchi, Koryak, Yupik) **14**

b) a front panel, a back panel, a left-side panel, and a right-side panel (Yukagir, Evenki, Koryak, Even, Nanai and other Amur region groups, Chukchi, Khanty, Mansi, Dolgan) **15**

c) a front panel, a back panel, two left-side panels, and two right-side panels (Yupik, Yakut, Evenki, Nenets, occasionally Nganasan) **7**

d) a front panel, a back panel, three left-side panels, and three right-side panels (Nganasan) **25**

Boot Tops

Tops of boot legs may be:

a) cut straight across (Yakut, Evenki, Even, Koryak, Chukchi, Even, Nanai, Yukagir, Dolgan, Nganasan, Enets, Orochi, Nivkhi, Negidal, Yupik, Ket) **1**

b) cut at a slant (Yupik, Altai Mountain group, Nenets, Khanty, Mansi, Evenki) **3**

c) cut with a piece removed at centre back (Buryat, Yakut) **13**

Gussets and Side Strips

There are a large number of variations in the use of side strips and gussets. The cultural groups identified below are those who most often use a particular style; however, some of these styles, with various combinations of soles and leg styles, are seen throughout Siberia and the Far East as well as in other areas of the circumpolar region.

Leg skin boots may be made:

a) without a side strip or gusset (Yupik, Altai Mountain group, Yukagir, Evenki) **16**

b) with a side strip that encircles the foot (Chukchi, Yupik, Koryak) **14**

c) with a side strip that almost encircles the foot, tapering to an end on each side at centre front (Nanai and other Amur region groups, Yukagir, Even, Evenki) 20

d) with a side strip that encircles the front part of the boot back to the edge of the back panel; sometimes another gusset is added at the side (Koryak, Chukchi, Yupik) 15, 18

e) with a side strip that extends from the side front to the edge of the back panel (Evenki) 21

f) with a side strip that extends from the side front to the edge of the front panel (Yakut, Evenki) 22

g) with one encircling side strip plus one short gusset that extends back to the edge of the front panel (Chukchi) 17

h) with one encircling side strip plus one gusset that extends back to the edge of the side panel (Enets, Nenets, Khanty, Mansi) 7

i) with one encircling side strip plus a strip that terminates at a point on each side of the centre front panel (Khanty, Mansi) 23

j) with one encircling side strip plus a strip that terminates at centre front on each side (Dolgan) 19

k) with two encircling side strips (Dolgan) 24

l) with two encircling side strips plus one gusset that extends back to the edge of the side panel (Nganasan, Enets) 25

Materials

Northern Siberian and Far Eastern footwear is made from many different materials. Further variety is created by treating skins with stain, dye, and smoke or by bleaching, dehairing, and cropping skins.

The main types of materials are:
a) reindeer skin (all Siberian groups)
b) fish skin (groups in coastal and river regions)
c) seal skin (groups in coastal regions)
d) moose skin (groups in taiga regions)
e) fabric (groups in mixed forest and southern taiga regions)
f) bird skin (interior, island, and coastal groups)
g) horsehide, cowhide, and the hide of other domestic animals (groups in mixed forest and southern taiga regions)

Decoration

Footwear is decorated with a wide assortment of hair and thread embroidery, skin mosaics, appliqué, metalwork, and beadwork. Hair embroidery is used throughout Siberia. Decorative techniques and designs are regionally distinct, although some designs are borrowed from or overlap with those of neighbouring groups. Photographs and illustrations in the preceding chapters provide examples of complex combinations of design elements and techniques that communicate cultural affiliation.

Footwear may be decorated with:
a) stylized geometric animals and other objects (Khanty, Mansi, Ket, Komi, Selkup, Nenets, Nganasan)
b) strips of contrasting skins or furs interwoven or sewn together (Koryak, Chukchi, Yupik)
c) beaded panels using linked circles, figure eights, arches, straight lines, and zigzags (Even, Evenki, some Yakut)
d) beaded panels using chevron designs (Dolgan)
e) heart-shaped designs in thread, hair, or metal embroidery (Yakut)
f) a panel of fabric folded over the top of the leg (Yakut)
g) welts of fabric (Nenets, Khanty, Even, Evenki, many other groups) or skin (Chukchi, Koryak, Yupik) sewn into the seams
h) fish, birds, bears, dragons, and other mystical beasts embroidered or trapuntoed onto the skin (Nivkhi and other Amur region groups)
i) metal pendants (shamans across Siberia)

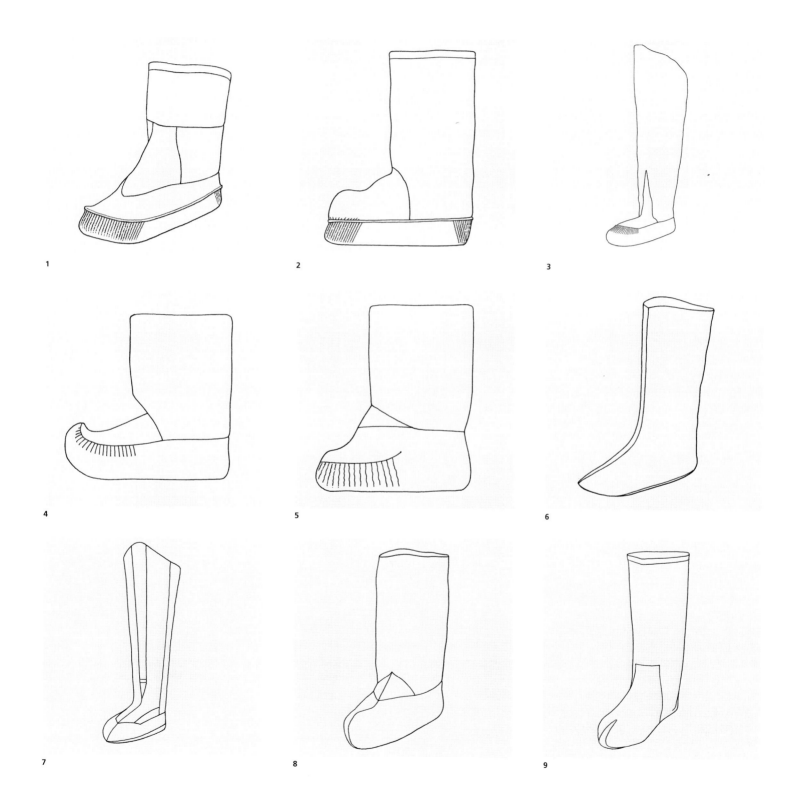

1

2

3

4

5

6

7

8

9

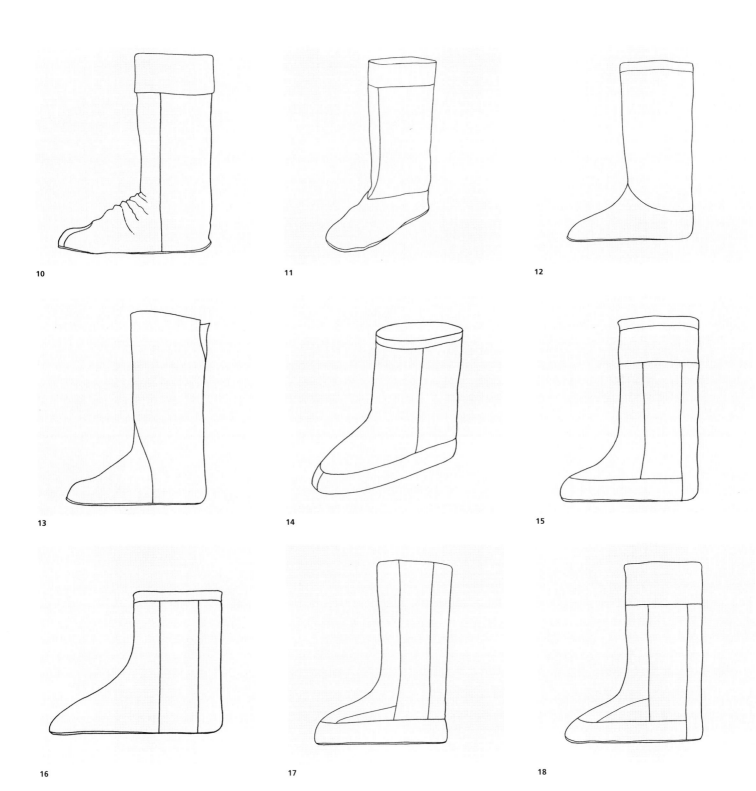

10   11   12

13   14   15

16   17   18

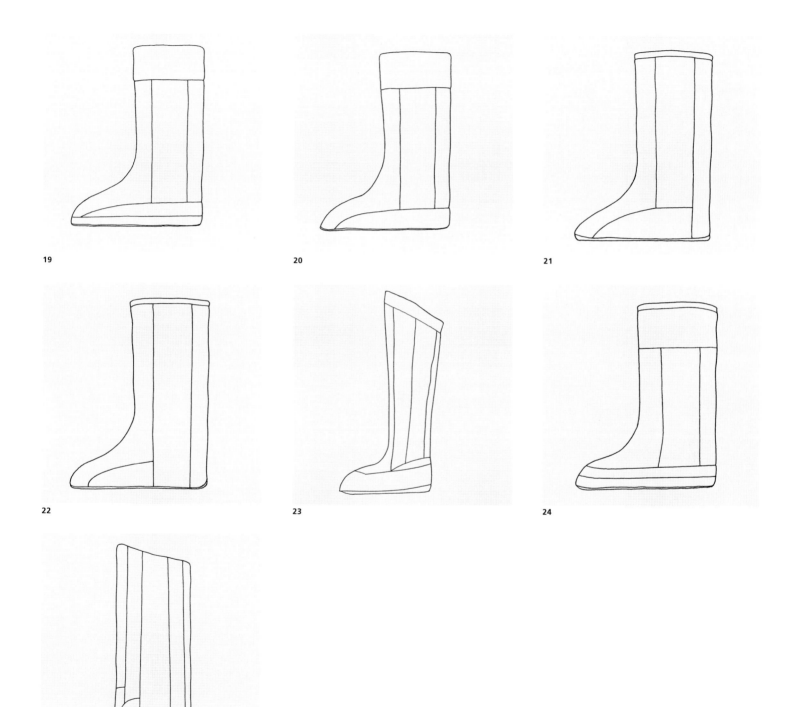

19

20

21

22

23

24

25

Indigenous Peoples of
Northern Siberia and the Far East

Official names, self-designations, and population size are taken from the last official Russian census, conducted in 1989 (Vakhtin 1992).

Aleuts (Unangans)	702
Chukchi (Luoravetlans, Oravedlans, Chawchuwats)	15,184
Chuvans	1,511
Dolgan (Sakhas)	6,932
Enets (Enneche, Yenisey Samoyeds, Madu)	209
Even (Lamuts)	17,199
Evenki (Orochons, Tungus)	30,163
Itelmen (Kamchadals)	2,481
Ket (Yenisey Ostyaks)	1,113
Khanty (Khante, Ostyaks)	22,521
Koryak (Nymylans, Chavchuvens)	9,242
Mansi (Voguls)	8,461
Nanai (Nani, Gol'ds)	12,023
Negidal (El'kan Beyenin, Elkembeys)	622
Nenets (Hasava, Yuraks, Samoyeds)	34,665
Nganasan (Nya, Tavgiyan Samoyeds, Tavgiyans)	1,278
Nivkhi (Gilyak)	4,673
Orochi (Orochili, Nani)	915
Oroks (Ul'ta, Ul'cha)	190
Saami (Lopars)	1,890
Selkup (Ostyak Samoyeds)	3,621
Udege (Udekhe, Ude)	2,011
Ulchi (Nani, Nanei)	3,233
Yakut (Sakha)	380,000
Yukagir (Oduls, Vaduls)	1,142
Yupik (Yupigyts, Yuits)	1,719

Skin Preparation Techniques in the Construction of Footwear

147

FIGURE 147
Nenets remove a reindeer skin by pulling it away from the body. The removal is done carefully to ensure that pieces of meat and fat remain on the carcass rather than on the skin.

Reindeer Skins

Skinning and Drying

Reindeer are skinned and their skins dried following ancient traditions that are culturally distinct. Nganasan dry their reindeer skins outside in the summer sun or slip them behind their tent poles in the winter. Nganasan, Chukchi, Koryak, and Yupik dry reindeer calf skins by hanging them outside on sticks or laying them out on the ground. Forehead and leg skins are stuck to flat surfaces while they are still wet and peeled off the surface after they have dried or frozen (Levin and Potapov 1956 [1964], Popov 1966 [1948]). Leg skins are then sewn together in pairs, fur sides facing, and hung outside in late winter; the skin becomes whitened by the bleaching action of the weather but the fur is protected. White-haired skins may be hung fur side out in the cold early spring sun to prevent them from turning yellow (Komtena 1996). In wet weather, Khanty stretch skins inside tents. Some Even and Koryak in the Far East allow the blood of newly slaughtered animals to sit on the skin for a few hours before being removed, to act as a softening agent (Hatt 1914 [1969]).

Scraping

Dried connective tissue, or fascia, on the flesh side of a reindeer skin is removed by scraping the skin from head to tail, then from side to side, and then again from head to tail. Once skins are scraped they are dampened, rolled into a bundle, and put aside for several hours or overnight. The process of scraping a skin, then dampening it, is repeated two or more times.

Each group has its own recipes for dampening agents. Some wipe scraped skins with damp moss; others smear a mixture of fish or bird eggs, boiled fish viscera, meat broth, wood pitch, or flour and water onto the skin before it is rolled up. Even and Evenki spread fermented fish liver, fish viscera, or reindeer liver on the skin and allow it to decompose for several days. Even also use a mixture of fish glue and boiled tea leaves or liver. Chukchi make a fermented mixture from urine and the fecal contents of a reindeer's large intestine; this is smeared onto the scraped skin, allowed to penetrate for an hour or two, then removed with a scraper. If the skin is still slippery and not pliable when it is unrolled, milk or more meat broth is rubbed in before the skin is rescraped.

Dampened skins are usually scraped on a board with a dull

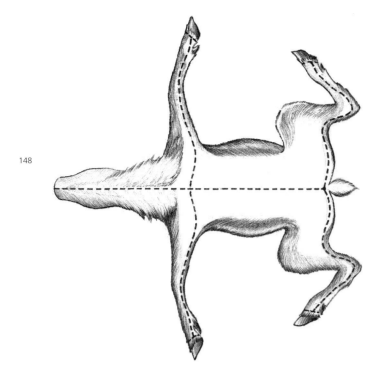

148

149

scraper. The edges are scraped first, while the rest of the skin is covered to prevent it from drying out. Edges that are too stiff to work, especially on leg skins, are hammered or chewed. Scrapers with wide blades are preferred for body skins, narrow-bladed scrapers for leg skins. The scraping process also stretches the skin, helping to make it soft and pliable. Skins may also be softened by being continually wrung by hand while women visit or supervise children (Karapetova 1997a, Oakes and Riewe 1996, Salender 1996c, Sem 1997, Vasilevich 1963a). Once skins are softened, they are gone over with a sharp scraper to remove all fascia and provide a smooth finish.

Dehaired Skins

Skins are dehaired by soaking them in either water or a mixture of boiled cedar needles until the hair begins to slip. A dull scraper is used to remove the hair before the skin is stretched onto a frame to dry (Sem 1997, Vasilevich, 1963a). Some groups cut off most of the hair before the skin is soaked; others freeze the skin so that hair is easier to remove. Dehaired skins are either smoked to make them water-repellent (which gives them a reddish-brown colour) or hung outside until they whiten. They are easily softened by hand-wringing (Kreynovich 1979). Sometimes macerated fish, reindeer viscera, and other mixtures are spread over dehaired skins and allowed to soak in before softening and smoking. To make dehaired skins even lighter and more flexible, they are boiled in water along with a decomposing reindeer brain. This fat-tanning process produces a piece of chamois that remains extremely pliable even after it gets wet (Popov 1966 [1948]).

Water-Repellent Skins

Reindeer skins provide excellent insulation but without treating have very little resistance to water. Haired and dehaired skins are made water-repellent through smoking, tarring, dying, or fat-tanning.

Smoked Skins

Large skins to be smoked are tucked behind tent poles with the fur facing away from the smoke. Leg skins and other small skins are either sewn together in pairs, with the hair to the inside, or combined to form a blanket, then placed behind tent poles. Sometimes strips of paper are placed over the hair

FIGURE 148
Reindeer skins are removed in one piece by cutting from the tail to the nose and from each hoof to the first cut line.

FIGURE 149
Some Indigenous people living in the mixed forest and southern taiga of Siberia stretch reindeer skins with sticks. Saami in northern Scandinavia also use this technique.
REM 5654.177

to further protect it from discolouration. July is the best month for smoking skins, because the hearth is always smouldering with green willow to ward off mosquitoes; winter fires produce more heat and less smoke. People living in wooden houses often set up a smoking tent.

Tarred Skins

In the past, groups living in the forest regions tarred reindeer skins and canvas to make them water-repellent. Tar is extracted from pine by cutting the wood into thin strips, then placing the upright strips tightly together in a pail. The pail is inverted over a strainer, which is then placed over another bowl that will collect the dripping pitch. The join between the pail, strainer, and collecting bowl is sealed with clay to keep heat and moisture inside. Hot coals are placed around the sides and top of the pail and tended for about one day. The pitch collected in this way may be used without further treatment. It may also be mixed with reddish-brown birch cambium (inner bark) that has been boiled for about an hour. The mixture of boiled cambium and pitch is simmered until it becomes a light reddish-brown colour; the powdered cambium is allowed to settle, and the remaining liquid is painted onto footwear. This paint may also be used for decorative purposes; hand-carved sticks are dipped into it and used to outline a design or to fill one in (Lazayamova 1996).

Dyed Skins

Reindeer skins are dyed with decoctions of plants and animal parts for increased flexibility, water resistance, decoration, and protection against evil spirits. Dyes are added either during the skin preparation process or after skins are made into clothing. Red is especially powerful because it is the colour of life; however, yellow (sun) and orange-brown (fire) are also commonly seen on footwear and clothing (Oakes and Riewe 1990, Sem 1997).

Different dye mixtures are used to create distinct colours. Evenki and Even use boiled chokecherry (yellow), alder (orange-brown), willow bark (orange-red), and a gluelike combination of simmered fish stomachs and ochre (red, blue, green, or orange), to which larch tree tar, powdered rotten wood, or ash and alder bark are sometimes added (Georgi 1799, Hatt 1914 [1969], Salender 1996c). After a skin has been

150

FIGURE 150
Leg skins are sewn together in pairs and hung in the tent until well smoked. Smoke acts as a mild tanning agent; clothing made from smoked skins is easier to soften if it gets wet.

smeared with reindeer rectal contents and urine, Chukchi, Koryak, and Yupik rub boiled alder bark into it to produce a reddish-brown colour (Oakes and Riewe 1990). Koryak produce a black dye by mixing alder bark shavings and iron-rich water from a grindstone trough. Yakut use larch bark or Icelandic moss for yellow; nettles, alders, or purple willows for red; and a mixture of either fat and soot (Hatt 1914 [1969]) or black lichens, fungi, cattle blood, fat, and wood pitch for black (Nosov 1955). Today, many people combine ink, ochre, and store-bought paint to make mauve and other colours painted on footwear for decorative purposes (Oakes and Riewe 1990, 1996).

Seal and Walrus Skins

The skins of ringed seal, bearded seal, and walrus, which are naturally water-repellent, are used by coastal peoples for rope, boats, clothing, and especially waterproof skin boots and boot soles (Hatt 1914 [1969]). Animals are skinned, then the fat is sliced off with a knife and the skin is rinsed in cold water. Clean skins may be treated with fatty substances and dyes before they are stretched out to dry on wooden frames. Some common mixtures are masticated or boiled fish liver or meat broth; alder or larch bark and aged urine; and ochre (red) or graphite (black) and fish eggs. Most mixtures are smeared over the skin and allowed to penetrate for a few days. Boiled alder bark mixtures are often poured into a bag made from the sewn skin; the skin sack is beaten with a wooden club, allowed to sit, then rebeaten until the alder bark stain permeates it, at which point the sack is taken apart and the skin is stretched to dry (Hatt 1914 [1969], Levin and Potapov 1956 [1964]). Ash from burned poplar trees mixed with alder bark is used to stain the hair of newborn and adult seal skins a reddish-orange (Boas 1937, Bogoras 1909 [1975], Hatt 1914 [1969]).

Dried seal skins are placed on a smooth wooden limb and worked with a dull scraper until soft. They may also be wrung by hand (Oakes and Riewe 1990). Occasionally they are smoked over the hearth or in a special smoking tent (Bogoras 1909 [1975], Hatt 1914 [1969], Vanstone 1985).

An ancient Chukchi legend cited by Bogoras (1902:591) implies that women miss the opportunity to scrape skins after they die.

A woman is shown the lower world through a hole in the ground of the upper one. She feels a yearning for her life in the lower world and drops a tear. The women below are busy scraping skins. They think it is raining, and hasten into their houses.

Dehaired Seal Skins

Hair is removed from seal skins either by slicing it off with a knife or by sprinkling ashes over the skin, then scraping it with the edge of a tin can lid, which takes the hair off without cutting into the epidermis or skin (Hatt 1914 [1969]; Murdoch 1892; Oakes and Riewe 1990, 1996). In another process, both the hair and the epidermis are removed from a seal skin by placing the skin in hot water until the hair slips and then rubbing it by hand or with a dull scraper (Hatt 1914 [1969]). This produces a yellowish or white skin. Dehaired skins are dried, smoked, or prepared with fatty mixtures.

Fish Skins

Depending on regional availability, skins from fish such as pike, burbot, salmon, carp, and catfish were used in the past for wind- and water-resistant summer clothing and footwear in western Siberia and year-round in the Far East (Georgi 1799, Hatt 1914 [1969]). Today, only a few people continue to prepare fish skins, which are dried flat in the sun or inside a heated dwelling (Black 1973). Flesh and fat is scraped off dried skins. Skins may be softened by hand-kneading or with a hinged or hammer-and-platform softener. Rotten willow wood or dry ash is sprinkled over skins to remove excess grease while they are being softened (Hatt 1914 [1969]). Khanty, Evenki, Nanai, Ulchi, Itelmen, and other groups rub masticated fish or bird eggs or fish stomachs into the skin and scrape the skin until soft (Hatt 1914 [1969], Vanstone 1985). Softened skins are then smoked and sewn into panels (Margolina 1997a).

Bird Skins

Historically, the fat and oil from the skins of swans, geese, ducks, and birds of prey were removed by sucking. Today, some women scrape the skin with a dull scraper instead; although this method is more likely to damage the tips of feathers, causing them to fall out, it is much easier. Pulp collected from rotten birch is then spread over each skin before the skin is rubbed gently but firmly over a smooth beam. Once skins are dry and soft, they are ready to be sewn (Hatt 1914 [1969], Oakes and Riewe 1996).

Horse, Cow, Dog, and Other Skins

Horse and cow hides are soaked in blood to soften, expand, and stain them. Skins are then rubbed with milk fat, scraped until soft, and smoked.

Dog skins are used to make clothing and footwear for damp conditions when seal skin is unavailable, because they are very durable and are not damaged by water. After skins are dried, the fat and fascia are removed with a knife or sharp scraper, then skins are covered with a mixture of rotten wood and fish eggs. Boiled alder bark mixed with ash from burned poplar trees is also rubbed into the skin, making it easier to soften and staining it orange (Hatt 1914 [1969]).

Muskrat, wolverine, otter, squirrel, and other skins are also used for hats, coats, and collars (Komtena 1996). All skins are prepared by removing the outer layer of fat, drying the skin, then softening the skin.

Glue Production

Several groups, particularly the Amur region peoples, make a glue from boiled fish heads or viscera that is used in clothing construction or as a pigment base (Black 1973, Georgi 1799, Salender 1996c). Yukagir cut antlers from young reindeer into short pieces and boil them in water for about a day; this gel is dried and used in winter to glue moose or spring-killed reindeer leg skins to the bottom of skis. Skis fitted with skins provide extra traction and are useful for stalking moose, because they are much quieter than skis without skins (Kreynovich 1979).

Shoe Grass

Grass for insoles is carefully selected to avoid species with sharp, cutting edges. Many groups use long fine grasses or sedges that grow near the water. Grass is cut in the fall, tied into bundles, and combed. The size and shape of combs vary regionally. Itelmen use a comb made from a seagull bone; Chukchi combs are made from wood or caribou or seal bone. Saami from Scandinavia employ similar techniques for preparing grasses.

A clump of combed grass is either wrapped around the foot or used as an insole. Grass wrapped around the foot is held in position with an arctic hare skin, an inner stocking, and an inner boot. Then a layer of coarser grass is wrapped around the foot before the foot is slipped into the outer boot (Hatt 1914 [1969], Salender 1996b). When grass is used as an insole it is split in half and placed with sharp ends alternating; both ends are folded under, then the insole is carefully inserted into the boot.

The importance of carefully arranged grass is underlined by a Yakut proverb: "A great beast pastures in a deep fold." When grass is prepared incorrectly, uncomfortable deep folds form under the foot. Walking on these folds creates a cutting action that makes the grass look as if a beast has been chewing it (Sem 1997, Solovieva-Oyunskaya 1992).

151

FIGURE 151
Shoe grass is split in half and flipped end for end to create flat, even boot insoles that keep feet dry and well insulated.

Aged skin   A skin, usually seal or caribou, from which the hair and epidermis have been removed by rotting or aging in water or fat.

Alder-barked skin   A skin, usually seal or caribou, which has been dyed a dark red with alder bark.

Ankle straps   Leather or cloth straps sewn to a skin boot which are tied around the ankle to secure footwear to the wearer's foot.

Appliqué   A cutout decoration fastened to a larger piece of material.

Awl   A hand-held tool used to make holes in thick or stiff skins.

Bleached skin   A dehaired skin that has been frozen and bleached white by the sun and the blowing snow; sometimes referred to as "freeze-dried skin."

Blubber   The fat of seals, whales, and walrus.

Boot leg   The part of the boot that extends above the ankle (Webber 1989). Referred to in this text as the leg section.

Bottom unit   A single piece of material, either soft or hard, comprising the bottom and upturned sides of a boot (Webber 1989).

Bow drill   An Eskimoan hand-held drill consisting of three parts: a drill shaft with a metal or stone point; a wooden or bone bow with a bowstring; and a bone, wood, or ivory socket that is held between the user's teeth.

Casing   A strip of material folded in half and stitched to the top of the leg section of a skin boot. A drawstring is usually threaded through the casing.

Chum   A tent used in Siberia which has a teepee structure and is made from reindeer skins or canvas.

Crampon   A piece of ivory, bone, or wood carved with a zigzag or tooth-shaped edge and worn over the boot sole to provide extra traction on icy surfaces.

Depilated skin   A skin from which the hair or fur has been removed, usually by means of a shaving or aging process.

Dermis   The sensitive, vascularized inner layer of the skin.

Embossed   A carved or moulded three-dimensional design in relief.

End scraper   An arm-length scraping tool with the scraping surface placed at one end.

Epidermis   The outer, nonsensitive, and nonvascular layer of the skin.

Fascia   A sheet of connective tissue that lies between the dermis and the muscles.

Gusset   A wedge-shaped inset often added at the ankle to provide extra room for easier movement.

Haired skin   A skin with the hair intact.

Handspan   One handspan equals the distance between the thumb-tip (first digit) and the tip of the outstretched middle finger (third digit).

Inner slipper   A slipper that is worn inside a pair of skin boots for added insulation.

Intestine scraper   A hand-held tool used to scrape the inner intestinal layer.

Leg section   The upper portion of a boot, which wraps around the leg.

Leg skin boots   Boots made from the skins of an animal's legs, usually reindeer, moose, caribou, dog, or wolf.

Ochre   A powdered, ferric mineral used as a pigment to stain skins.

Oesophagus   The passage through which food passes from the mouth to the stomach. Dried and scraped, it is often used for decorative trim by people living in the Far East.

Over boots   A pair of boots worn over another pair of boots for additional insulation.

Over shoes   Footwear worn over boots for extra insulation and traction.

Overcast stitch   A slanting stitch used over cut edges or open parts.

Radius   The thicker and shorter bone of the forearm of a mammal or bird.

Rick rack   A zigzag-shaped trim.

Running stitch   A linear stitch that runs parallel to the seam allowance.

Scraper   A hand-held tool with either a sharp or a dull edge, used for different steps in skin preparation.

Seam allowance   The width of material beyond the seam line.

Shaved skin   A skin on which the hair, but not the epidermis, has been shaved off.

Side strip   A piece of skin sewn between the sole and vamp of a pair of skin boots.

Sinew   Dried animal tendons used as sewing thread.

Skin presser   A hand-held tool used to press skin soles into shape.

Slashed dart   A technique used to fit material closely to a three-dimensional shape and remove excess material.

Smoked skin   A depilated skin, often caribou, reindeer, moose, fish, or seal, which has been cured by smoking.

Snow beater   A wooden, ivory, or antler stick used to beat snow off skin boots or other clothing.

Sole   The bottom, bottom unit, or under-surface of a shoe or boot (Webber 1989).

Stick painting   A process in which designs are applied using a carved stick as a "paintbrush."

Tibia   The larger of the two bones of the vertebrate hind limb between the femur and the tarsus.

Topstitching   A visible line of sewing done with small, even, short passes of the needle through two pieces of material to join them together.

Ulna   The inner of the two bones of the forelimb of a mammal or bird.

Ulu   A semicircular knife used primarily by women.

Upper   The part of a boot that includes the apron (vamp), the boot leg (leg section), and the upper part of the bottom unit (sole) (Webber 1989).

Vamp   The front section of an upper, covering the toes and part of the instep.

Welt   A strip of skin or fabric placed in a seam before the seam is sewn together. Welts provide extra strength and protect stitches from being exposed to excessive wear.

Yuranga   A tent used mainly in eastern Siberia which has a dome-shaped silhouette and is made from reindeer skins or canvas.

Aburtina, L. 1990. Chukchi medical doctor, Bilibenoe, Chukotka. Personal communication.

Ackerman, R. 1984. Prehistory of the Asian Eskimo zone. In Dumas, D. (Ed.). *Handbook of North American Indians, Vol. 5. Arctic* (pp. 106–118). Washington, D.C.: Smithsonian Institution.

Ackerman, R. 1988. Settlements and sea mammal hunting in the Bering-Chukchi Sea region. *Arctic Anthropology* 25(1):52–79.

Afanasev, V., and Y. Pitkzu. 1987. *Lyudi Dolgoi Vesni*. Magadanskoe: Knishnoe Izdatelstvo.

Agche, E. 1990. Chukchi brigade leader, Kraseno, Chukotka. Personal communication.

Alekseyev, M. 1941. *Sibiri v izvestiyakh zapadnoyevt.ropeyskikh oputeshestvennikov i pisateley* [Siberia in the reports of West European travellers and writers]. Irkutsk.

Alekseyev, V. 1979a. Anthropometry of Siberian peoples. In Laughlin, W., and A. Harper (Eds.). *The First Americans: Origins, Affinities, and Adaptations* (pp. 57–90). New York: Gustav Fisher.

Alekseyev, V. 1979b. The genetic structure of Asiatic Eskimos and Coastal Chukchis compared to that of American Arctic populations. *Arctic Anthropology* 16(1):147–164.

Alexandra, L. 1996. Nenets seamstress, Tazovsky Collective Farm. Personal communication.

Anderson, D. 1991. Turning hunters into herders: A critical examination of Soviet development policy among the Evenki of southeastern Siberia. *Arctic* 44(1):12–22.

Anisimov, A. 1958. *Religion of Evenks*. Leningrad.

Anisimov, A. 1963a. The shaman's tent of the Evenks and the origin of the shamanistic rite. In Michael, H. (Ed.). *Studies in Siberian Shamanism* (pp. 84–123). Toronto: Arctic Institute of North America, Anthropology of the North Translations from Russian Sources. No. 4.

Anisimov, A. 1963b. Cosmological concepts of the peoples of the North. In Michael, H. (Ed.). *Studies in Siberian Shamanism* (pp. 157–229). Toronto: Arctic Institute of North America, Anthropology of the North Translations from Russian Sources. No. 4.

Anonymous. n.d. *Khudozhestvennie iedeleya narodov severa Sibiri*. Moscow.

Antonovitch, K. 1996. Khanty reindeer herder, Roskinsky region. Personal communication.

Antropova, V. 1971. *Kultura i bit Koryakov* [Culture and way of life of the Koryak]. Institute of Ethnography, Academy of Science, Leningrad.

Antropova, V., and V. Kuznetsova. 1964. The Chukchi. In Levin, M., and L. Potapov (Eds.). *The Peoples of Siberia* (pp. 799–835). Chicago: University of Chicago Press.

Apassingok, A., W. Walunga, and E. Tennant (Eds.). 1985. *Lore of St. Lawrence Island: Echoes of Our Eskimo Elders*. Vol. 1. Unalakleet: Bering Strait School District.

Apassingok, A., W. Willis, R. Oozevaseuk, and E. Tennant (Eds.) 1987. *Lore of St. Lawrence Island: Echoes of Our Eskimo Elders*. Vol. 2. Unalakleet: Bering Strait School District.

Armstrong, T. 1965. *Russian Settlement in the North*. Cambridge: Cambridge

University Press.

Armstrong, T. 1968. Farming on the permafrost. *The Geographical Magazine* March:961–967.

Armstrong, T. 1980. Who are the "northern peoples" of the USSR? In Muller-Wille, L., P. Pelto, L. Muller-Wille, and R. Darnell. *Consequences of Economic Change in Circumpolar Regions*. Edmonton: Boreal Institute for Northern Studies.

Armstrong, T. 1989. *Northern Peoples of the USSR, 1989*. Cambridge: Scott Polar Institute.

Arpen, R. 1989. *Tundra Taiga*. Québec: Musée de la Civilisation.

Arutiunov, A. 1988a. Even: Reindeer herders of Eastern Siberia. In Fitzhugh, W., and A. Crowell (Eds.). *Crossroads of Continents: Cultures of Siberia and Alaska* (pp. 35–38). Washington, D.C.: Smithsonian Institution.

Arutiunov, A. 1988b. Chukchi: Warriors and traders of Chukotka. In Fitzhugh, W., and A. Crowell (Eds.). *Crossroads of Continents: Cultures of Siberia and Alaska* (pp. 39–41). Washington, D.C.: Smithsonian Institution.

Arutiunov, A. 1988c. Koryak and Itelmen: Dwellers of the smoking coast. In Fitzhugh, W., and A. Crowell (Eds.). *Crossroads of Continents: Cultures of Siberia and Alaska* (pp. 31–34). Washington, D.C.: Smithsonian Institution.

Arutiunov, A., and W. Fitzhugh. 1988. Prehistory of Siberia and the Bering Sea. In Fitzhugh, W., and A. Crowell (Eds.). *Crossroads of Continents: Cultures of Siberia and Alaska* (pp. 117–129). Washington, D.C.: Smithsonian Institution.

Arutiunov, S., I. Krupnik, and M. Chlenov. 1979. "Kitovaia alleia"—drevneeskimosskii kul'tovyi pamiatnik na ostrove Ittygran [The "Whale alley," an early Eskimo ritual memorial centre on Ittygran Island]. *Sovetskaia Etnografiia* 4:12–28.

Bakhrushin, S. 1935. *Ostyatskiye i vogulskiye knyazhestva v XVI-XVII vekakh*. Leningrad.

Balzer, M. 1980. The route to eternity: cultural persistence and change in Siberian Khanty burial ritual. *Arctic Anthropology* 17(1):77–89.

Balzer, M. 1981. Rituals of gender identity: Markers of Siberian Khanty ethnicity, status, and belief. *American Anthropology* 83(4):850–867.

Bartels, D., and A. Bartels. 1986. Soviet policy toward Siberian Native people: Integration, assimilation or russification? *Culture* VI(2):15–31.

Birket-Smith, K. 1953. The Chugach Eskimo. *Nationalmuseets Skrifter, Etnografish Raekke* 6. Copenhagen.

Black, L. 1973. The Nivkh (Gilyak) of Sakhalin and the Lower Amur. *Arctic Anthropology* 10(1):1–110.

Black, L. 1979. Notes on Yukagir linguistics and method of text transcription. *Arctic Anthropology* 16(1):179–186.

Black, L. 1988. Peoples of the Amur and Maritime Regions. In Fitzhugh, W., and A. Crowell (Eds.). *Crossroads of Continents: Cultures of Siberia and Alaska* (pp. 24–30). Washington, D.C.: Smithsonian Institution.

Bliss, L. 1990. Environmental and ecological evaluation of the gas fields in the Tyumen Region, USSR. Botany Department, University of Washington, Seattle. Unpublished report.

Bliss, L., O. Heal, and J. Moore (Eds.). 1981. *Tundra Ecosystems: A Comparative Analysis. International Biological Programme 25*. Cambridge: Cambridge University Press.

Boas, F. 1933 [1973]. Relationships between North-west America and North-east Asia. In Jenness, D. (Ed.). *The American Aborigines: Their Origin and Antiquity* (pp. 355–370). Published for presentation at the Fifth Pacific Science Congress, Canada, 1933. Reprinted New York: Cooper Square Publishers.

Boas, F. 1937. Waldemar Bogoras. *American Anthropologist* 39:314–315.

Bockstoce, J. 1977. *Eskimos of Northwest Alaska in the Early Nineteenth Century*. Oxford: Pitt Rivers Museum.

Bodenhorn, B. 1990. "I'm not the great hunter, my wife is." *Études Inuit Studies* 14(1–2):55–74.

Bogoras, W. 1901. The Chukchi of Northeastern Asia. *American Anthropologist* 3:80–108.

Bogoras, W. 1902. Folklore of Northeastern Asia as compared with that of Northwestern America. *American Anthropologist* 4:577–683.

Bogoras, W. 1909 [1975]. The Chukchee, 1904–1909. *The Jesup North Pacific Expedition 7, Memoirs of the American Museum of Natural History*. Leiden. Reprinted New York: AMS Press.

Bogoras, W. 1910 [1975]. Chukchee Mythology. *The Jesup North Pacific Expedition 8(1), Memoirs of the American Museum of Natural History*. Leiden. Reprinted New York: AMS Press.

Bogoras, W. 1913 [1975]. The Eskimo of Siberia. *The Jesup North Pacific Expedition 8(3), Memoirs of the American Museum of Natural History*. Leiden. Reprinted New York: AMS Press.

Bond, A. (Chair) 1991. Panel on Siberia: Economic and territorial issues. *Soviet Geography* 32(6):363–432.

Buijs, C. 1984. The Nivkh and the Oroch, two changing Siberian peoples. In Nooter, G. (Ed.). *Life and Survival in the Arctic* (pp. 45–65). The Hague, Netherlands: Government Publishing Office, National Museum of Ethnology.

Burch, E. 1988. War and trade. In Fitzhugh, W., and A. Crowell (Eds.). *Crossroads of Continents: Cultures of Siberia and Alaska* (pp. 227–240). Washington, D.C.: Smithsonian Institution.

Buschan, G. *Die Sitten der Völker* [Customs of the people]. Third volume. Stuttgart, Berlin, Leipzig: Union Deutsche Verlagsgesellschaft.

Bychkov, O. 1994. Russian hunters in Eastern Siberia in the seventeenth century: Lifestyle and economy. *Arctic Anthropology* 31(1):72–85.

Capochena, L. 1996. Khanty seamstress, Roskinsky. Personal communication.

Caseburg, D. 1993. Religious practice and ceremonial clothing on the Belcher Islands, Northwest Territories. Unpublished Master of Arts thesis, University of Alberta, Edmonton.

Chance, N., and E. Andreeva. 1995. Sustainability, equity, and natural resource development in Northwest Siberia and Arctic Alaska. *Human Ecology* 23 (June).

Charrin, A. 1984. The discovery of the Koryaks and their perception of the world. *Arctic* 37(4): 441–445.

Chaussonnet, V. 1988. Needles and animals: Women's magic. In Fitzhugh,

W., and A. Crowell (Eds.). *Crossroads of Continents: Cultures of Siberia and Alaska* (pp. 209–226). Washington, D.C.: Smithsonian Institution.

Chaussonnet, V. 1995. Crossroads times. In Chaussonnet, V. (Ed.) *Crossroads Alaska: Native Cultures of Alaska and Siberia* (pp. 48–97). Washington, D.C.: Smithsonian Institution.

Cherkasov, A. 1982. The native population of the Soviet North: Language, education, and employment. *Musk-Ox* 30:65–73.

Chernetsov, V. 1948. Ornament lentochnogo tipa u Obskikh Ugrov. *Sovetskaya Etnografiya* 1:139–152.

Chernetsov, V. 1963. Concepts of the soul among the Ob Ugrians. In Michael, H. (Ed.), E. Dunn and S. Dunn (Trans.). *Studies in Siberian Shamanism* (pp. 3–45). Toronto: Arctic Institute of North America, Anthropology of the North Translations from Russian Sources. No. 4.

Chernov, Yu. 1985. *The Living Tundra*. Cambridge: Cambridge University Press.

Chlenov, M., and I. Krupnik. 1984. Whale Alley: A site on the Chukchi Peninsula, Siberia. *Expedition* 26(2):6–15.

Chubarova, L. 1985. Bicer. *Severnie Prostori*. January-February 1:43–44.

Chubarova, L. 1988. "Kerker"—Chukotski Kombinezon. *Severnie Prostori*. November-December 6:42–43.

Clark, R., and J. Finlay. 1977. Effects of oil spills in arctic and subarctic environments. In Malins, D. (Ed.). *Effects of Petroleum on Arctic and Subarctic Marine Environments and Organisms* (pp. 411–476). Vol. II. New York: Academic Press.

Crowell, A. 1988. Dwellings, settlements, and domestic life. In Fitzhugh, W., and A. Crowell (Eds.). *Crossroads of Continents: Cultures of Siberia and Alaska* (pp. 194–208). Washington, D.C.: Smithsonian Institution.

Czaplicka, M. 1914. *Aboriginal Siberia: A Study in Social Anthropology*. Oxford: Clarendon Press.

Dahl, J. 1990. *Indigenous Peoples of the Soviet North*. International Workgroup for Indigenous Affairs, Document No. 67.

Dall, W. 1881. On the so-called Chukchi and Namollo people of Eastern Siberia. *American Naturalist* 15(10):857–868.

DeBardeleben, J. 1990. Economic reform and environmental protection in the USSR. *Soviet Geography* 31(4):237–256.

Dikov, N. 1965 [1964]. The stone age of Kamchatka and the Chukchi Peninsula in the light of new archaeological data. *Arctic Anthropology* 3(1):10–25. [Trans.]

Dikov, N. 1968 [1967]. The discovery of the Palaeolithic in Kamchatka and the problem of the initial occupation of America. *Arctic Anthropology* 5(1):191–203. [Trans.]

Dioszegi, V. 1968. The problem of the ethnic homogeneity of Tofa (Karagas) shamanism. In Dioszegi, V. *Popular Beliefs and Folklore Tradition in Siberia*. Budapest.

Dioszegi, V., and M. Hoppal (Eds.). 1978. *Shamanism in Siberia*. (Trans. S. Simon.) Budapest: Akademiai Kiado.

Dmytryshin, B., E. Crownhart-Vaughan, and T. Vaughan (Eds.). 1985. Russia's conquest of Siberia, 1558–1700: A documentary record. *To Siberia and Russian America: Three Centuries of Russian Eastward Expansion*. Vol 1. Portland, Oregon: Western Imprints.

Dolgikh, B. 1957. The Origin of the Nganasan: Preliminary remarks. In Michael, H. (Ed.). *Studies in Siberian Ethnogenesis* (pp. 220–299). Toronto: Arctic Institute of North America, University of Toronto Press.

Dolgikh, B. 1965. Problems in the ethnography and physical anthropology of the Arctic. *Arctic Anthropology* 3(1):1–9.

Dubin, L. 1987. *The History of Beads from 30,000 B.C. to Present*. New York: Harry N. Abrams.

Faegre, T. 1979. *Tents: Architecture of the Nomads*. Garden City, New York: Anchor.

Federal Service of Geodesy and Cartography of Russia. 1995. *Peoples of Russia and Adjacent Countries* [Map]. Moscow: The Russian Humanitarian and Scientific Fund, Fund for the National and Cultural Revival of the Russian Peoples.

Fitzhugh, W. 1988. Eskimos: Hunters of the frozen coasts. In Fitzhugh, W., and A. Crowell (Eds.). *Crossroads of Continents: Cultures of Siberia and Alaska* (pp. 42–51). Washington, D.C.: Smithsonian Institution.

Fitzhugh, W. 1995. Ancestral times. In Chaussonnet, V. (Ed.). *Crossroads Alaska: Native Cultures of Alaska and Siberia* (pp. 36–47). Washington, D.C.: Smithsonian Institution.

Fitzhugh, W., and A. Crowell (Eds.). 1988. *Crossroads of Continents: Cultures of Siberia and Alaska*. Washington, D.C.: Smithsonian Institution.

Fitzhugh, W., and S. Kaplan. 1982. *Inua: Spirit World of the Bering Sea Eskimo*. Washington, D.C.: Smithsonian Institution.

Fondahl, G. 1985. Native peoples of the Soviet North. *The Northern Raven*. 5(1):14.

Fondahl, G. 1995. The status of Indigenous peoples in the Russian North. *Post-Soviet Geography* 36(4):215–224.

Forsyth, J. 1992. *A History of the Peoples of Siberia: Russia's North Asian Colony, 1581-1990*. New York: Cambridge University Press.

Fortier, E. 1978. *One Survived*. Anchorage: Alaska Northwest Publishing Company.

Gachilov, A. 1996. Selkup linguist and professor, Hertzen Institute, Department of Northern Peoples, University of St. Petersburg. Personal communication.

Garena, N. 1989. Pletenie iz besera. *Severni Prostori* Mai(3): 38–39.

Georgi, J. G. 1799. Opisaniye vsekh obitayushchikh v Rossiyskom v gosudarstve narodov [Description of all the peoples inhabiting the Russian Empire]. St. Petersburg.

Golovnev, A. 1994. From one to seven: Numerical symbolism in Khanty culture. *Arctic Anthropology* 31(1):62–71.

Gorbacheva, V. 1997. *Traditional Footwear of Chukchi, Koryak, and Yupik*. St. Petersburg: Russian Museum of Ethnography.

Gracheva, G. 1987. Balok-zimnee schilishe Dolgan [Dolgan winter housing]. *Severni Prostori* 3 (May-June):40–44.

Gurvich, I. 1979. *Novi materiali o traditionnoi kultura Chukchii* [New material on traditional Chukchi culture]. *Sovietskaiia Etnografiia* 2:95–105.

Gurvich, I. (Ed.). 1980. *Semeinaia obriadnost' narodov Sibiri* [Family rituals of the peoples of Siberia]. Moscow: Nauka.

Gurvich, I. 1987. Novye dannye po traditsionnoi obriadnosti koriakov. *Traditsionnye verovaniia i byt narodov Sibiri* [New data on the traditional rituals of the Koriak. In *Traditional Beliefs and the Life of the Peoples of Siberia*]. Novosibirsk.

Gurvich, I. 1988a. The Northern Native groups in the USSR. *Inuktitut* 68 (fall-winter):29–40.

Gurvich, I. 1988b. The languages of the Northern Peoples. *Inuktitut* 68 (fall-winter):41–50.

Hajdú, P. 1968. *The Samoyed Peoples and Languages*. The Hague, Netherlands: Indiana University, Bloomington Mouton & Co.

Hallowell, A. 1926. Bear ceremonialism in the northern hemisphere. *American Anthropologist* 28:1–173.

Hatt, G. 1914 [1969]. Arctic skin clothing in Eurasia and America: An ethnographic study. *Arctic Anthropology* 5(2):1–132. [Trans. from J. Schultz, *Forlagsboghandel Graebes Bogtrykkeri*.]

Hatt, G. 1916. Moccasins and their relation to arctic footwear. *Memoirs of the American Anthropological Association* 3(3):147–250.

Hatt, G. 1934. North American and Eurasian culture connections. *Proceedings of the Fifth Pacific Science Congress* (pp. 2755–2763). Toronto: University of Toronto Press.

Hsio-Yen S,. 1963. A Chinese shell-inlay motif. *1962 Annual*. Toronto: Art and Archaeology Division, Royal Ontario Museum, University of Toronto.

Hughes, C. 1984. Asiatic Eskimo: Introduction and Siberian Eskimo. In Dumas, D. (Ed.). *Handbook of North American Indians, Vol. 5. Arctic* (pp. 243–246, 247–261). Washington, D.C.: Smithsonian Institution.

Ilyina, L. 1990. Senior research geographer, Institute of Geography, Academy of Sciences of the USSR. Personal communication.

Iokelson, V. 1990. Koryaki iz nayuchnovo naslediya. *Severnie Prostori*. 3 (May-June) 3:38–41.

Issenman, B. 1985. Inuit skin clothing: construction and motifs. *Études Inuit Studies* 9(2):101–119.

Issenman, B. 1997. *Sinews of Survival: The Living Legacy of Inuit Clothing*. Vancouver: U.B.C.Press

Istomen, K. 1990. *Prazdneki i obryadi narodnostei chukotki*. Magadan: Magadanskoy Kneshnoy Izdatelstvo.

Ivanov, S. 1937. Medved'v religioznom i dekorativnom iskusstve narodnostei Amura. *Pamiati V. G. Bogoraza (1865–1936)* [The bear in the religious and decorative art of the peoples of the Amur. In *In Memory of W. G. Bogoras (1865–1936)*]. (pp. 1–45). Moscow: Institut Etnografii.

Ivanov, S. 1954. Materialy po izobrazitel'nomu iskusstvu narodov Sibiri XIX–nacgaka XXv [Material on the depictive art of the peoples of Siberia, 19th and early 20th centuries]. *Trudy Instituta Etnografii* n.s.22. Moscow: ANSSSR.

Ivanov, S. 1963. Ornament narodov Sibiri kak istoricheskii istochnik [Ornamentation of the Siberian peoples as a historical source]. *Trudy Instituta Etnografii* n.s.81. Moscow: ANSSSR.

Ivanov, S. 1970. *Odezhda narodov Sibiri*. Akademiia Nauk SSSR, Leningrad.

Ivanov, S., and V. Stukalov. 1975. *Ancient Masks of Siberian Peoples*. Leningrad: Aurora Publishers.

Jochelson, W. 1905–1908 [1975]. The Koryak. *The Jesup North Pacific Expedition 6, Memoirs of the American Museum of Natural History*. Leiden. Reprinted New York: AMS Press.

Jochelson, W. 1907. Past and present subterranean dwellings of the tribes of Northeastern Asia and Northwestern America. *Congrès International des Américanistes, 15ème Session, Québec* (pp. 115–128).

Jochelson, W. 1926a. The ethnological problems of Bering Sea. *American Museum Journal* 26(1):90–95.

Jochelson, W. 1926b [1975]. The Yukaghir and the Yukaghirized Tungus. *The Jesup North Pacific Expedition 9, Memoirs of the American Museum of Natural History*. Leiden. Reprinted New York: AMS Press.

Jochelson, W. 1928. *Peoples of Asiatic Russia*. New York: American Museum of Natural History.

Jochelson, W. 1933. The Yakut. *Anthropological Papers of the American Museum of Natural History* (p. 106). New York City: American Museum of Natural History.

Jonaitis, A. 1978. Reconciliation of complementary opposites: The Yakut shaman costume. *Anthropology* 2(1):61–66.

Kairaiuak, L., and D. Orr. 1995. Yupik. In Chaussonnet, V. (Ed.). *Crossroads Alaska: Native Cultures of Alaska and Siberia* (pp. 12–13). Washington, D.C.: Smithsonian Institution.

Kalashnikova, N. 1990. *National Costumes of the Soviet Peoples*. Moscow: Planeta Publishers.

Karapetova, I. 1997a. *Traditional Boots of Nganasan and Enets*. Russian Museum of Ethnography: St. Petersburg.

Karapetova, I. 1997b. *Traditional Footwear of Nenets*. Russian Museum of Ethnography: St. Petersburg.

Karapetova, I. 1997c. *Traditional Footwear of Dolgans*. Russian Museum of Ethnography: St. Petersburg.

Karapetova, I. 1997d. *Traditional Footwear of Sel'kups*. Russian Museum of Ethnography: St. Petersburg.

Khudyakova, O. 1996. Chief curator, Khanty-Mansisk Museum of Regional Studies. Personal communication.

Klimova, N. n.d. *Folk Embroidery of the USSR*. Scientific Research Industrial Arts Institute. New York: Van Nostrand Reinhold.

Kocheschov, N. 1989. *Etnicheskie Traditsii v Dekorativnom Iskusstve Narodov*. Leningrad: Academiya Nayk SSSR.

Komtena, Ekaterina N. 1996. Museum curator and Khanty seamstress in Roskinsky. Personal communication.

Konakov, N. 1993. Ecological adaptation of Komi resettled groups. *Arctic Anthropology* 30(2):92–102.

Konakov, N. 1994. Calendar symbolism of Uralic peoples of the pre-Christian era. *Arctic Anthropology* 31(1):47–61.

Kos'ven, M. 1962. Iz istorii etnografii koriakov v XVIII v [History of the ethnography of the Koryak in the 18th century]. *Sibirskii Etnograficheskii Sbornik 4. Trudy Instituta Etnografii* n.s.74:276–291. Moscow: ANSSSR.

Kraseninnikov, S. 1755. *Opisanija zemli Kamcatki*. St. Petersburg.

Kreynovich, E. 1979. The tundra Yukagirs at the turn of the century. *Arctic Anthropology* 16(1):187–216.

Krupnik, I. 1985. The male-female ratio in certain traditional populations of the Siberian Arctic. *Études Inuit Studies* 9(1):115–140.

Krupnik, I. 1995a. Even. In Chaussonnet, V. (Ed.). *Crossroads Alaska: Native Cultures of Alaska and Siberia* (pp. 30–31). Washington, D.C.: Smithsonian Institution.

Krupnik, I. 1995b. Amur River peoples. In Chaussonnet, V. (Ed.). *Crossroads Alaska: Native Cultures of Alaska and Siberia* (pp. 32–33). Washington, D.C.: Smithsonian Institution.

Krupnik, I. 1995c. Siberian Yupik. In Chaussonnet, V. (Ed.). *Crossroads Alaska: Native Cultures of Alaska and Siberia* (pp. 24–25). Washington, D.C.: Smithsonian Institution.

Krupnik, I. 1995d. Chukchi. In Chaussonnet, V. (Ed.). *Crossroads Alaska: Native Cultures of Alaska and Siberia* (pp. 26–27). Washington, D.C.: Smithsonian Institution.

Krupnik, I. 1995e. Koryak. In Chaussonnet, V. (Ed.). *Crossroads Alaska: Native Cultures of Alaska and Siberia* (pp. 28–29). Washington, D.C.: Smithsonian Institution.

Krupnik, I., and M. Chlenov. 1979. Dinamika etnolingvisticheskoi situatsii u asi-atskikh eskimosov (konets XIX v.–1970-e gg) [Trends in the ethnolinguistic situation of the Asiatic Eskimos (late 19th century to the 1970s); English summary]. *Sovetskaia Etnografiia* 2:19–29.

Krushanov, A. (Ed.). 1987. *Istoria i kul'tura Chukchei* [Chukchi history and culture]. Leningrad: Nauka.

Kuz'mina, L. 1988a. The clothing, crafts and applied arts of Soviet native people. *Inuktitut* 68:51–59.

Kuz'mina, L. 1988b. Chukchi and Inuit folklore. *Inuktitut* 68:51–59.

Lapsoy, T. 1996. Nenets seamstress, Antipayota. Personal communication.

Laufer, B. 1902 [1975]. The decorative art of the Amur Tribes. *The Jesup North Pacific Expedition 4, Memoirs of the American Museum of Natural History.* Leiden. Reprinted New York: AMS Press.

Lazayamova, Z. N. 1996. Khanty seamstress, Khanty-Mansisk. Personal communication.

Lebedev, V. 1988a. Siberian Peoples: A Soviet view. In Fitzhugh, W., and A. Crowell (Eds.). *Crossroads of Continents: Cultures of Siberia and Alaska* (pp. 314–318). Washington, D.C.: Smithsonian Institution.

Lebedev, V. 1988b. Education, employment, economic organizations and health services in the USSR Far North. *Inuktitut* 68:92–103.

Levin, M. 1958. Etnicheskaia antropologiia i problemy etnogeneza narodov Dal'nego Vostoka [Ethnic anthropology and problems of ethnogenesis of the peoples of the Far East]. Moscow. Anthropological types of the Northeastern Paleoasiatics and the problems of ethnogenesis. *Proceedings of the 32nd Congress of Americanists* (pp. 607–616).

Levin, M. 1963. *Ethnic Origins of the Peoples of Northeastern Asia.* Michael, H. (Ed.). Translated from Transactions of the Northeastern Expedition II. Physical Anthropology and Ethnogenetic Problems of the Peoples of the Far East, published in Trudy Instituta Etnografi im. N.N. Miklukho-Maklaya, n.s., XXXVI, 1958. Toronto: Arctic Institute of North America.

Levin, M., and L. Potapov. 1956 [1964]. *The Peoples of Siberia.* Dunn, S. (Trans. Ed.). Chicago: University of Chicago Press. [Orig. pub. *Narody Sibiri.* Moscow: ANSSSR.]

Levin, M., and L. Potapov. 1961. *Istoriko-etnograficheskii atlas Sibiri* [Historico-ethnographic atlas of Siberia]. Institut etnografii. Moscow-Leningrad: ANSSSR.

Levin, M., and D. Sergeev. 1964. The penetration of iron into the Arctic: The first find of an iron implement in a site of the Old Bering Sea Culture. In Michael, H. (Ed.). *The Archaeology and Geomorphology of Northern Asia: Selected Works* (pp. 310–326). Toronto: Arctic Institute of North America. Anthropology of the North Translations from Russian Sources. No. 5.

Levin, M., and B. Vasil'yev. 1956 [1964]. The Evens. In Levin, M., and L. Potapov. *The Peoples of Siberia* (pp. 670–684). Chicago: University of Chicago Press.

Luick, J. 1978. *Reindeer, Horse, and Yak Production in Yakutia USSR.* Juneau: U.S. Dept. of the Interior Bureau of Indian Affairs.

Lukena, N. 1979a. *Alvbum Khantiskii ornamentov* [Album of Khanty ornament]. Tomsk.

Lukena, N. 1979b. Materiali po olenevodstvi vostochnikh Khantov [Material on eastern Khanty reindeer herders]. *Sovietskaiia Etnografiia* 6:110–121.

Lukena, N. 1992. *Ornament narodov zapadnoi seberi.* Tomsk.

Manning, D., J. Cooper, I. Stirling, C. Jones, M. Bruce, and P. McCausland. 1985. Studies on the footpads of the polar bear (*Ursus maritimus*) and their possible relevance to accident prevention. *The Journal of Hand Surgery* 10-B(3):303–307.

Margolina, N. 1997a. Summary of the Nivkhi. St. Petersburg: Russian Museum of Ethnography.

Margolina, N. 1997b. Summary of the Odegie. St. Petersburg: Russian Museum of Ethnography.

Margolina, N. 1997c. Summary of the Nanaits and Ulchi. St. Petersburg: Russian Museum of Ethnography.

Mark, J. 1988. *Ethnic Jewellery.* London: British Museum.

Mason, O., and S. Gerlach. 1995. Chukchi hot spots, paleo-polynyas, and caribou crashes: Climatic and ecological dimensions of north Alaska prehistory. *Arctic Anthropology* 32(1):101–130.

Menovshchikov, G. 1964. The Eskimos. In Levin, M., and L. Potapov. *The Peoples of Siberia* (pp. 836–850). Chicago: University of Chicago Press.

Michael, H. (Ed.). 1963. *Studies in Siberian Shamanism.* Dunn, E., and S. Dunn (Trans.). Toronto: Arctic Institute of North America, University of Toronto Press.

Michael, H. (Ed.). 1961–1974. *Anthropology of the North: Translations from Russian Sources.* Montreal: McGill-Queen's University Press.

Michael, H. 1984. Absolute chronologies of late Pleistocene and Early Holocene cultures of Northeastern Asia. *Arctic Anthropology* 21(2):1–68.

Michael, H., and J. Vanstone (Eds.). 1983. *Cultures of the Bering Sea Region: Papers from an International Symposium.* New York: International Research and Exchanges Board.

Milovsky, A. 1991. Sea hunters of Sireniki. *Natural History* 1:31–36.

Mitlyanskaya, T. 1976. *Kudoshniki Chukotki.* Moskva: Izobrazitelnoe Iskusstvo.

Mitlyanskaya, T. 1983. *Selskomy Ychitelu O Narodnick Khydoschestbennik Remeclak Sibiri i Dalnebo Bostocka.* Moskva: Prosbeschenie.

Mitryukova, L. 1988. Eskimosk tapochki. *Severni Prostori* 4:42–44.

Mochanov, I. 1969. The Ymyiakhtakh Late Neolithic culture. *Arctic Anthropology* 6(1):115–118.

Moore, R. 1923. Social life of the Eskimo of St. Lawrence Island. *American Anthropologist* 25(3):339–375.

Morrow, P. 1984. It is time for drumming: A summary of recent research on Yup'ik ceremonialism. *Études Inuit Studies* 8 (special issue):113–140.

Mote, V. 1995. Siberia. *Compton's Encyclopedia and Fact Index*. Chicago: Compton's Learning Company.

Muldanova, T. 1979. *Album Khantyskik ornamentov* [Album of Khanty designs]. Tomsk: University Press.

Muldanova, T. 1992a. Ozori lokotok lisisti i sheyr otki gogolya. *Yugra* 8 (August):54–55.

Muldanova, T. 1992b. Ornamentalnoe iskchsstvo namdov kanshi i manei. *Yugra* 1 (January):26–27.

Muldanova, T. 1992c. Yuzor "sovoli." *Yugra* 2 (February):48–49.

Muldanova, T. 1992d. Yuzor "berezovaya vetb." *Yugra* 3 (March):56–58.

Muldanova, T. 1992e. Ornament "chelyust loshadi." *Yugra* 5 (May):13.

Muldanova, T. 1992f. Ornamenti "krest," "oleni roga" i bryugie. *Yugra* 9 (September):51.

Muldanova, T. 1992g. Ornament "tryasogyuzka." *Yugra* 10(October):54–55.

Muldanova, T. 1992h. Ornament "krilya chaiki." *Yugra* 6 (June):17–18.

Muldanova, T. 1992i. Razne ornamenti. *Yugra* 7 (July):55–56.

Muldanova, T. 1993. Ornament "Soletsye." *Yugra* 4 (April):50–52.

Muldanova, T. 1994. Nachivanie i nizanie beserom ornamenta "golovka." *Yugra* 7 (July):54–55.

Muldanova, Timothy. n.d. Chastnoy olenevodstvo v Khanty-Mansiyskom avtonomeom okryuge [Private reindeer herding in Khanty-Mansisk]. Unpublished paper. Khanty-Mansisk.

Muldanova, Timothy. 1996. Khanty cinematographer and ex-herder living in Khanty-Mansisk. Personal communication.

Murashko, O., and N. Krenke. 1996. Burials of Indigenous peoples of the Lower Ob region: Dating, burial ceremonies, and ethnic interpretations. M. Bonnichsen (Trans.). *Arctic Anthropology* 33(1):37–66.

Murdoch, J. 1892. Ethnological results of the Point Barrow Expedition. *9th Annual Report, Bureau of American Ethnology*. Washington, D.C.

Mytnie, A. 1992. Lude Severa: Kto Oni? [Northern peoples: Who are they?]. Centr Molodeshneik Ennovashii [Centre for Youth]. Moscow.

Nagishkin, D. 1980. *Folktales of the Amur: Stories from the Russian Far East*. New York: Harry N. Abrams/Leningrad: Aurora Art Publisher.

Nelson, E. 1899 [1983]. The Eskimo about Bering Strait. *Bureau of American Ethnology Annual Report* 18:1–518. Washington, D.C.: Smithsonian Institution. Reprinted with introduction by W. Fitzhugh in *Classics of Smithsonian Anthropology Series*, 1983. Washington, D.C.: Smithsonian Institution Press.

Nelson, R. 1969. *Hunters of the Northern Sea Ice*. Chicago: University of Chicago Press.

Noble, J., and J. King. 1992. *USSR: A Travel Survival Kit*. Berkeley: Lonely Planet.

Nobmann, E., F. Mamleeva, and E. Klachkova. 1994. A comparison of the diets of Siberian Chukotka and Alaska Native adults and recommendations for improved nutrition: A survey of selected previous studies. *Arctic Medical Research* 53:123–129.

Northern Affairs. 1993. The Indigenous peoples of the Russian North. *Circumpolar Notes* 2(1):6–8.

Nosov, M. 1955. Clothing and adornment of Yakut clothing from the end of XVIII century to 1920s. *Collection of research articles by Yaroslavskii Yakut Republican Museum of Local Lore*, 2: 116–169.

Oakes, J., and R. Riewe. 1989. Field notes. Alaskan Yupik and Inupiat. University of Manitoba, Winnipeg.

Oakes, J., and R. Riewe. 1990. Field notes. Northern Far East of Russia. University of Manitoba, Winnipeg.

Oakes, J., and R. Riewe. 1996. Field notes. Northwestern Siberia. University of Manitoba, Winnipeg.

Oakes, J., and R. Riewe. 1997. *Culture, Economy and Ecology: Case Studies in the Circumpolar Region*. Millbrook: The Cider Press.

Okladnikov, A. 1965. *The Soviet Far East in Antiquity: An Archaeological and Historical Study of the Maritime Region of the USSR*. Michael, H. (Ed.). Toronto: Arctic Institute of North America, University of Toronto Press.

Okladnikov, A. 1970. *Yakutia before its Incorporation into the Russian State*. Michael, H. (Ed.). *Anthropology of the North*. Montreal: Arctic Institute of North America, McGill-Queen's University Press.

Okladnikov, A. 1981. *Ancient Art of the Amur Region/Art of the Amur, Ancient Art of the Russian Far East*. Leningrad: Aurora Art Publisher.

Osherenko, G. 1995a. Indigenous political and property rights and economic/environmental reform in Northwest Siberia. *Post-Soviet Geography* 36(4):225–237.

Osherenko, G. 1995b. Property rights and transformation in Russia: Institutional change in the Far North. *Europe-Asia Studies* 47(7):1077–1108.

Osherenko, G. 1995c. Photographic exhibition and written communications. Dartmouth College.

Pelikh, G. 1972. *Origin of the Sel'kups*. Tomsk.

Pelyrmagen, S. 1990. Chukchi mayor of Krasnoe, Chukotka. Personal communication.

Pentikäinen, J. 1992. Finno-Ugric minorities in Siberia: Extinction or survival? *Language Problems and Language Planning* 15(3):297–298.

Petrov, A. 1997. *Yakuts Footwear*. St. Petersburg: Hertzen Institute, Department of Northern Peoples, University of Russia.

Pika, A. 1996. Reproductive attitudes and family planning among the Aboriginal peoples of Alaska, Kamchatka, and Chukotka: The results of comparative research. *Arctic Anthropology* 33(2):50–61.

Pika, A., and D. Bogoyavlensky. 1995. Yamal Peninsula: Oil and gas development and problems of demography and health among indigenous populations. *Arctic Anthropology* 32(2):61–74.

Pitul'ko, V. 1993. An early Holocene site in the Siberian High Arctic. *Arctic Anthropology* 30(1):13–21.

Pitul'ko, V., and A. Kasparov. 1996. Ancient Arctic hunters: Material culture and survival strategy. *Arctic Anthropology* 33(1):1–36.

Poelzer, G. 1995. Devolution, constitutional development, and the Russian North. *Post-Soviet Geography* 36(4):204–214.

Pokaychev, V. 1996. Khanty herder, Roskinsky region. Personal communication.

Popov, A. 1966 [1948]. *The Nganasan: Material Culture of the Tavgi Samoyeds.* Bloomington: Indiana University. [Trans. E. Ristinen Nganasany: Material'naya Kul'tura. (Nganasan: Material Culture.)] Trudy Instituta Etnografi im. N. N. Miklukho-Maklaya, novaya seriya vol 3. Moscow.

Popov, A. 1984a. *The social device and beliefs of the Nganasan.* Leningrad.

Popov, A. 1984b. The family life of the Dolgans. In Dragadze, T. (Ed.). *Kinship and Marriage in the Soviet Union: Field Studies* (pp. 192–219). London: Routledge & Kegan Paul.

Popova, U. 1981. *Eveny Magadanskoi oblasti; ocherki istorii i kul'tury evenov Okhotskogo poberezh'ia 1917-1977gg* [The Magadan District Even, sketch of the history and culture of the Okhotsk Sea Coast Even, 1917–1977]. Moscow: Nauka.

Prokhorov, A. (Ed.) 1976. *Great Soviet Encyclopedia.* A translation of the third edition. New York: Macmillan.

Prokofyeva, E. 1963. The costume of an Enets shaman. In Michael, H. (Ed.), E. Dunn, and S. Dunn (Trans.). *Studies in Siberian Shamanism* (pp. 124–156). Toronto: Arctic Institute of North America, Anthropology of the North Translations from Russian Sources. No. 4.

Prokofyeva, E. 1964. The Sel'kups. In Levin, M., and L. Potapov (Eds.). *The Peoples of Siberia.* Chicago: University of Chicago Press.

Prokofyeva, E. 1971. Shamanskie kostiumy narodov Sibiri [Shamanistic costumes of the peoples of Siberia]. *Sbornik Muzeia Antropologii i Etnografii* 27:5–100. Leningrad: ANSSSR.

Prytkova, N. 1970. *Clothing of the People of Siberia.* St. Petersburg: Nauka.

Prytkova, N. 1976. Odezhda Chukchei, Koriakov i Itel'menov. *Material'naia kul'tura narodov Sibiri i severa* [Chukchi, Koryak, and Itelmen clothing. In Vdovin, I. (Ed) *The Material Culture of the Peoples of Siberia and the North*] (pp. 5–88). Leningrad: Nauka.

Riewe, R. 1991. Inuit use of the sea ice. *Arctic and Alpine Research* 23(1):3–10.

Riewe, R. 1992. The demise of the great white North: Environmental impacts on the circumpolar Aboriginal peoples. *Information North* 18(4):1–7.

Rudenko, S. 1961. *The Ancient Culture of the Bering Sea and the Eskimo Problem.* Michael, H. (Ed.), Tolstoy, P. (Trans.). Toronto: Arctic Institute of North America, University of Toronto Press.

Rudenko, S. 1970. *Frozen Tombs of Siberia: The Pazyryk Burials of Iron Age Horsemen.* (Trans. M. W. Thompson.) Cambridge: Cambridge University Press.

Rultineut, E. 1989. *Chukotskie i Eskimosskie Tantsi.* Upravlenie Kulturi Magadanskovo Oblispolkoma.

Salender, L. 1996a. Nenets herder and seamstress, Antipayota region. Personal communication.

Salender, M. 1996b. Nenets herder and seamstress, Antipayota region. Personal communication.

Salender, T. 1996c. Nenets herder, Antipayota region. Personal communication.

Sapronov, V. 1985. Whaling and nutritional needs of the aboriginal population of the Chukotka Peninsula. *The Arctic Policy Review* 3(3):5–8.

Sartagov, V. 1996. Khanty elder and seamstress, north of Roskinsky. Personal communication.

Saunders, A. 1990. Poisoning the Arctic skies. *Arctic* 1(2):22–31.

Savoskul, S. 1978. Social and cultural dynamics of the peoples of the Soviet North. *Polar Record* 19(119):129–152.

Schuster, C. 1951. Joint marks: A possible index of cultural contact between America, Oceania, and the Far East. *Royal Tropical Institute* 39:4–51. Amsterdam.

Schuster, C. 1964. *Skin and Fur Mosaics in Prehistoric and Modern Times.* Munchen.

Sem, T. 1993. Idea of cosmic communication in attributes of Even shamans. *Ethnosemiotics of Ritual Objects Used by Even Shamans* (pp. 127–140). St. Petersburg.

Sem, T. 1997. *Traditional Footwear of Evenki and Even.* St. Petersburg: Russian Museum of Ethnography.

Semeonovna, E. 1997. *Traditional Footwear of Even from Magadan Region.* St. Petersburg: Hertsen Institute, Department of Northern Peoples, University of Russia.

Seraskovoi, T. 1996. Khanty seamstress, Katawoosh. Personal communication.

Serov, S. 1988. Guardians and spirit-masters of Siberia. In Fitzhugh, W., and A. Crowell (Eds.). *Crossroads of Continents: Cultures of Siberia and Alaska* (pp. 241–255). Washington, D.C.: Smithsonian Institution.

Shrenk, L. von. 1883–1903. *Ob Inorodtsakh Amurskogo Kraia.* Russian version of *Reisen und Forschungen im Amur Lande in den Jahren 1854-1856. Vol 3. Peoples of the Amur Region.* St. Petersburg.

Shternberg, L. 1904. Gilyaki. *Etnograficheskoe Obozrenie* 1:1–42.

Shternberg, L. 1931. Ornament iz olenyego volosa i igol dikoobrazov [Decoration in reindeer hair and porcupine quills]. *Sovetskaia Etnografiia* (3–4):103–121.

Shternberg, L. 1933. *Giliaki, Orochi, Gol'dy, Negidaltsy, Ainy.* Khabarovsk.

Siikala, A. 1978. *The Rite Technique of the Siberian Shaman.* Helsinki: Academia Scientiarum Fennica.

Sirelius, U. 1904. *Ornamente auf Birkenrinde und Fell bei den Ostjaken und Wogulen.* Société Finno-Ougrienne, Travaux ethnographiques, II. Helsinki.

Smolyak, A. 1988. The clothing, crafts, and applied arts of Soviet Native people. *Inuktitut* 68:73–91.

Sokolova, Z. 1982. *Puteshestviye v Yugru.* Moscow.

Sokolova, Z. 1983. *Sotsial'naia organizatsiia khantov i mansi v XVIII-XIX vv* [Social organization of the Khanty and Mansi in the XVIII–XIX centuries]. Moscow.

Sokolova, Z. 1988. The contemporary economy of the Northern people. *Inuktitut* 68:105–119.

Solovieva, K. 1997a. *Traditional Khanty Footwear.* St. Petersburg: Russian Museum of Ethnography.

Solovieva, K. 1997b. *Traditional Mansi Footwear.* St. Petersburg: Russian Museum of Ethnography.

Solovieva-Oyunskaya, S. 1992. *Puzzles of Yakut People.* St. Petersburg.

Sopochina, Lydia. 1996. Director, Centre for National Culture, Roskinsky. Personal communication.

Susoi, E. 1994. *Is Golubini Vekov.* Institut problem osvoeniya Severa SO RAN. Tumen.

Susoi, E. 1996. Nenets author and historian, Salekhard. Personal communication.

Sverdrup, H. 1978. *Among the Tundra People.* M. Sverdrup (Trans. from 1939). San Diego: University of California.

Swadesh, M. 1962. Linguistic relations across Bering Strait. *American Anthropologist* 64:1262–1291.

Symmons-Symonolewicz, K. (Trans. and Ed.). 1972. *The Non-Slavic Peoples of the Soviet Union: A Brief Ethnographical Survey.* Meadville, PA: Maplewood Press.

Szathmáry, E. 1984. Human biology of the Arctic. In Dumas, D. (Ed.). *Handbook of North American Indians, Vol. 5., Arctic* (pp. 64–71). Washington, D.C.: Smithsonian Institution.

Taksami, C. 1967. *Nivkhi.* Leningrad: Nauka.

Taksami, C. 1970. Odezhda Nivkhov [Nivkhi clothing]. In Ivanov, S. (Ed.) *Odezhda narodov Sibiri* (pp. 166–195). Leningrad: Akademiya nauk SSSR.

Taksami, C. 1990. Opening speech at the Congress of Small Indigenous Peoples of the Soviet North. *Indigenous Peoples of the Soviet North.* IWGIA Document 67:23–44. Copenhagen.

Tein, T. 1994. Shamans of the Siberian Eskimos. *Arctic Anthropology* 31(1):117–125.

Turner, G. 1976. Hair embroidery in Siberia and North America. *Occasional Papers on Technology 7.* Oxford: Pitt Rivers Museum, University of Oxford.

UNESCO. 1983. *The Arctic / L'Arctique.* Paris: UNESCO.

Vakhtin, N. 1992. Native peoples of the Russian Far North. 1992. *Minority Rights Group International Report 92/5.* Manchester Free Press.

van Deusen, K. 1994. Oral traditions of Chukotka: Contemporary language issues. *Fourth National Student Conference on Northern Studies: Conference Programme and Abstracts* (p. 120). Ottawa: Association of Canadian Universities for Northern Studies and Department of Indian and Northern Affairs.

Vandimova, E. 1996. Khanty seamstress, Katawoosh. Personal communication.

Vanstone, J. 1983. Protective hide body armor of the historic Chukchi and Siberian Eskimos. *Études Inuit Studies* 7:3–24.

Vanstone, J. 1985. An ethnographic collection from Northern Sakhalin Island. *Anthropology* (8). Chicago: Field Museum of Natural History.

Vanstone, J. 1988. Hunters, herders, trappers, and fishermen. In Fitzhugh, W., and A. Crowell (Eds.). *Crossroads of Continents: Cultures of Siberia and Alaska* (pp. 173–182). Washington, D.C.: Smithsonian Institution.

Vanynto, M. 1996. Nenets seamstress and herder, Tazovsky region. Personal communication.

Varjola, P. 1990a. *Alaska-Russian America.* Helsinki: National Board of Antiquities.

Varjola, P. 1990b. *The Etholén Collection.* Helsinki: National Board of Antiquities.

Vasilevich, G. 1963a. *Tipi obovi narodov sibiri* [Boots of Siberia]. Sbornik Muzeya Antropologi i etnographi XXI [Museum of Anthropology and Ethnography]. Academy of Science, USSR.

Vasilevich, G. 1963b. Early concepts about the universe among the Evenks (Materials). In Michael, H. (Ed.). *Studies in Siberian Shamanism* (pp. 46–83).

Toronto: Arctic Institute of North America, Anthropology of the North Translations from Russian Sources. No. 4.

Vasilevich, G., and A. Smolyak. 1964. The Evenks. In Levin, M., and L. Potapov (Eds.) *The Peoples of Siberia* (pp. 620–654). Chicago: University of Chicago Press.

Vasil'evskii, R. 1969. The origin of the ancient Koryak culture on the Northern Okhotsk coast. *Arctic Anthropology* 6(1):150–164.

Vokueva, M. 1996. Khanty seamstress, Katawoosh. Personal communication.

Wallen, L. 1990. *The Face of Dance: Yup'ik Eskimo Masks from Alaska.* Calgary: Glenbow Museum.

Weber, A. 1989. *North American Indian and Eskimo Footwear: A Typology and Glossary.* Toronto: University of Toronto Press and Bata Shoe Museum.

Wissler, C. 1933 [1973]. Ethnological diversity in America and its significance. In Jenness, D. (Ed.). *The American Aborigines: Their Origin and Antiquity* (pp. 165–216). Published for presentation at the Fifth Pacific Science Congress, Canada, 1933. Reprint ed. New York: Cooper Square Publishers.

Yemelyanova, N. 1988. Chuchki life, new and old. *Inuktitut* 68(Fall-Winter):17–21.

Yudin, A., Y. Dobriakov, and J. Luick. 1979. *Preparation, Preservation and Medicinal Uses of Reindeer Antler.* Fairbanks: University of Alaska Institute of Arctic Biology.

Zakharova, I. 1974. Winter work footwear of Evens of Okhotsk coast. *Historical Material on the Far East* (pp. 278–280). Vladivostok.

Zhornitskaya, M. 1988. Music, song and dance in the North and Far East. *Inuktitut* 68 (fall-winter):60–71.

Zimmerly, D. 1986. *Qajaq: Kayaks of Siberia and Alaska.* Juneau: Division of State Museums.

In large part, this book was developed from the extensive body of knowledge shared by the curators of the Russian Museum of Ethnography; Indigenous professors from the University of Russia in St. Petersburg and Academy of Science in Moscow and Circumpolar Health in Moscow; and the many Indigenous Siberian people who offered their perspectives and hospitality during our field work (1990 and 1996) in northern Siberia.

The following people are thanked especially for their willingness to share traditional knowledge and their warm hospitality:

Among the Khanty: Nadja, Simon, Daniel, Darya, and Vaseli Pokaychev; Varvara, Michel, and Constantine Sartagov; Tatyana, Vetra, Oleg, Vladymir, Evan, and Sasha Aevaseda; Ruthiana and Clavdi Averyanovoi; Martha Sjazi; Tatyana Seraskovoi; Tatyana Serasnova; Anastasia Sainahova; Matrena Vokueva; Zoya Lazanmova; Dyana Greshnov; and Ludmela Alexandranov.

Among the Nenets: Milya, Lena, Sara, and Sergie Vanynto; Zoya Russkina; Ekaterina Komtina; Antaki Lapsui; Galena Ettovna; Valody and Galyna Vanyto; the Yardne family; and Natasha, Vanya, Timothy, Milya, and Lydia Salender.

Among the Even: Tefonova Alexondrovina, Galena Darchova, Maria and Ekaterina Demyanckaya, Vetra Demyanskii, George Goryachkin, Svetlana Budnikova, Galena Lougovaia, Elena Sherbakova, Elena Eraemeeva, and Bereskina Kyrillovna.

Among the Chukchi: Edward Agache; Sergee Pelyrmagen; Victor and Val Timofeevich; Elena Naychkike; Alexsie Kychnarev; Juravliov Matveevich; Anne and Ivanovna Judina; Mikhaylovna Kamil'girgina; Egorovna, Mitrjukhina, Olga, and Dyachkova Nikolaevna; Dem'janskaya Petrovna; Karamzina Illarionovna; Nishnya Kykashka; Svetlana Grigorevna; Monakhova Semenovna; Mishin Tikhonovich; Rytikai Vazsilevna; Svetlana Okro; Olga Omritval; Darchkova Kontantinovna; Galena Mashtakova; Dolganova Sergeenva; Tatyana and Andrew Mogilevskim; and Sergie Mikhailovich. Thanks to Ludmila Ilyna and Pavel Zaifudin for their contacts across Siberia.

We would like to thank Larrisa and Misha Aburtina, Chukchi Medical Unit, and Arkadi Gachilov, State Pedagogical University of Russia, for their tremendous hospitality, their invitation to study in northern Siberia, and their willingness to share their many contacts throughout the North, including their own Chukchi and Selkup families. Multimedia research, including photographs, drawings, videos, and audio recordings, were generously shared by David Anderson, University of Alberta; Kira van Deusen, Antioch University; Bryan and Cherry Alexander; Bruce Grant, Strathmore College; Maja-Leena Kaasalainen, National Board of Antiquities, Helsinki; Jouko Aaltonen and Ullimo Oy, Helsinki; Tatyana Pika and the late Alexandra Pika, Russia; Gail Osheranko, Dartmouth College; Asen Balikci, Bulgaria; Natalie Firnhaber, Department of Anthropology, Smithsonian Institution; Atsushi Yoshida, Academy of Science, Moscow; and the archivists at the Russian Museum of Ethnography Archives, St. Petersburg.

Researchers from museums and universities throughout North America, Europe, and Russia shared insights drawn from their Siberian collections and field work, including Garth Taylor, Canadian Museum of Civilization, Ottawa; Betty Issenman, Montreal; Tom Svensson, Ethnographic Museum, Institute and Museum of Anthropology, University of Oslo; Jonathan King and Phillip Taylor, Department of Ethnography, Museum of Mankind, The British Museum, England; Claudius Müller, East Asian Department, and Peter Bolz, Department of North American Indians, Museum für Völkerkunde, Berlin; Cunera Buijs, National Museum of Ethnology, Leiden; Irina Karapetova, Nina Margolina, Karina Solovieva, Tatyana Sem, Valentina Gorbacheva, and Natalia Kalashnikova, Russian Museum of Ethnography, St. Petersburg; Olga Khudyakova and Tatyana and Timothy Muldanova, Khanty-Mansisk Museum of Regional Studies, Russia; curators at the Magadan Museum of Ethnography, Magadan, Russia, and the Museum of Ethnography, Anadyr, Russia; Pirjo Varjola, Ildiko Lehtinen, and Saija Sarkki, National Museum of Finland, Helsinki; Stephan Augustin, Museum für Völkerkunde, Herrnhut; Renate Wente-Lukas and Rosita Neeno, Deutches Ledermuseum, Offenbach; Gillian Crowther, Cambridge University Museum of Archaeology and Anthropology, Cambridge; Jeremy Coote, Pitt Rivers Museum, University of Oxford; Henning Siverts, Ethnographic Museum, University of Bergen; Heinz Israel, Museum für Völkerkunde, Dresden; curators at the Alaskan State Museum, Anchorage, Alaska, and the Regional Museum, Nome, Alaska; Alexander Petrov, Arkadi Gachilov, and Elrika Semeonova, Department of Northern Peoples, at the A. I. Hertsen Russian State Pedagogical University, St. Petersburg; National Museum of Denmark, Copenhagen; Elena Susoi, Salekhard; curators at the Museum of Ethnography, Salekhard, Russia; Lydiya Sopochina, Centre for Native Culture, Roskinsky; curators at the Roskinskya Museum, Roskinsky; and Ludmila and Sergei Chubarova, Academy of Science and Circumpolar Health, Moscow.

Staff members and volunteers of the Bata Shoe Museum are gratefully acknowledged, especially Antony Vecera for his photographic skills; Sarah Beam for keeping photograph, text, and correspondence files organized, updating inventories, and tracking down missing information; Sharon McDonald and Jonathan Walford for co-ordinating various aspects of this project; Ada Hopkins for testing boot patterns; Ada Hopkins and Saundra Reiner-Moffatt for sharing valuable insights gained while conserving Siberian artifacts; and Hanna Pelnar for translations. Research conducted by Gail Fondahl, University of Northern British Columbia; Elaine Simpson, Canadian Circumpolar Library; Shannon Ward and Shawn Charlebois, University of Manitoba; and members of the International Arctic Social Sciences Association was extremely useful. Field notes from Christine Bata-Schmidt and references from William (Skip) Koolage were also appreciated. Basil Rotoff, Cecelia Fomina, Orysia Tracz, Olga and Peter Zhilkin, Marta Darczewski, and Alexandra Sosnowski are thanked for their professional translation services. Nina Rabkin is thanked for her translating and for expediting in the field. Editorial advice and co-ordination from Barbara Pulling, Douglas & McIntyre, are also gratefully acknowledged, as is Val Speidel's design. Thank you to Heather Warkentin and Frank Kazmerowich for working with us to create the maps and illustrations. Drs. William Fitzhugh, Igor Krupnik, and Stephen Loring, Arctic Studies Center, Smithsonian Institution, are thanked for critically reviewing the manuscript.

We gratefully acknowledge the Bata Shoe Museum Foundation and the Social Sciences and Humanities Research Council of Canada for exhibit and research funding; and Tyumen Aviation and Far East Flying Medical Services for support in kind.

PHOTOGRAPHY AND ILLUSTRATION CREDITS

All illustrations by Frank Kazmerowich

Maps by Heather Warkentin and Isabelle Swiderski

Numerals for photographs below refer to figure numbers.

Title page
Rick Riewe; inset photo Rick Riewe

Opposite Foreword
Rick Riewe

Preface
1: Rick Riewe

Introduction
2, 3: Russian Museum of Ethnography (REM)
4: Maria Stenzel/National Geographic Image Collection
5, 6: Rick Riewe
7, 8, 9: Antony Vecera
10: Rick Riewe
11: Antony Vecera
12, 13, 14: Rick Riewe

Chapter 1
17: *Die Sitten der Völker*/Georg Buschen
18, 19: Rick Riewe
20: Alexandra Pika
21: Antony Vecera
22: Rick Riewe
23, 24: Vladimir Dorokhov
25, 26, 27, 28: Antony Vecera
29: Vladimir Dorokhov
30: Antony Vecera

Chapter 2
31, 32: Rick Riewe
33: REM
34: Rick Riewe
35: Antony Vecera
36: Vladimir Dorokhov

37: Rick Riewe
38: Vladimir Dorokhov
40, 42, 43, 44, 45, 46: Antony Vecera

Chapter 3
47, 48: REM
49: Vladimir Dorokhov
50: REM
51, 52: Antony Vecera

Chapter 4
54: REM
55: Rick Riewe
56: REM
58, 59, 60, 61, 62, 63: Antony Vecera
64: Vladimir Dorokhov

Chapter 5
65: REM
66: David Anderson
67, 68: Vladimir Dorokhov
69: REM
71, 72: Antony Vecera
73: Vladimir Dorokhov

Chapter 6
74: REM
75: Rick Riewe
76: Vladimir Dorokhov
77, 78: Antony Vecera
79: David Anderson
80, 81: Antony Vecera

Chapter 7
82, 83: REM
84: *Die Sitten der Völker*/Georg Buschan
85: Vladimir Dorokhov
86: Antony Vecera
88, 89, 90: Dietrich Graf, Museum für Völkerkunde, Berlin
91: Antony Vecera

Chapter 8
92: REM

93: Rick Riewe
94, 95: Vladimir Dorokhov
97: Rick Riewe
99, 100, 101: Antony Vecera

Chapter 9
102: Image 542, courtesy Dept. of Library Services, American Museum of Natural History
103: Rick Riewe
105: Antony Vecera
106: REM
109, 110, 111: Antony Vecera
112: Vladimir Dorokhov
113: Dietrich Graf, Museum für Völkerkunde, Berlin
114: Vladimir Dorokhov

Chapter 10
115: Alexandra Pika
116: Kira van Deusen
117, 118: Alexandra Pika
119, 123: Vladimir Dorokhov
124, 125, 126: Antony Vecera
127: British Museum

Chapter 11
128: Kira van Deusen
129, 130: Antony Vecera
131: REM
132: Vladimir Dorokhov
133: REM
134: Vladimir Dorokhov
136, 137, 138, 140: Antony Vecera
141: Antony Vecera
142, 143, 144: Antony Vecera

Chapter 12
146: REM

Appendix II
147: Rick Riewe
149: REM
150, 151: Rick Riewe

INDEX

References to page numbers are in roman type; references to figure numbers are in *italic type*.

Welts, types of: 22, 186

Whale, 19, 151: bone, 126, 150, 166; carving of, 151; tail (decoration), 152, 156, 162. *See also* Beluga whale; Bowhead whale; Hunting; Muktuk

Willow, 10, 27, 87, 193, 194: bark, 75, 193; symbolism of, 44

Wolf, 10, 12, 31, 64, 73: fur, 139; skin boots, 115; tail skin, 126. *See also* Hunting

Wolverine, 12: fur, 139; skin, 195

Woodworking, 165

Yak: herding, 110

Yakut, 109–22: ancient history, 112; beliefs, traditional, 112; clothing, traditional, 75, 113, 115, *85*; contact with other groups, 110, 116; death rites, 112; decoration, 113, 115, 122, *85, 90*; footwear, 115–17, 122; homelands, 110, *map 8*; horses, 110; lifestyles, traditional, 110; loon skin boots, *91*; medieval history, 110; moose hide boots, *86*; patterns, 87; population, 110; reindeer leg skin boots, 66, 115–16, *88–90*; reindeer leg skin boots, dehaired, *82*; scrapers, 14; sewing, 19, 115; skin preparation, 194; skin softeners, 15; slippers, loon skin, 117; stockings, 115

Yakutsia, 110

Yamal-Nenets region, *35*

Yenisey River, 10, 24, 32, 40, 64, 86, 90, 92, 182

Yukagir, 112–13: ancient history, 112; clothing, traditional, 115; contact with other groups, 112, 117, 182; decoration, 115, 116; footwear, 117, 122; homelands, 110, *map 8*; lifestyles, contemporary, 113; lifestyles, traditional, 113; population, 110; recent history, 113; reindeer leg skin boots, 66, 96–97, 116–17; reindeer leg skin boots, dehaired, 117

Yupik, Alaskan, 157, *120, 124*

Yupik, Siberian, 149–62: beliefs, traditional, 151–52; clothing, contemporary, 153; clothing, traditional, 140, 152–55; decoration, 22, 152, 155, 156, 162, *124, 127*; footwear, 155–62, 184; homelands, 150, *116, map 11*; importance of footwear to, 155; knives, *7*; lifestyles, contemporary, 136, 150; lifestyles, traditional, 150; population, 150; prehistory, 16; red seal skin boots, 157, 162; reindeer leg skin boots, 22, 155; "runner" boots, 157; seal skin boots, dehaired, 155–57, 162, *126*; seal skin boots, haired, 156–57; sewing stitches, 22; skin preparation, 191, 194; slippers, 162; stockings, 162; taboos, 155; trade with Chukchi, 138; ulus, 14

Yurangas, 126, 138, *103*